AF272933

Strategy and the Military
A Propaedeutic Approach to Military Science
Wolfgang Peischel (Ed.)

Strategy and the Military

A Propaedeutic Approach to Military Science

edited by
Wolfgang Peischel

2023

Carola Hartmann Miles-Verlag Berlin

Bibliographical information in the German National Library
The German National Library (Deutsche Nationalbibliothek) lists this publication in the German National Bibliograpy; detailed bibliographic information can be accessed at: http://www.dnb.de.

© 2023 Carola Hartmann Miles-Verlag, Berlin
www.miles-verlag.jimdo.com
email: miles-verlag@t-online.de

Cover illustration: Ares © Marie-Lan Nguyen/Wikimedia.org/CC-Lizenz 2.5 (artistic adaptation) | Athene © Wikimedia.org/PD (artistic adaptation)

Printing: Books on Demand, Norderstedt
Editorial work: Dr. Laurenz Fürst, Diana Jilek, Bertram Mayer
Translation: Language Institute of the Austrian Armed Forces
Cover design: Stefan Lechner, BA

Printed in Germany

ISBN 978-3-96776-062-0

Contents

Chapter 0: Objective of the Propaedeutic Approach to Military Science, Editor's Preface

BG (retd.) MMag. Wolfgang Peischel, PhD

In order to ensure its long-term survival, every society and every state needs to take forward-looking precautions at all times during its existence, on the one hand in order to build up the potential for development required to pro-actively gain an advantage over emerging political actors and possible future opponents and, on the other hand, in order not to be defencelessly exposed to threats in the more distant future. It is precisely this proactive, long-term forward-looking assurance of the state's freedom of action that defines the concept of strategy on which this propaedeutic approach is based.

The problem hiding beneath this understanding of the term is that failures to build the required strategic capability are not visible or directly perceptible in the political fair-weather phases in which European democracies have lived until recently, and that exhortations to develop credible strategies are dismissed as prophesies of doom.

Strategic capability requires sacrifices and limitations in terms of long-term security as early as in the fair-weather phase (i.e. at a time when the requirement for action is not yet identified) due to the inherent long-term nature of the concept of strategy resulting from the long lead time for the development of strategic capabilities and the long time span over which strategically significant developments take place.

Western pluralist democracy is based on the fundamental principle of the will of the majority, which is regularly expressed through electoral decisions on which the elected representatives of the people depend for their political objectives for the next legislative period. If voters do not learn the hard way how essential it is to take strategic precautions during the fair-weather phase, it is hardly possible to find a majority here and now to agree on restrictions in favour of a strategic assurance of the future because it is currently not felt to be necessary. A security policy that is dependent on voter acceptance will therefore have to focus less on strategic threats and necessarily more on short-to medium-term threats, i.e. threats whose effects are immediately perceptible and for whose defence majorities can be won and for which the confirmation of government action through the citizens can be expected. It is questionable whether a security policy based on the short-lasting will of the electorate would at least be able to take substantial steps towards a credible strategic capability if an existential strategic threat were already clearly visible on the horizon – but even if it were, these approaches would probably come too late. Consequently, security policy research, which should, firstly, serve the political decision-making level, which is in turn obliged to follow the will of the majority and therefore also has a rather short- to medium-term understanding of strategy and which, secondly, forms the scientific basis for the security-political actions of the state, will tend to have to focus more on the reactive management of short- to medium-term threat situations.

In order to break through the possibly resulting systemic strategic inhibition of Western pluralist democracies, a science policy is needed that focuses on long-term objectives with regard to the security of the state's survival and whose central functional principle and essential structural factor justifying its performance is the overlapping of policy areas, because it is precisely the latter that represents the prerequisite for the overall quality of its research results. This science should not be driven by the will of the voting majority, but should be able to derive capabilities from an unbiased, objective strategic assessment that are necessary to give the state an advantage over competing actors in the future beyond the legislative period and to guarantee security from possible opponents, i.e. to secure long-term strategic freedom of action for the state or the confederation of states or the alliance. The spectrum of capabilities derived from, and further developed by, this science would also have to include the use of armed forces in the sense of the state's ultima ratio. Consequently, one facet of this science would lie in giving advice to the political leadership on the strategic orientation of the state in questions of long-term security of survival and a second facet in the scientific underpinning of military operational command. Both task qualities would have to be thought of as an organic unity because the escalation chain for controlling vital threats in an emergency ranges from advice on the strategic purpose to operational implementation planning to tactical implementation, and frictions can only be avoided, at least to a large extent, if both – strategic advice and operational implementation – remain in one hand. If only because the scientific elaboration of the fundamentals of operational armed forces command can only be carried out by researchers who come from a military service environment, it is *military science* that satisfies the claim derived here and is predestined to cover both task qualities simultaneously. This Janus-faced disposition of military science is reflected in Greek mythology, which knows two deities of war – Athena, the goddess of strategy and wisdom, and Ares, the god of actual, 'operational' warfare. The overall security and survival of the polis, however, was understood to depend on the complementary, synergistic work of both related deities. The choice of this book's cover image was intended to emphasise both this context and the two principal dimensions of military science.

Military science sees itself neither in competition nor in opposition to security policy research, but as its necessary dialectical complement. However, in order to be able to make a substantial contribution to such an overall national synthesis, an institutionalised military science is required that qualitatively equals the standard at a university and thus enjoys the same academic recognition as the civilian disciplines.

However, the fact that military science, in contrast to security policy research, does not have to take into account the social acceptance of sacrifices necessary for strategic capability as a primary basis for assessment in the elaboration of its results, but rather would have to conduct an uninfluenced factual strategic threat analysis based on military assessment logic, must by no means be interpreted as an 'undemocratic' momentum for two reasons in particular. Firstly, because the results of military science research can only be strategic *advice in preparation* for a decision, and the actual decision in the sense of the primacy of politics is in any case reserved for the elected representatives. Secondly, because the results of military science should only serve to inform the elected representatives of the people about the strategic threat situation and to convince them of the factual necessity of developing certain strategic capabilities - it would, however, remain the sole task of politics to raise the electorate's voluntary and convinced allegiance for strategic measures that would demand a certain restriction of prosperity here and now, although also a postponement of pending strategic decisions (not to be confused with 'strategic patience') would not, for the moment, result in any immediately perceptible adverse consequences for the electorate.

A future **military science** can only provide the indispensable and unsubstitutable benefit for the security of society derived here if it starts from an **understanding of strategy** that is based on long-term purpose (i.e. on the question of `what for´) and not on the short- to medium-term implementation of already predetermined decisions (i.e. on the question of `how´) and develops its strategic advisory contribution on the basis of a specifically military assessment logic derived from abstracted leadership principles, i.e. developed from **military** leadership practice.

This dependency gives rise to the conceptual triad in the title of the book, in which the connection between strategy, the military and military science is analysed and conclusions for the development of new military science capabilities are to be derived. The actual unique achievement, the added value of this propaedeutic approach, lies in demonstrating that the military can provide an indispensable and irreplaceable benefit for the strategic security of the state, given a certain understanding of strategy and a corresponding thematic and structural orientation of military science.

Now that it is being realised that the political fair-weather phase Europe has enjoyed in the recent decades during which little was invested in building strategic capabilities and reducing unilateral dependencies is likely to come to an end, it is beginning to be remembered that strategic researchers from the field of military science already started to point out the need for strategic action immediately after the end of the bloc confrontation. They have attempted to heighten public awareness of the evidence that reaping an excessive (and not temporally dependent on the enemy's resurgence) profit from the peace dividend leads to the fact that the Western democracies (especially the ones in Europe) and also Europe as a whole may not only miss out on developing any outward-looking strategic power, but rather could also lose their defensive assertiveness against emerging autocratic/authoritarian challengers – and thus run the risk of jeopardising the Western value order as a whole. Military science has also not become tired of pointing out the dangers that arise when states, in order to keep defence spending low, equip themselves for probable threats instead of maintaining credible military capabilities even for less likely but highly intense threat scenarios. At the latest with the Russian attack on Ukraine, which has shown how limited the European possibilities are as regards working substantially towards a rapid end of the war or even falling back on prepared alternative resource options, with which it could be prevented that the permitted one-sided energy dependence on Russia endangers its own economy and social peace, the thesis of a systemic strategic inhibition of Western pluralist democracy can no longer be so easily refuted – namely, the thesis that a long phase of prosperity without a foreseeable strategic threat within one legislative period leads to the fact that political approaches that advocate restrictions with regard to the creation of strategic capabilities do not find a democratic majority. Indirectly, this thesis could also be supported by the fact that in some states on the eastern periphery, i.e. those that tend to have a higher threat perception, there are electoral decisions that welcome 'quasi-authoritarian' moments of government action in the sense of an increased resilience capacity.

In general, the call for strategy is now also getting louder – without, however, there being a precise idea of what kind of strategy it would have to be in order to increase the long-term security of the state. Should it be a short- to medium-term strategy, guided by the question of how (i.e. what `ways´ there are), and based exclusively on the logic of security policy assessment, on the politics of what is feasible, and which recognises peace as the natural condition which, with good conduct, can be maintained even without a permanent exertion of force? This understanding has led to Europe's limited strategic capacity today.

A new understanding must therefore be created, one that makes it possible to comprehend that the underlying concept of strategy does not simply offer a better semantic definition, but describes a functional principle that is capable of attaining and permanently guaranteeing self-assertiveness and global power as a precondition for the preservation of the Western order of values.

Military science (in the potential structure of an institutionalised military science to be created, specifically the core subject 'strategic thinking' of the branch of strategy science) is concerned precisely with the definition of such a concept of strategy, and with the derivation and further development of functional principles of strategy, with the help of which the long-term survival of the state can be guaranteed. The military science definition of strategy aimed at this purpose (including not only the definition of the term, but above all the functional principles of strategy), which partly goes beyond the understanding of strategy in security policy-dominated academic disciplines or differs from it in perspective and therefore in a certain sense represents a unique achievement of military science strategy research, can be described by way of example via the following cornerstones and constitutive principles of action[1]:

- Strategy is a capability category that belongs to the sphere of `thinking´ rather than `acting´and therefore focuses more on finding the strategic purpose (`ends´-orientation) than on its implementation (`ways´-orientation).

- It is `long-term proactive/prophylactic´ rather than `reactive/symptomatic´ in orientation.

- Strategy is a function of will. Accordingly, it must not be reduced to the implementation of what is politically feasible at the moment, but should rather make feasible what is necessary for security. If it is recognised that the will is the essential constitutive moment of strategy and that this will almost regularly leads to the development of the corresponding strategic capability, then the assessment of emerging enemy actors should not be limited exclusively to their available potential. Military history teaches us that great defeats, some of which were even accompanied by the downfall of cultures (see the example of the Battle of the Teutoburg Forest), were often due to the fact that the emerging strategic quality of the opponent's actions was underestimated or recognised too late.

- Although it does not embody a `win-win´ principle and is therefore fundamentally *confrontational*, its creative and visionary moment can nonetheless liberate it from the inevitable compulsion to *physically violent conflict resolution*.

---

[1] These cornerstones and principles of action, which are used to define the understanding of strategy on which the introduction is based, are elaborated in more detail in Chapter 1.

- Due to its long-term nature, the successes or failures of a strategic purpose usually only become apparent after the term of office of those who have set a strategic direction has expired. This places particularly high demands on the moral and ethical integrity of the representatives of the strategic decision-making level, but also on the strategically advising staff.
- In the sense of Weber's ethics of responsibility, strategic capability demands an above-average degree of humanistic education rolled out across all socio-economic strata – on the one hand, because this is the basis for the duty of resistance of implementing intermediate levels against any form of possible ideologisation and thus, in particular, strengthens the democratic-political reliability of armed forces and, on the other hand, because this promotes the rationally based insight of the voter that certain restrictions may be necessary here and now with regard to the long-term security of the state.
- Because strategy has to maintain and defend the canon of values of the respective society as its innermost core of identification, it is necessarily specific to the cultural area, i.e. it is also decisively determined by the canon of values underlying the respective cultural area. The postmodern change in values of Western pluralist democracies could lead to a decreasing willingness to contribute to the community or the security of subsequent generations. This could put Western democracy in a position of strategic inferiority vis-à-vis authoritarian challengers (this could be seen as a further indicator of an emerging `systemic strategic inhibition´ of Western pluralist democracy). Strategy would therefore have to aim at strengthening value consciousness and reviving community values.
- Strategy can be understood as a weighing up of long-term security of survival against the restrictions governing the here and now that must necessarily be accepted for this. Because the consequences of a wrong or missing strategy are not immediately noticeable, democratic majorities for the necessary tightening of the belt are hard to find. The strategic assurance of the future would therefore have two fundamentally different dimensions:
  - a professional expert assessment of possible threats or development opportunities, uninfluenced by the possibilities of political feasibility, and the derivation of capabilities necessary to exploit the latter (this would be the task of strategy research within the framework of a military science to be developed)
  - and the democratically legitimised decision on the strategic purpose, among other things on the basis of the above expert assessment, as well as the enlistment of voluntary and convinced followers for this

purpose and the sacrifices to be made to achieve it (primacy of politics).

- The most essential, performance-generating functional principle of the strategy lies in its horizontal cross-policy assessment capability (`comprehensiveness`). The most common etymological derivation of the concept of strategy is based on the translation of the underlying στρατός ἄγειν as `leading the army`, according to which strategy would on the one hand represent a military domain and on the other hand be limited to the implementation of the political purpose by military means. Thus, there would be no overall added value for the long-term security of a state's society. Now, στρατός could also mean `class`, the class of merited citizens who were appointed to the college of strategists for a limited period of time in order to guide the political fortunes of the Attic polis there, entrusted with different areas of responsibility. Military officers were represented in this college, but by no means in a prominent or dominant role. The scope of the college went far beyond the leadership of armed forces and encompassed all areas of politics in the sense of a holistic leadership. It could also be understood as a forerunner of a modern government consisting of ministers responsible for specific departments – with the difference, however, that it was precisely the cross-departmental leadership, i.e. the concordance across the entire στρατός, and therefore also `strategic` purpose, that probably constituted the clout of the polis. For this very reason, a study that wants to introduce to the relationship between strategy and the military must cover all essential, strategy-relevant thematic areas, present them in a structure in which they could be depicted in the teaching of strategy at tertiary military educational institutions, and finally explain their mutual interrelationship so that the student gains a first insight into the functional principles of strategy.
- In this publication, strategy is deliberately distinguished from the term military strategy, because the latter means the implementation of a military sub-task assigned to the armed forces from the overall strategic decision-making level, it has little cross-policy area reference and is primarily oriented towards the implementation of strategic objectives (the conditions under which military strategy actually assumes a strategic character are explained in Chapter 4).

The present work aims to introduce an understanding of strategy defined by the above-mentioned key points, which can be used to proactively strengthen the long-term security of the state. During the research preceding this publication, an attempt was made to identify thematically related, constitutive subareas of strategic thinking, to capture their interrelationships and to translate both into a working structure that is also suitable as a possible subject structure for a military science which is to research and teach strategic thinking. With this structure, an attempt was made to do justice to the inherent cross-domain and multispectral nature of the concept of strategy. The chapters of this book reflect this structure in a simplified form, which should further facilitate first steps into a study of military science.

For many years, the International Society of Military Sciences (ISMS) has been systematically engaged in building the foundations of the further development of a military science that meets today's requirements and is capable of making a unique contribution to the strategic security of the state (the confederation or the alliance).

In 2019, the year in which I had the honour of holding the presidency, ISMS gave me the opportunity to place the annual conference to be held at the National Defence Academy in Vienna under the topic *Building Military Science for the Benefit of Society* and to publish the results in 2020 in the Carola Hartmann publishing house under the same title in the name of ISMS. The society had thus taken a substantial step towards providing the thematic and structural foundations of a core subject-oriented military science recognised at the university level, with which students could be provided with a valuable basic military science apparatus.

Based on these initial approaches of the ISMS, the Norwegian Defence University College launched the *Handbook of Military Sciences* in 2020, an authoritative open access, living reference work on military sciences, published online under Springer Nature Reference – Living Edition. The editor-in-chief of the work, Lieutenant Colonel Dr. Anders McD Sookermany, PhD, has succeeded in a pioneering manner in presenting a comprehensive thematic introduction to the broad spectrum of sub-disciplines of military science and in providing an overview of the existing approaches that attempt to describe, understand and explain military topics. A major achievement of this *Handbook of Military Sciences*, which cannot be overestimated in terms of its value for the study of military science or for professional engagement with military issues, is that it addresses a very broad target group, ranging from students of military science, students from the security sector in the broader sense, pupils at schools preparing for a military career, political functionaries and decision-makers with a connection to military issues, professional military personnel, contractors of armed forces, representatives of NGOs involved in international operations, to journalists who write about military-related issues. In this way, the complex *black box* of military thinking and military leadership contexts, which has so far been difficult to see inside, is made accessible to the entire social education sector in a highly professional manner and with a quality and multidimensionality that has never been achieved before. The success formula, with the help of which it was possible to familiarise readers with the principles of military science quickly and in an instantly understandable way, irrespective of their professional background or their original scientific discipline, is probably on the one hand that the contributions focus on applied scientific findings rather than on too profound basic theoretical derivations or on the development of new theoretical approaches. On the other hand, the individual articles are written independently of each other (in such a way that each article can be read on its own), which means that the reader can choose topics according to his or her specific interest and jump straight to them without having to read through the work's overall structure or work through the mutual cross-relationships between the individual essays. Of course, as the editor of this brief propaedeutic approach, I do not feel in any way called upon to judge such a comprehensive and landmark work as the *Handbook of Military Sciences* – the above assessment merely reflects the enthusiasm and respect it must inevitably inspire in a reader coming from a military science background.

This propaedeutic approach to military science is intended to offer a third attempt, based on the work of the ISMS and serving its fundamental purpose, which could be understood in some way as an optional addition to the first two.

As the broad-brush assessment in this preface shows, military science, in order to provide a unique, overall national security benefit, must represent a *strategic* and an *operational* science discipline, the simultaneous mastery of which represents its unique achievement. The discipline of strategy aims at the overall strategic advisory capacity of the senior military leadership at the interface with the political decision-making level (Clausewitz speaks in *On War*, Third Book, Chapter 1, in a different context of "... the highest regions of strategy ... where it borders on politics and statecraft or rather becomes both itself"). It is based on a concept of strategy whose central functional principle is the horizontal interdisciplinarity of policy areas and the reciprocal linking of core and subsidiary subjects of military science. Because it must further develop existing theoretical approaches in order to adapt them to current threat scenarios or because it must create new theories in order to maintain the state's strategic freedom of action even in the face of possible future challenges, a careful derivation from basic theory is an indispensable prerequisite. This segment of the strategic science dimension of military science, which has to cover the interface between strategic decision-making and strategic advice prior to decisions as well as the dependence of the latter on strategic research – i.e.

the relationship between strategy, the military and military science – could not be conveyed with the systematics used in the *Handbook of Military Sciences*, because the necessary overlapping of policy areas or subjects would diametrically oppose the independent readability of individual chapters, because the main benefit is derived from the development of new strategic approaches and the focus can therefore not lie on the presentation of currently applied strategic concepts, and finally, because the derivation of new approaches would not be scientifically permissible without a sufficiently profound basic theoretical derivation. In addition, the required basic knowledge in the areas of core and subsidiary subjects of military science and certain basic theoretical approaches would mean that parts of the target group of the handbook would not be able to derive any corresponding benefit from such an orientation.

For this reason, the propaedeutic approach at hand is intended to highlight the relationship between strategy, the military and military science as a core topic of the strategic dimension of military science and, among other things, to offer it as an optional thematic supplement to those readers of the *Handbook* who want to go beyond the study of the individual chapters and also deal with the embedding of the military science sub-disciplines in an overall strategic context. The publication is to be understood as a basic theoretical, holistic introduction to strategic thinking and the purpose of military science, which should contribute to gaining an overview of the military science subjects and understanding their interaction.

In principle, this propaedeutic introduction is intended as an offer, aimed at students of military science or civil security studies and at future strategic decision-makers or decision-preparers from the military, political, private-sector corporate leadership and operational organisations.

A number of outstanding, highly renowned Austrian and international strategy experts and military scientists were won for the preparation of this work, and I would like to seize this opportunity to thank them for their contribution and commitment. The individual contributions do not represent isolated perspectives on the topic, but rather have emerged on the basis of a common basic understanding of strategy, which could develop because the authors have been actively involved over the years in the strategy development platform created with the Vienna Strategy Conference series and have also exchanged views on this platform. In this context, it must be explicitly pointed out that the statements of all authors are their personal views and research results, which do not necessarily have to be in accord with the opinion of the respective defence departments or educational institutions.

Thanks are also due above all to the ISMS, whose activities provide the starting point and breeding ground for the further development of military science and have paved the way for publications such as *Building Military Science for the Benefit of Society, Handbook of Military Sciences* or *Strategy and the Military. A Propaedeutic Approach to Military Science.*

The Clausewitz Society and the Clausewitz Network for Strategic Studies are to be given thanks for their authorial support of the publication and for their substantial contribution to the development of the book's content through their participation in the Vienna Strategy Conference Series.

The Commandant of the National Defence Academy, Lieutenant General Mag. Erich Csitkovits, and his Chief of Staff, Brigadier General Mag. Reinhard Schöberl, are thanked for their untiring efforts to promote research into the further development of military science, for supporting the representation of the Academy on the Board of the ISMS and for providing the publication project with the necessary personnel support.

The Language Institute of the Austrian Armed Forces also contributed substantially to the quality of the publication by providing the translation into English. Heartfelt thanks are extended to the translators, Dr. Walter Wintschalek, MMag. Heidemarie Lenz, MA, Mag. Gernot Fridum, and Mag. Christopher Schönberger.

Dr. Laurenz Fürst and Bertram Mayer deserve sincere praise and sincere thanks for the editorial preparation of the book, for accompanying the contributions from the initial idea through the numerous coordination steps to the final editing and for the substantive input to individual contributions – because the publication would not have been possible without their highly ambitious commitment.

I would also like to thank the chief graphic designer of the Austrian Military Journal, Stefan Lechner, BA, for the graphic design of the book cover.

I wish all readers an insightful read that stimulates strategic thinking and a fundamental overall understanding that should arouse curiosity and open the door to the study of military science.

Chapter 1: Strategy and the Military: Concept, Functional Principles, Basics of Strategic Theory

BG (retd.) MMag. Wolfgang Peischel, PhD

Keywords: Military Strategy; Philosophy of Military Strategy; Strategic Theory; Military Science; Strategic Thought; Principles of Strategy;

0. Abstract

This chapter develops the foundations of the relationship between strategy and the military, i.e. between securing the long-term survival of the state as a whole, across all policy areas, through its democratically legitimised political leadership on the one hand, and the military in its capacity as strategic advisor and as the body realising the operational implementation of the strategic objectives on the other. The military could make this contribution to strategy development and implementation by developing a core subject-led, organic, interdisciplinary and institutionalised military science which ensures academically recognised research and teaching for both the discipline of strategic thought and applied military command – the embedding of strategic thought in military science is explored against this background.

The overall theme of this publication was structured according to leading research questions, derived from the analysis presented in this chapter, which precedes the further articles of the book. This structure is reflected in the topics of the following individual contributions and in the areas where they come into contact – the 'path through the study' outlined here as an introduction is intended to facilitate understanding.

The theories of strategy put forward are categorised by area of application, level of legitimacy, origin of the underlying functional principles and cultural region – but above all with regard to the dichotomy between the focus on ends and implementation. The approach taken by Carl von Clausewitz is highlighted because he was the first to base his theory on the need for simultaneity between strategic policy advice and applied operational command theory.

The functional principles of strategic thought abstracted from military command theory or derived from military evaluation logic form the basis for the consultation of national political decision-makers by the senior military leadership (and thus essentially determine the relationship between strategy and the military). Due to the high degree to which they are abstracted, they can also be applied in an adapted form to decision-making at lower echelons.

1. The purpose of this propaedeutic approach to military science

The guiding question for this and all other chapters of the study presented here, is *How can the phenomenon of strategy be understood/explained – what is strategy in relation to the military and how do we study this relation.*The follow-up goal for students will lie with a holistic understanding of military science - this book aims to create an entry-level understanding of military science by first focusing on the relationship and interaction between strategy and military science.

This strategy and its relationship to the military is neither a strategy reserved for political decision-makers nor limited to military strategy, and it is certainly not an attempt to assign a role to the military that conflicts with the primacy of politics. The theme of Strategy and the Military was deliberately chosen to set itself apart from the above-mentioned perceptions and instead focus on what strategic thought derived from military science and abstracted from military command principles can achieve for the long-term security of the democratically constituted state and its citizens. Strategic thought is, therefore, understood to be the functional core of military science serving the long-term security of the state, based on abstracted military command principles.

With regard to the *power to take decisions* (i.e. the power to define/stipulate and order its implementation), *strategy* is to be understood as a dimension of state action assigned to the sovereign, i.e. the democratically legitimised political level, spanning all areas of politics and life, which in western pluralistic democracies is to be perceived in a value-based and responsible manner and which is geared towards ensuring the long-term survival of the state. The political leadership defines the strategic ends, initiates the operational implementation, makes resources available and bears or is responsible for the risk taken. It is assumed that strategy must be geared primarily towards the question of what *ends* political action serves (*why/for what purpose?*), because this is the most effective way of ensuring the long-term survival of the state. Theories which restrict the concept of strategy to the question of the *ways* in which the identified ends are to be implemented and achieved run the risk of being put on the defensive against an opponent who plans strategically for the long term and are, thus, likely to be the main reason for the current inhibition to develop/incapacity to pursue a strategy (see Peischel 2017b, p. 139) in many areas of European politics in particular, but also in private business management. The ends-led understanding of strategy is, therefore, key to the relationship between strategy and the military, because strategic thought, which should enable military science to provide responsible advice to policymakers on security issues, would have to be geared towards it.

As long as the creation of a position of power as a rational precondition for the enforcement of interests against the will of competing actors serves this survival, the concept of strategy, on which this publication is based, applies. An offensive action against other political actors which cannot be rationally justified by a state's survival and which has irrational motives (e.g. revanchism, nationalistic/ideological claims to superiority, fantasies of world domination) should not, however, be subsumed under the concept of strategy as considered in this study.

Strategic thought as the functional core of military science serving the long-term security of the state would have to cover the entire breadth of the *content* of the concept of strategy defined above – in contrast to the policy-making level, however, not in a decision-making capacity, but only in an advisory capacity that prepares the way for decisions; its tasks to guide military science in terms of content and structure and to enable it to provide a unique benefit for society are derived from this. The strategic thought of the senior military command, therefore, does not differ from strategy in terms of content, i.e. with regard to the subject matter to be assessed (in terms of content, this thought is just as ends-led, cross-policy and whole-of-nation as the strategy it is intended to serve), but only in that the result of strategic thought, in contrast to the political decision-making on the strategic ends, is only of a quality that is suitable for *preparing* for decisions.

Strategic thought determines the relationship between the military and strategy with regard to three capability categories:

a) Perception of the role of a controlling body via core and subsidiary subjects and via the security-related contributions of civilian disciplines, as a prerequisite for organically structured military science, which is only able to deliver its unique social benefit, as a result of this understanding;

b) Making a substantial contribution to decision preparation and providing advice on overall strategy on questions concerning the long-term security of the state at the level where it meets political decision-making;

c) Creation of the academic basis for the implementation of the military part of national strategy (operational command science).

It is important to note that b) can only stem from a) and that only the ability to cope with b) and c) simultaneously and synergistically constitutes the actual unique benefit of military science.

Carl von Clausewitz creates the basis for this need for simultaneity by combining the tasks of policy advice and operational implementation under one strategy concept. He separates both bundles of capabilities neatly in terms of definition so that they can be clearly distinguished at any point in the work, but subsumes them under one and the same term *strategy* in order to indicate that they must be thought of in the context of military science as a pair of two mutually dependent factors.

Reducing the publication's subject matter to *military strategy* would have made it impossible to cover the entire spectrum of strategic thought and to demonstrate its substantial contribution to military science serving the security of the state. Above that, a lack of clarity about the purpose of strategic thought, which is also partly related to specific cultural regions, has led to such a variety of contradictory concepts of military strategy that this command level can only be dealt with after a basic understanding of strategic thought that serves the military science, and thus the security of the state.

In the absence of such a basic understanding, it would not be possible to define clearly whether military strategy means

- the content-related strategic, advisory activity of the senior military command, in preparation for decisions, at the interface with the political decision-making (`strategic thinking of the military´ that would be based on an understanding of strategy that is focused on `ends´),
- the performance of the tasks of national strategy assigned to the military – i.e. de facto, the implementation of the political purpose into operational military planning (ways- based understanding of strategy), or
- the control and distribution of forces, resources and risks between several major war theatres, by the senior military command within the framework of one and the same overall strategic objective, on behalf of the state.

It is precisely because military strategy represents a constitutive element of strategic thought, but its concept must simultaneously have such controversial connotations due to the fundamentally different underlying perceptions of strategy, that the nature and functional principles of strategy and the relationship between the latter and the military will first be analysed, and conclusions about military strategy only then drawn in a separate chapter.

When analysing the functional logic of strategy, the question to ask is not which perception of strategy is the more appropriate (it can be assumed that every area and level of social reality defines its concept of strategy in such a way that it provides the optimum benefit for it, and thus despite all the differences vis-à-vis others, is legitimate in its own right, within the bounds of its scope of application) but rather according to how strategy and strategic thought in the military's scope of application *should* be defined, understood and structured in order to bring about military science which is in turn capable of providing a unique added value for the long-term security of the state.

This added value for the long-term survival of the state, which arises from military strategic thought, should also be the critical factor for the student's independent evaluation of strategic approaches. Together with the criteria of a living definition of strategy, abstracted from military command principles and geared towards this purpose, the student should be able to independently and critically evaluate strategic approaches, theories, thinkers and self-developed draft strategies, but ultimately also this publication.

In the course of the study, a wide variety of doctrinal opinions on issues such as the direction of purpose or implementation with regard to the understanding of strategy, the approaches of various strategic thinkers, the cultural region-specific aspects of strategy or the relationship between strategy and doctrine will become visible. The introductory chapter is intended to familiarise the readers with the different views and approaches and to introduce them to the academic discourse – the book as a whole is intended to provide the basic understanding that enables the reader to evaluate the different schools of thought and doctrines by means of their own judgement and without bias.

2. Structure and ductus of this publication

The structure of this propaedeutic introduction to military science resulting from the leading research questions, derived in detail in particular in paragraphs 4, 5, and 6 of this chapter, as well as the interaction between the individual papers, should be presented, thus providing a path through this book that will allow the complexity of the overall subject matter to be comprehended holistically. What all the papers have in common is the didactic requirement of creating an understanding of *what is to be studied and how it can be taught*.

In the introductory chapter `*Strategy and the Military: Concept, Functional Principles, Basics of Strategic Theory*´ in addition to explaining the structure and ductus of the study, an attempt is made to grasp the nature of strategy and its interface with strategic thought in the military, to show how strategic thought is embedded in military science and to explain the core of the relationship between strategy and the military by means of military science-based advice at the point where it interfaces with political decision-making. The derivation of functional principles of strategic thought, which make such a strategic advisory function possible at all, implicitly leads to an initial discussion proposal for a contemporary concept of strategy. In addition, a categorised overview of strategy theories (in the broadest sense) is provided for students and it is explained which of these theories provides a basis for the understanding of this approach to strategy on which the book is based.

Because Clausewitz's `*Zweck-Ziel-Mittel*´- *Relation* and its more recent *ends-ways-means perception* require, *inter alia*, fundamentally different roles of military command within the strategic decision-making process, and because it is precisely this role assignment that represents an essential criterion for the strategy-military relationship, chapter 2 `Strategy, Politics, and the Use of Force in Europe´ presents a more in-depth analysis of chapter 1 in this respect (in addition, an interface with the analysis of the relationship between ends, ways, means from a philosophical point of view is provided here in chapter 3). It also deals with the comprehensive strategy approach. In the presentation of the relationship between politics and national interest/national strategy, there is an interface with chapter 4, `Military Strategy´.

The cultural space-specific nature of strategy/strategic thought and in particular the evaluation logic underlying the strategic decision-making process is largely determined by the prevailing philosophical approaches. For this reason, chapter 3, `Strategy and Philosophy, War Theory´, examines the philosophical/war-theory foundations of strategy, addresses the aspect of `strategy and responsibility – cultural space-specific, ethical dimension of strategic thought´ and sheds light on the role of polemology as a war prevention science. By analysing the relationship between ends, ways and means from a philosophical point of view, this creates a bridge to chapter 1 and chapter 2. The approach to the theory of war results mainly from the examination of the philosophical and methodological foundation of Clausewitz's work On War.

Chapter 4, `Military Strategy´ deals with the relationship between military strategy and military doctrine and explains the hierarchical embedding of the former. The presentation of the relationship between national strategy and military strategy provides an interface to chapter 2, which introduces the military-strategic dimension of naval warfare, aerial warfare, space warfare and the challenges of cyberspace, covering the global commons factors that are to be thought of as a strategic unit. The bridge to the operations perspective is created by presenting the interface between military strategy and operational command.

Chapter 5, `The Historical Evolution of Strategic Theory´ provides a conceptual overview of the main school of thoughts, strategic thinkers, perspectives or discourses related to the study of strategy in relation to the military, structured by time periods. This continues the categorisation of theories of strategy from Chapter 1. Geostrategic and contemporary approaches are addressed. The processing of the strategy theories structured according to time periods implicitly leads to the nature and possibilities of a history of strategy.

Chapter 6 explains the basics, functional principles, theoretical approaches (strategic culture theories, concepts) of `Strategic Culture´ and aims to awaken an understanding of the cultural space-specific aspects of strategic thought. The chapter thus offers an introduction to the field of research and an introduction to the study of strategic culture.

Because economics is one of the most effective instruments of an interest-driven government strategy, chapter 7, `Strategy and Economics´, presents the most important theoretical approaches in this regard and deals with the economic policy aspects of geostrategy and geoeconomics. In addition, the difference between whole-of-nation, ends-led perception of strategy and the implementation-led perception of strategy often found in the private sector is presented. In the course of the comparison, however, the approaches of major powers in particular, which see the economy as an instrument of overall strategic objectives, are also dealt with. Finally, the economic policy dimension of the ends-ways-means-risks relationship and thus an interface with the themes of chapter 1 and chapter 3 is dealt with.

Chapter 8, `Military Strategy and Technology´ analyses the importance of the strategic factors *artificial intelligence, robotics, autonomous platforms, cyberspace* which are new to the existing (force-time-space-information-technology), including their ethical dimension. In addition, the technical dimension of the Global Commons discussed in chapter 4, emphasising the strategic dimension of space, as well as the history, theories and further development of the Revolutions in Military Affairs (RMA) and the importance of offset strategies in connection with the C4ISR (meanwhile extended to C5ISTAR) approach will be highlighted. It concludes with an assessment of threats posed by future disruptive technologies.

`Strategic communication´ is interpreted in chapter 9 as an instrument of strategic influence directed towards political purpose and thus, in contrast to the current understanding, as a tool accompanying the operational implementation. Furthermore, it will be specified on the basis of strategic examples from recent history. The psychological dimension of strategic communication and thus its basic functional mechanism is explained via the logic of narratives.

3. Embedding strategic thought in military science

However, an independent military science, which the book is intended to introduce is only justified in existing if it is capable of providing a unique, whole-of-nation added value/benefit for society for which there is no substitute. This demand is especially true for the field of military science that is concerned with research on strategic thought, because the latter can also play the role of a content-related steering body for the individual subjects of military science. The purpose of the study of the relationship between strategy and the military is, above all, to ascertain which requirements military science must meet in order to provide a unique, non-substitutable benefit for the security of the state – and how the subject of strategic thought must be structured and directed in order to enable military science to provide such a service[1]. It follows from this that the question of what strategic thought can do for military science is the decisive factor in the relationship between strategy and the military.

If one starts off by considering strategy described above as a democratically legitimised (especially with regard to decision-making powers), whole-of-nation, cross-policy dimension of action to ensure long-term survival, then its relationship to the military, or more precisely to military science, and vice versa, the contribution of military science to the strategic planning/implementation of the state, can be presented in two possible forms with which the student should be familiarised:

(1) Security policy-led approach

- The thematic focus is on the security-relevant aspects of various, mainly non-military scientific respectively political areas.

- Although the security policy focus implies a whole-of-nation approach, it concentrates on the implementation of the overall political strategic ends into *security* policy goals and can therefore offer only limited advice with regard to the overall strategic ends. By contrast, the military-scientific research is the only component that can think through the chain of action from setting the strategic ends to the possible deployment of the armed forces and that is able to feed-back the influence of resource requirements and the risk taken on the strategic ends setting - however, is not represented at the same academic quality level and neither equally involved in the assessment process as civilian experts. This is one of the reasons why, in practice, the security policy-led approach often tends towards short to medium-term assessment results, recommendations or forecasts.

- The focus on a short/medium-term quality of findings increases the visibility and relevance of the approach for the solution of current security policy problems, but leads to a stronger focus on strategy implementation (ways), whereby the core subjects of military operational command science are rarely integrated to the necessary extent.

---

[1] This connection can be described with a comparison that may be oversimplified, but is nevertheless meaningful. Just as military science is supposed to contribute to the long-term security of the state, the fire brigade is required to rescue people from a burning house. It can only fulfil this task if the commander of the fire-fighting vehicle gets the operators of the pump, compressor, water tank, turntable ladder, pressure hoses, etc. to work together smoothly and ensures that the fire-fighting vehicle actually reaches the scene of the fire by giving clear instructions to the driver. Similarly, strategic thought would have to first bring together the subjects of military science to create a synergistic result and then, building on this, to steer military science as a whole towards an overall strategic advisory service at the interface with political decision-making.

- Since the main focus is on security policy issues, the teaching/research staff mostly draw their basic academic qualifications from civilian academic disciplines. The subjects of strategy- and operational command science are not raised to the same university level of recognition, which is why academic qualification in military science core subjects is only possible at a few European defence universities. This leads to the fact that strategic assessment and operational implementation competence of the military is seldom reflected at the same university quality level that civilian disciplines achieve, and thus also to the result that the two strategic assessment components which are interdependent and therefore urgently need to be simultaneously assessed, namely the strategic advisory and military-implementation aspects, are not researched and taught in the sense of an organic unit.
- The security policy-led approach correlates with a military science structure, which can be described by using the Marquee Model (see Sookermany 2020, pp. 53-73). This understanding of military science starts from the assumption that researchers from different civilian university-level educational institutions who, within the framework of their faculty's research mandate, deal *inter alia* with questions relevant to security, form a loose cooperation in which also researchers of military tertiary educational institutions are included, but which is neither structured nor geared towards a common, military scientific research purpose (i.e. comprehensive long term state security) by a military scientific steering body.
- The conceptual/theoretical foundations are mostly political science (security policy), economic science and, occasionally, theories of international relations.
- The security policy-led approach supports *complementary*[2] policy advice based on a high degree of scientific interdisciplinarity with high relevance especially for current (short to medium-term) issues of security policy.

(2) Strategic thought as the functional core of military science based on abstract military command principles and evaluation logic

- Strategic thought covers the entire range of the concept of strategy defined above (the only difference is that its results can only be used in an advisory capacity in preparation for decisions) and includes not only all policy areas, but also the deployment of armed forces as the *ultima ratio*

---

[2] 'Complementary' because the security policy focus often means that the investigation of long-term strategic objectives takes a back seat and because the aspects of strategy- and military operational command science in the course of strategy implementation analyses are not carried out in organic synergy with security-political research.

of strategy implementation in the assessment of long-term, security-related objectives.

- The focus on long-term objectives (ends-led approach) includes the treatment of strategy implementation (ways) as a dialectical antithesis, which is concurrently necessary. The ability to advise on strategic objectives and the simultaneous requirement for the ability for operational implementation are understood as interdependent fields of research, which are represented as a synergetic unit in organically structured military science.

- The focus on primarily long-term findings, together with the stronger focus on the theme of strategic ends, justifies the relevance of the approach for security-related policy advice. The core subjects of strategy- and military operational command science are integrated to the necessary extent and ensure the essential feedback from demand for resources and the risk to be taken for strategic ends.

- The framework for this approach would be an organically structured military science which is characterised by a high degree of interdisciplinarity, but which is guided by a `steering instance´ strategic thought, whose core subjects are taught up to a university-recognised level of quality (doctorate) and which reflects the ability to provide overall strategic advice in synergy with the requirements of operational command science, thus ensuring the scientific support of the entire chain of action from the strategic objective and operational implementation to the determination of the necessary resources and the risk to be taken, as well as the feedback to the starting point of the strategic assessment. This structural model of military science correlates with the *Sailors and Helmsman Model* (cf. Peischel 2020, pp. 17-52), which is based upon the understanding of military science as the synergetic interaction of core and ancillary subjects including researchers from civilian disciplines working on topics relevant to security, but contrary to the Marquee Model, geared towards a holistic societal benefit, towards a common military scientific research purpose, by a military-scientific steering body – strategic thought.

- This approach is largely under-represented in theory. For the purpose of conceptual underpinning, geopolitical theories are mostly used, although they are based on a very narrow understanding of strategy. The central theory of a comprehensive, ends-led understanding of strategy is presented by the work of the Prussian war theorist Carl von Clausewitz, *On War*.

- The strategic thought approach supports *substantial, security-related* policy advice based on a high level of scientific interdisciplinarity, albeit guided by core subjects, which *cannot be substituted by civilian disciplines*, while *at the same time* scientifically supporting the operational implementation of the strategic ends, which is the actual *unique benefit of military science for the security of the state*.

The steering function of this strategic thought via the subjects of military science becomes necessary only if it is assumed that substantial, ends-led, security-related advice for policymakers is part of the spectrum of tasks involved in strategic thought. Conversely, such a substantial advisory contribution is only possible if the steering influence of strategic thought produces organically structured military science that enables this service.

The answers to the questions of whether strategy should be understood as focused on the political objective, and whether strategic thought should reflect this understanding in terms of content and make a substantial contribution to consultancy, the added value of which is based on the fact that it also covers the scientific underpinning of military operational command and steers the subjects of military science towards a unique, non-substitutable benefit for the security of the state, represent the essential criteria for determining the relationship between strategy and the military.

Whether strategy is now primarily understood as being ends-led (leading question: "What for; what purpose does political action serve?") or implementation-led (leading question: "How; in what way is the specified objective implemented?") is the essential preliminary decision from which all further questions can flow and which divides the current theories of strategy into two basic schools of thought. The characteristic distinction between the security policy approach and the strategic thought approach described above also reflects to some degree the dichotomy between ends-led and implementation-led approaches.

Only if strategy is understood as being guided by a long-term, national ends-led approach, can the military make its advisory contribution at the interface with political decision-making – in other words, only then can we speak of a mutual relationship between strategy and the military, i.e. of strategic decision-making on the one and strategic thought on the other hand.

Starting out from an ends-led understanding of strategy could result in a developing relationship between strategy and the military which is defined by the following key points:

- The political leadership has the undivided decision-making responsibility for defining the strategic ends of the state, its implementation, the resources needed to achieve them and the risks to be accepted. In defining the strategic ends, the political leadership will seek advice from senior military commanders in preparation for decisions. It also incorporates the military's feedback on the derived resource requirements or the identified residual risk in its iterative assessment cycles.

- The senior military command advises the political leadership in preparation for decision-making with regard to the definition of the strategic ends. It is suitable for this purpose due to its cross-policy evaluation logic abstracted from military command principles and a core subject-controlled, interdisciplinary military science[3]. In contrast to other university disciplines, it is the only one that covers the entire escalation arc, from strategic policy advice and operational implementation planning to the deployment of the armed forces as the *ultima ratio* of state survival.

If the state's escalation track were not conceived up to and including conflict resolution through physical force or the deployment of the military defence component, there would be no holistic strategy. If the escalation track was thought through to the end, but the military was not consulted (especially in the case of physical conflict), the political decision regarding the strategic ends could not be made on the basis of the results of the implementation planning, the resource-related feasibility assessment from a military point of view, or the determination of the residual risk[4]. Coordinating the strategic ends, the resources required for implementation and the risk to be taken could then hardly be achieved in the quality of the iterative assessment cycles Carl von Clausewitz envisages in his *ends-ways-means* and in the hermeneutic circle he derives from Hegel's dialectics.

With his work *On War*, the Prussian war theorist Carl von Clausewitz provides the central theoretical basis for the strategic advisory role of the military leadership with regard to political decision-makers, which must necessarily be considered simultaneously with the ability to scientifically underpin applied operational command. For this reason and because there is no alternative to the basic idea of a military science that strives to provide a unique and non-substitutable benefit for society, the work of Clausewitz is particularly emphasised in the presentation of the theoretical strategy approaches.

---

[3] The military could make this contribution to strategic planning and implementation by developing a core subject-led, organic, interdisciplinary and institutionalised military science which ensures university-level recognised research and teaching for both the discipline of strategic thought and applied armed forces command.

[4] In this case, the military would have no choice but to implement the military part of the overall strategy, i.e. a clear limitation to the implementation dimension, which would no longer have anything to do with strategy in the whole-of-nation sense. Even if this task were to be semantically defined in terms of a strategic quality, it would essentially remain implementation without any substantive contribution to the strategic ends. Consequently, there would be no more interaction at the interface with political decision-makers and, thus, no more relationship between strategy and the military. The necessity of an interdisciplinary approach to military science research and teaching which is geared towards policy areas could thus no longer be justified.

Even in the case of a strategic concept that does not provide for the military to contribute to the strategic ends and thus limits the military leadership to the implementation of the given strategic ends, it remains an inherent task of commanders and staffs, simply because of the hybrid character of armed conflicts; the aim is to make an interdisciplinary assessment, to identify the enemy's long-term strategic objectives and, due to the *ultima ratio* character of armed forces, to think through the entire escalation chain from the definition of the strategic ends to actual deployment. Strategic thought will thus remain the core content of military command training, regardless of whether or not the military leadership is involved in the definition of the strategic ends. Because the principles of this strategic thought must be formulated at a very high level of abstraction in order to support independent mission command instead of restricting it through rigid recipes for action, some of them, as Ångström and Widén explain in their work *Contemporary Military Theory* (2015, p. 36), are not bound to a specific understanding of strategy or a specific command echelon, but can be applied in an adapted form in a useful way, for example at operational or tactical level.

4. Strategy theories

In the course of gaining an insight into military science, the study of classical theories of strategy initially aims to provide a broad overview, then to distil the elementary functional principles of strategic ideas common to most approaches, and finally to identify those approaches that have hardly any overlaps with the theories that are characterised by similar principles. Each strategy theory and its underlying understanding of strategy has its justification for the relevant area of application.

However, as this publication is concerned with the relationship between strategy on the one hand and the military, and in particular military science, on the other, and since the latter primarily serves an understanding of strategy that aims to ensure the long-term survival of the state and its society across all policy areas, the further derivation of determining functional principles of strategic thought will be founded on theories that are based on precisely this understanding of strategy and that emanate from the state as a strategic actor.

4.1. A possible categorisation of approaches to strategy theory

The following categorisation is intended to make it easier for students of military science to gain an overview of the broad field of strategy theories (also of those theories which nominally operate under the term strategy theory but which do not correspond to the understanding of strategy on which this study is based, i.e. strategy theories in a broader sense). These strategy theories in a broader sense can be classified according to the following criteria:

- **According to the respective operator/user:**

Strategic actors include, for example, the state or society, private management, public administration, emergency services, scientific disciplines, and diplomats (right down to the individual in terms of their personal life planning).

- **According to the content characteristics of strategic thought:**

Strategic thought can focus *either on the strategic ends or on the operational or tactical implementation* of the set strategic ends (operational management concepts in private sector management would be an example of an implementation-led strategy).

One special form is made up of approaches which do not seek to find specific ends and which are only geared indirectly at the implementation of the set ends, but which instead offer a toolbox of techniques, methods and ruses (stratagems) which are intended to serve the bare preservation of power (instrumental logic of preservation of power) without asking about the moral legitimacy of the set ends. These categories include, for example, Sun Tzu over long stretches of his work *The Art of War*, Machiavelli and his *Il Principe* and *Discorsi* as well as Gracián's aphorisms in *The Art of Worldly Wisdom*.

- **According to the hierarchical level of legitimacy of the strategic ends:**

Depending on the political system of the state/alliance/group of states, the following strategy hierarchies can be identified: *National Interest-Grand Strategy, Grand Strategy-National Strategy, (National) Comprehensive Strategy-Sub-Strategies.* The hierarchy *vision-mission-corporate strategy* is frequently encountered in private business management.

If strategy is interpreted as a system's original ends-defining echelon, making decisions in a holistic and cross-policy manner, then any subordinate strategy level would be a *contradictio in adiecto*. This contradiction is resolved if the subordinate levels of strategy are only granted limited cross-policy areas and/or competence to set objectives and have to focus more on the implementation aspect (ways) of strategy. By definition, only the top level of the hierarchy can meet the requirement of the original, holistic purpose.

- **According to the origin of the underlying, abstracted functional principles or according to the scientific discipline from the perspective of which the theory was developed:**
  - The political science/security policy approach manifested in the theories of international relations: theories in this category serve as preparatory advice to political decision-makers – in contrast to the military-scien-

tific approach, however, they lack expertise in the area of operational implementation, planning and command in the deployment of armed forces as the *ultima ratio* of the strategic escalation track. The military-scientific approach, on the other hand, is based on the simultaneous ability to think strategically and to implement operations, and also provides the necessary, technically sound feedback to political decision-makers in the iterative strategic decision-making process with regard to resource requirements and the resulting residual risk. A distinction can be made between positivist (realism and liberalism, both including their respective further developments) and constructivist theories.

o   Geopolitical/geostrategic theoretical approaches: these approaches were developed as a special form of the realist approaches in the bipolar world order period after World War II, and often tend to narrow strategic thought to the pursuit of territorial gain and hegemonic power. In the absence of alternative approaches, they therefore almost inevitably lead to strategic options that result in a physically violent conflict, or they are instrumentalised/abused to legitimise arguments for such a path (for example, Huntington's *Clash of Civilisations* could be deliberately misinterpreted as a call for a cultural war).

o   Economic theory approaches (also known as operational management concepts in private enterprise management): this category includes ends-led theories which make statements about the influence of the economy on the overall strategic development of the state (for instance, Friedrich August Hayek, winner of the 1974 Nobel Prize in Economics), but also those which focus on the implementation aspect of strategy and therefore actually produce operational management concepts (i.e. vision, mission or management concepts which implement the strategic corporate ends).

o   The military-scientific approach based on functional principles abstracted from military command theory and military assessment logic: many of these theoretical approaches, in accordance with the underlying understanding of strategy (or the role assigned to the military in the state decision-making process), tend to focus on the operational implementation aspect of strategy, i.e. primarily on answering the question of how to implement the given strategic ends. As a result, they often have only limited relevance for the whole-of-nation-strategic level – and contribute little to explaining the relationship between strategy and military. Examples of theories in this category, which are *nevertheless aimed at the ends* or the ends in conjunction with operational implementation, include the approaches of Ångström and Widén (*Contemporary Military Theory*) and Carl von Clausewitz (*On War*).

Strategic approaches to naval warfare (Geoffrey Till, Julian Stafford Corbett, Alfred Thayer Mahan) and air warfare (Giulio Douhet, Hugh Montague Trenchard) often interact closely with geopolitical/geostrategic theories.

- According to the respective cultural region:
  - e.g. Confucian, Hindu, Western Occidental and Islamic cultural regions.
- According to the time of origin:
  - Greek and Roman thinkers. This category often combines state theory, military and geostrategic approaches. Due to their high degree of abstraction, they can still be highly relevant today. Thucydides' abridged statement, for example, that the exaggerated fear of an established, powerful strategic actor (Athens) in the face of an emerging challenger of limited power (Sparta) would lead to a long-lasting, terrible war (the Peloponnesian War), is reflected in the Chinese (deliberately misleading and misinterpreted) narrative underlying today's tensions with the USA (see Graham Allison's *Destined for War*).
  - Epoch-related strategic theories
  - Contemporary strategic theories

As the theme of the publication is the relationship between strategy and the military, and as such a relationship begins to exist only when a whole-of-nation understanding of strategy and an ends-driven competence in strategic thought and advisory roles on the part of the military leadership are assumed, the ultimate derivation of functional principles of strategic thought has to be based on those theoretical approaches in which the state is the strategic actor, which focus on determining strategic ends, are supported by the national interest, are based on the evaluation logic of military science, and have been developed for the Western cultural region.

4.2. Sample strategy theory approaches for selected categories

- For the category of Greek and Roman thinkers[5], the following approaches can be given as examples. Aeneas (textbook of strategy, focuses more on the implementation aspect of strategy, has parallels with Sun-Tzu), Asklepiodotos (deals mainly with the aspects of army organisation, structure and armament of formations), Polybios (evokes the political purpose), Caesar, Onasander, Flavius Vegetius Renatus (discuss the distinction between direct and indirect strategy), Leo the Wise, Thucydides, Xenophon, Pericles, Alexander.
- For the military-scientific approach

---

[5] For a description of the Greek and Roman thinkers, see Stahel 1996.

o Carl von Clausewitz *On War*: the most essential theoretical basis, which, based on a specifically military assessment logic, starts from an ends-led understanding of strategy and sees the task of senior military leadership and of military science as a whole in the simultaneous provision of advice to policymakers and the operational implementation of the strategic ends set by the policymakers. Apart from a few more recent approaches, such as that of Ångström and Widén (*Contemporary Military Theory*), this field appears to be entirely under-theorised. A separate explanatory subchapter is therefore devoted to Clausewitz's theoretical approach.

o Ångström and Widén *Contemporary Military Theory*: their approach to military theory is thematically broader than strategic theory in the strict sense, but it contains essential, profound statements and derivations that are essential for a comprehensive understanding of strategy and for determining a contemporary relationship between strategy and the military.

o Approaches to maritime strategy: Julian Stafford Corbett, *Some Principles of Maritime Strategy*. London, Longmans, Green and Company, 1911. Alfred Thayer Mahan, *The Influence of Sea Power upon History, 1660–1783*, 1890. Alfred Thayer Mahan, *The Influence of Sea Power upon the French Revolution and Empire, 1793–1812*, 1892. (Jomini of naval strategy) Geoffrey Till, *Modern Sea Power: An Introduction London*, Brassey's Defence, 1987.

o Basil Henry Liddell Hart, *Strategy,* second revised edition, London, Faber and Faber, 1967.

o Rupert Smith, *The Utility of Force*, London, Penguin Books, 2005.

o Antoine-Henri Jomini, *Précis de l'Art de la Guerre: Des Principales Combinaisons de la Stratégie, de la Grande Tactique et de la Politique Militaire*, Brussells, Meline, Cans et Compagnie, 1838.

o Trevor Nevitt Dupuy, *A genius for war: The German army and general staff, 1807-1945*, 1977.

- For the economic approach
o Henry Mintzberg, *The rise and fall of strategic planning*.

o Hinterhuber, Hans H., *Strategische Unternehmungsführung*, third edition, de Gruyter, Berlin, 1984.

o Harvard principle: Fischer, Roger and William Ury, *Getting to Yes: Negotiating Agreement Without Giving In: The Secret to Successful Negotiation*, 1981.

- For approaches concerning instrumental logic of power maintenance

- o Sun Tzu, *The Art of War* (largely focused on techniques of power acquisition/maintenance – strategic where war is the last resort)
- o Harro von Senger, *Strategeme. Lebens- und Überlebenslisten der Chinesen – die berühmten 36 Strategeme aus drei Jahrtausenden*, Bern, 1979.
- o Niccolò Machiavelli, *Discorsi sopra la prima deca di Tito Livio*, 1517, *Il principe*, 1532
- o Baltasar Gracián y Morales S.J., *The Art of Worldly Wisdom*, 1647.
- For geopolitical/geostrategic approaches as a starting point for later theories of realism
  - o Thucydides, *The Peloponnesian War*, fourth century B.C.
  - o Halford John Mackinder, *The Geographical Pivot of History*, 1904 The rimland-heartland theory is still a key factor in the strategic power relations between Russia, China, the EU and the USA today, because a rapprochement between the continental powers (pivot) would risk marginalising the transatlantic policymakers, which could ultimately lead to a confrontation between the USA and China (cf. Gompert et al. 2016)
  - o Carl Schmitt, *Land and Sea*, Plutarch Press, 1997. (original year of publication: 1954)
  - o Carl Schmitt, *The Nomos of the Earth in the International Law of the Jus Publicum Europaeum*, Telos Press, 2003. (Original year of publication: 1950)
  - o John Joseph Mearsheimer, *The Tragedy of Great Power Politics*, New York, Norton, 2001. Mearsheimer represents the offensive variety of neo-realism and could provide the theoretical basis for the current US position on offshore balancing.
  - o Samuel Phillips Huntington, *The Clash of Civilization and the Remaking of World Order*, 1996.
  - o Samuel Phillips Huntington, *The Soldier and the State: The Theory and Politics of Civil-Military Relations*, 1957.
  - o Edward Nicolae Luttwack, *Strategy: The Logic of War and Peace*, Cambridge, Massachusetts, 1987.
  - *The Grand Strategy of the Roman Empire from the First Century AD to the Third*, Baltimore, Johns Hopkins University Press, 1976; with his approaches concerning predatory capitalism he is also at the interface with economic theories.
- For the political science approach (IR theories)

- o Realism theory: Morgenthau, Hans Joachim, *Politics Among Nations. The Struggle for Power and Peace*, New York, Alfred A. Knopf. Carr, Edward Hallett, *1939. The Twenty Years' Crisis, 1919–1939. An Introduction to the Study of International Relations*, London, Macmillan, 1948
- o Neo-realism: Waltz, Kenneth Neal, *Man, the State, and War*, New York, Columbia University Press, 1959. *Theory of International Politics*, Reading, Addison-Wesley, 1979
- o Precursor to liberalism: Locke, John, *Two Treatises of Government*, 1690. Immanuel Kant, *Zum Ewigen Frieden. Ein philosophischer Entwurf*, 1795.
- o Neo-liberalism: Keohane, Robert Owen, *After Hegemony. Cooperation and Discord in the World Political Economy*, Princeton University Press, 1984.

  Nye, Joseph Samuel, *Bound to Lead: The Changing Nature Of American Power*, New York, Basic Books, 1990.
- o Constructivism: Critical security research: Buzan, Barry, Wæver, Ole, & De Wilde, Jaap, *Security. A new framework for analysis*, Lynne Rienner Publishers, 1998.
- ▪ Concerning strategy and responsibility: Maximilian Carl Emil Weber, "Politik als Beruf", in, *Geistige Arbeit als Beruf. Vier Vorträge vor dem Freistudentischen Bund. Zweiter Vortrag*, Munich, 1919. Niklas Luhmann, *Introduction to Systems Theory*, 1984.

4.3. The theoretical approach of Carl von Clausewitz[6]

With his work *On War*, the Prussian war theorist Carl von Clausewitz created the basis for military science based on interdependence or the need for simultaneity between the two capability strands *strategic advice* and *applied operational command*. It is therefore based on a concept of strategy which takes into account the above-mentioned need for simultaneity, but which can easily confuse especially non-German speaking readers. His concept of strategy includes both overall strategic thought for the purpose of advice at the interface

---

[6] Regarding the entire subchapter 5.3. see Peischel 2020 (pp. 17-52), where the Prussian war theorist's trend-setting approaches to strategic thought are presented in more detail and in a larger context.

with political decision-making[7],[8] as well as applied operational command[9]. As can be seen clearly and without contradiction in the context at each point, both strands are different in content, but are only assigned one and the same semantic term. This may be the starting point for the fact that many contemporary approaches only draw upon the implementation aspect (ways-orientation) of his concept of strategy and think they can refer to Clausewitz with this limited interpretation.

---

[7] "Even so, it is only in the highest realms of strategy that intellectual complications and extreme diversities of factors and relationships occur. At that level there is *little or no difference between strategy, policy and statesmanship*, and there, as we have already said, their influence is greater in questions of quantity and scale than in forms of execution" (von Clausewitz 1989, p. 178), even clearer in the original German text: "Aber auch bei diesen [geistigen Kräften] sind die Geistesentwicklungen und die große Mannigfaltigkeit der Größen und Verhältnisse nur in den höchsten Regionen der **Strategie** zu suchen, da, wo sie **an Politik und Staatskunst grenzt oder vielmehr beides selbst wird**" (von Clausewitz 1980, p. 347) – Clausewitz not only means that at this level there is hardly any difference between strategy, politics and statecraft, but explicitly that strategy itself *becomes* politics and statecraft.

[8] "The first, the supreme, the most far-reaching act of judgment that the statesman and commander have to make is to establish by that test **the kind of war on which they are embarking**; neither mistaking it for, nor trying to turn it into, something that is alien to its nature. This is the **first of all strategic questions and the most comprehensive**" (von Clausewitz 1989, p. 88) – German original: "Der erste, der großartigste, der entschiedenste Akt des Urteils nun, welchen der Staatsmann und Feldherr ausübt, ist der, **daß er den Krieg, welchen er unternimmt, in dieser Beziehung richtig erkenne**, ihn nicht für etwas nehme oder zu etwas machen wolle, was er der Natur der Verhältnisse nach nicht sein kann. Dies ist also **die erste, umfassendste aller strategischen Fragen**" (von Clausewitz 1980, p. 212).

[9] „It follows that the *strategist* must go on campaign himself. Detailed orders can then be given on the spot, allowing the general plan to be adjusted to the modifications that are continuously required" (von Clausewitz 1989, p. 177). The German original: „... so folgt von selbst, dass *die Strategie* mit ins Feld ziehen muß, um das Einzelne an Ort und Stelle anzuordnen und für das Ganze die Modifikationen zu treffen, die unaufhörlich erforderlich werden. Sie kann also ihre Hand in keinem Augenblick von dem Werke abziehen" (*von Clausewitz 1980, Seite 345*).[10] Hartmann describes that Clausewitz achieves this synthesis by means of a procedure based on the "hermeneutic circle" already considered by Schleiermacher and Hegel (cf. Hartmann 1998, pp. 102-106). This procedure can be applied to the iterative coupling of a pragmatic (operational forward planning from the present point in time into the future) with a visionary (backward planning from a strategic ends "projected" into the future, i.e. from a strategic ends that has been anticipated back to the present planning point in time) approach and represents the basis of the operational management procedure, which is based on a working hypothesis determined a priori rationally, with subsequent empirical proof in staff work and which was presented in the conference proceedings for the Vienna Strategy Conference 2016.

The main reasons why Clausewitz's approach points the way forward for the relationship between strategy and the military:

- because he sees military science more clearly than other thinkers under the aspect of the simultaneous need for strategic thought (for the purposes of advising policymakers) and scientifically supported operational command;

- because he expands upon Jomini's doctrine, which is based on the belief that war can be understood mathematically and is bound by rules, to include the spiritual respectively humanistic dimension of military command;

- because he bases his theory on a dialectical approach, to be found via a hermeneutical circle, from *a priori* rational thought and abstracted empirical findings;

- because, carrying on from Helmuth von Moltke the Elder, he clearly defines the boundaries between strategic ends, planning and independent command (`sense´ of judgement; in the original German version: `Takt des Urteils`) of commanders at all echelons;

- because, although he assumes a clear primacy of politics (*the continuation of politics by other means*) with his ends-ways-means relationship, he nevertheless provides for strategic advice from senior military leadership, which is geared towards defining the state's purpose and thus inevitably goes beyond mere operational implementation (the prevailing perception of the ends-ways-means relation in the NATO context bases indeed on a literal translation of the Zweck-Ziel-Mittel Relation which, however, in contrast to Clausewitz's approach, limits the military and military science to the operational implementation component, i.e. to a ways-dominated understanding of strategy);

- because he calls for mental abilities, especially creative ingenuity and *a priori* rational thought from military commanders in order to do justice to the intellectual as well as ethical dimension of war, *inter alia* by enabling them to assess the content of strategic objectives, which is a fundamental difference from theories that merely offer toolboxes of techniques, pragmatic instructions for action and stratagems for maintaining power (Sun Tzu, Machiavelli and Gracián, mostly).

The fact that Clausewitz's theoretical understanding (on which the present study is also based) is a normative one is evident in his attempt to analyse a blueprint behind the phenomenon of war, i.e. the interaction of its key factors and functional principles, in order to be able to direct and control it in such a way that it serves to ensure the long-term survival of the state.

The following two pairs of seeming opposites, which he actually works through in a dialectical rather than antagonistic relationship to each other, support his understanding of theory:

- the reciprocal relationship between theory and practice, which dissolves dialectically because, on the one hand, the purpose of his theory lies in the shaping of reality (which also represents the practical relevance of his theory) and because, on the other hand, practical experience from Prussia's defeats by Napoleon (above all the battle of Jena and Auerstedt, under the influence of which the Four Main Deficits emerged, which are almost timelessly valid and can still be held responsible for the failure of armies) flows into the theory he developed, and
- the reciprocal relationship between theory and empiricism, more precisely the relationship between *a priori* rational and empirically guided theory formation which only seems antagonistic because Clausewitz, for the purpose of empirical validation, couples his theorems, derived *a priori* rationally in an iterative process (the hermeneutic circle) with the knowledge he has gained from abstracted analyses of battles, i.e. shorn of epochal reference.

It is precisely because Carl von Clausewitz explores both strands of his concepts of strategy (strategic thought, applied operational command) in their interdependence that he succeeds in developing a theory that goes far beyond a theory of *warfare* – that is actually more of a *strategic* theory and can thus form the basis for a military science that provides an non-substitutable security benefit for society. His understanding of theory might be based on the ancient Greek θεωρέειν, which initially describes the consideration of truth through pure thought and, in contrast to knowledge gained empirically, focuses on understanding gained through thought. The normative (as opposed to explanatory) character of his theoretical approach is demonstrated by the fact that his theory creates an image, a model of reality, investigates why which key factors function according to which principles, in order to become effective in shaping reality from this knowledge. Following Kant's model, Clausewitz recognises in the *a priori* rational approach a source of theory formation which is to be evaluated as being at least as important as the empirical one. As mentioned above, he resolves the apparent antagonism between the *a priori* rational and empirical approaches by means of a hermeneutic circle corresponding to Hegel's dialectic[10]. This iterative oscillation between a theoretical and

---

[10] Hartmann describes that Clausewitz achieves this synthesis by means of a procedure based on the "hermeneutic circle" already considered by Schleiermacher and Hegel (cf. Hartmann 1998, pp. 102-106). This procedure can be applied to the iterative coupling of a pragmatic (operational forward planning from the present point in time into the future) with a visionary

an empirical approach, which at the same time also correlates with the relationship between a visionary and a pragmatic approach, is not only reflected in the operational decision making processes of the Prussian armed forces, but is also likely to represent the essential achievement of Clausewitz's military science methodology. By transferring his original split between theory and empiricism into a planned methodology, the result of which is a normative theory resulting from the dialectical synthesis of both approaches, Clausewitz developed a fundamental functional principle of strategic thought. The fact that this approach, primarily in the German-speaking world, has become a leading approach is one of the proofs of the cultural region-specific aspects of strategic thought. In contrast, Ångström and Widén assume an understanding of theory that includes both "statements that are not yet entirely proven and those that, through a great number of experiments and/or observations, have proven to be valid" (Angstrom & Widen 2015, p. 4), but in both cases gives greater weight to the fundamental necessity of empirical validation and does not explicitly call for the *a priori* rational theory-construction approach. Derived from this, the relationship between theory and practice is described as an antagonistic one that forces military theory to choose between practical and explanatory utility (Angstrom & Widen 2015, p. 4) – a dialectic bridging between theory and practice pursuant to Hegelian patterns is not explicitly considered in the first approach. If one now recognises an essential functional principle of strategic thought in the methodology of theory construction, it becomes clear to what extent, from the perspective of the respective command philosophy, military theory and the strategy approaches resulting from it can be justified and yet at the same time differ from one cultural region to another, even within continental Europe, and how enriching a comparison and scientific discourse on the strategic evaluation logic that can be derived from it would be.

The dialectical contrast between theory and empiricism is also reflected in the military-scientific methodology that runs through *On War* (cf. Peischel 2017b, pp. 138-170). An essential functional principle exemplary for strategic thought can be recognised in the constant oscillation between the two worlds of thought (which must by no means be interpreted as a contradiction) and in the fact that Clausewitz, up to and including the revision of the First Book of *On War*, did not decide on one or the other, but formed his theory as a dialectic synthesis of both poles. This approach is also characteristic of the

---

(backward planning from a strategic ends "projected" into the future, i.e. from a strategic ends that has been anticipated back to the present planning point in time) approach and represents the basis of the operational management procedure, which is based on a working hypothesis determined a priori rationally, with subsequent empirical proof in staff work and which was presented in the conference proceedings for the Vienna Strategy Conference 2016.

predominant continental European scientific methodology. Clausewitz analyses the theoretical approaches of Kant, Hegel, Fichte and Schleiermacher on the one hand, and on the other hand he also examines some 125 battles in order to be able to use them, freed from historical references, to prove his theoretical approaches empirically. On this basis, he *inter alia* develops his theory on the Absolute War and the Paradoxical Trinity (in the German original: 'Die wunderliche Dreifaltigkeit'), in order to finally reach again the practical applicability of this theory. Clausewitz's repeated change of perspective between theoretical and empirical approach must not be interpreted as fickleness or as an attempt to find the better of the two approaches, but rather as the synthetic coupling of both approaches for the purpose of creating a theory, a scope and significance unknown up to that point, the application of which can also achieve overall strategic assessment and practical command superiority on the battlefield. As in the course of empirically guided theory formation, Clausewitz examines battles for regularly recurring successes/failures under the same conditions. However, he goes beyond a purely statistical evaluation, because he filters out and excludes factors from theoretical considerations that can only be relevant from the perspective of a specific epoch. Moreover, his form of *a priori* rational thought also enables him, from just a few battles sifted out according to the above criteria, or even from a single battle, i.e. without a broader sample, to draw conclusions on generally valid theoretical doctrines - just as he used his experiences in the twin battles of Jena and Auerstedt to determine the `Four Main Deficits´ of Prussian top-down, dogmatic, lectern-based teaching applied at that time and thus the systemic reasons for the catastrophic defeat. In this way, he also derives very fundamental deficits, whose abstract validity still convinces today, and which illustrate the still widespread cardinal vices or symptoms of subpar military or civil command structures. In the *a priori* rational part of Clausewitz's theorising, the idea of Faust in the study comes to mind, for whom a table, a piece of paper, a quill, some ink and the pale glow of a candle are enough to understand whatever binds the world's innermost core together, and who trusts that he carries the essential principles of thought necessary for his judgement in his head from birth on, even without extensive empirical evidence. There is nothing new about the process in which a possible theory explaining the phenomenon is inferred inductively from a large number of observations and then the attempt is made to deductively arrive at predictions for future individual cases. The innovative aspect of Clausewitz's approach is that it arrives at the theory via two initially largely independent approaches (the theoretical and the empirical), which are subsequently synthesised. The dialectic between the separation and subsequent synthesis of theory and empiricism includes the added value of strategic performance that military science can offer beyond the military sphere. In Uwe Hartmann's (cf. 1998, pp. 9-13) work, this connection is illustrated in the metaphor of a roof which represents Clausewitz's theory of war, or his military-scientific method, and which rests on two pillars, namely theory and empiricism. In contrast to this, the concept of strategy as represented by Piehler and Houston does not contain an *a priori* rational path to theory formation, but derives the qualification for military tactics, operations and strategy[11] mainly from a solid understanding of military history, which suggests a primarily empirical approach. The fact that military history is declared to be an essential basis for military science, including the operational and tactical levels of command, leads to the assumption that this is indeed the analysis of historical battles – as Clausewitz had done in order to cover the empirical proof of his theory formation – but without accompanying this empirical part with an *a priori* rational, theoretical approach. The implied proximity to battle analysis provides a further indication that strategy here does not refer to cross-policy, overall strategic thinking, and that instead of focusing on the ends, it is more likely to focus on the implementation of strategic thought.

Beyond the dialectically linked pairs of terms *theory & practice* and *theory & empiricism*, which are described in detail above, the guiding function of Clausewitz's work can be explained in more detail by means of the following further core statements, which ultimately lead to the constitutive functional principles of strategic thought in the sense of an understanding of strategy to be proposed:

- **"Practical experience versus a priori rational thought":**
the example of Clausewitz's methodological approach teaches that an overestimation of experience as a factor can limit the scope for systematic scientific research into strategic command/decision-making processes and often leads to an `*unsystemic*´ lessons-learned approach, i.e. an approach which does not ask whether a failure arises from a fundamentally inadequate structure/process control or an unsuitable functional principle (i.e. whether the probability of the failure happening again can be reduced by changing the system parameters), or whether it is a matter of more or less statistically distributed, random events. It was precisely with his battle analyses, in which he was not primarily concerned with accumulating a wealth of experience, i.e. collecting data that can be evaluated statistically, but rather with the theory-based derivation of principles that are supposed to apply generally and detached from histrorical

---

[11] „Military Tactics, Operations, and Strategy – This aspect of the discipline, grounded in a solid understanding of military history, addresses the military and the use of organized coercive force …" (Piehler & Johnson 2013, p. 884);

reference points, that Clausewitz laid the foundations for a systemic lessons-learned process and thus for an accurate follow-up to strategic assessment and decision-making processes, intended to accompany the process. With a view to a possible overestimation of experience in strategic and operational command, Frederick the Great, when his officers questioned the value of military studies and in return emphasised their extensive combat experience, is said to have once stated ironically: "If experience alone (...) were sufficient to form great commanders, the mules of Prince Eugene would have been such commanders" (as cited in Demeter 1965, p. 78).

- **"Inductive versus a priori rational theory construction":**
Clausewitz contrasted the inductive method, still predominant in the Anglo-American world today, with an a priori rational approach oriented towards the search for the essence of things. He combined both insofar as he carried out a theory-based derivation of universal principles from his war-historical examples on the one hand and, on the other hand, tried to validate his theoretical approaches by means of empirical findings. In this, of course, he built on foundations already created inter alia by Kant and Hegel – the concrete application to the military-scientific dimension is, however, undoubtedly to be attributed to him. With this, a tool had been found with which the induction problem later addressed by Popper could be overcome.

- **Critical-analytical thought versus operational creativity:**
this distinction refers to the command performance-enhancing value of separation (separation in the sense of a chronological staggering or the assignment of tasks to different staff cells) on the one hand between strategic ends definition and operational implementation planning, and on the other hand between the operational-creative identification of possibilities and the critical-rational corroboration/falsification of the working hypothesis given by the commander. Operational creativity is one of the most important prerequisites for the development of proposals for strategic ends planning that prepare the ground for decisions, particularly for the capability strand in military science geared towards consultation on a national level at the interface with political decision-makers, i.e. for the area of strategic thought.

- **Action versus thought:**
in this pair of opposites, action would be understood as a more experience-led ability geared towards the actual execution of tasks, correlating to the operational implementation level. The civilian concept of management is also based on implementation on behalf of another with a limited element of discretion (see *manu agere* – leading the horse into the stable at the master's behest – or *mansionem agere* – running the house of the absent master at his behest). *Planning* correlates with action in so far as it thinks ahead into the future by

means of experience-based command thinking and thus creates the basis for the implementation (*ways*) of the strategic ends set by the policymakers. By contrast, *thinking* builds on operational (as opposed to expressive) creativity and *a priori* rational talent and thus points to the strategic level, i.e. to the question of the purpose (*ends*) of political action. In order to be able to unfurl its full potential in the category of thought reserved for it, the strategic level passes on the ends resulting from the assessment to the operational level for implementation after a resource-related feasibility study has been carried out, and then steps aside itself. Thought correlates with leading in the strategic sense, i.e. by identifying ends. Clausewitz also makes this conscious distinction between strategic ends and operational implementation – without, however, introducing a separate term for the two qualities. Clausewitz interprets strategy, as described in the introduction, to mean, on the one hand, the quality of leading committed to thought, operational creativity and the political goal as well as the operational implementation of the strategically defined purpose – but without, as already noted, introducing a separate term for each of the two qualities.

- **Pragmatic instructions for action versus the `sense of judgement':** pragmatic instructions for action dominated in armed forces in which enlightened, humanistic education was not rolled out to the lowest echelons of the command hierarchy, so that leaders could be assumed to make a situational decision in a given combat situation or could have been expected to do so. As a rule, this was the case with armed forces which were either so strong in manpower that this training would not have been affordable, or so strong in material that they did not need such compensation for numerical inferiority. Martin van Creveld's (cf. 1982, Chapter 6) judgement on the size and effectiveness of US planning staffs in the Second World War and the contingency plans they drew up shows the problem of instructions for action created with foresight particularly clearly. One of the main driving forces behind the development of Clausewitz's theory of strategy is probably the recognition that the approach of viewing war deterministically and treating it as a phenomenon that can be grasped and controlled in numbers and algorithms inevitably leads to a fatal misjudgement – namely, that it can be calculated mathematically in advance and can therefore be directed by instructions for action and contingency plans. One of the most outstanding proponents of this thesis was the Swiss theorist Jomini. The result of this perception was that military science, and thus military command theory, was limited to the tactical and operational level and had to abstain from the topic of strategic thought and thus political advice, because it simply had no answers to questions of the intellectual dimension of warfare, friction and chance, the meeting of independent opposing wills and the independent ability of commanders at all levels to judge the given situation (sense of judgement, martial genius, divinatory component, *coup d'oeil*)[12] for themselves. Jomini's approach of treating war as a phenomenon that could be understood mathematically and abstaining from the task of strategic advice was in keeping with the Prussian equestrian spirit, not least because political strategy was regarded as less than honourable and therefore not worthy of the officer class and because pragmatic instructions for action relieved them of the task of making complex assessments of the situation – and thus cleared their minds for the actual battle. But Jomini could not be quoted in good conscience because he was the theoretician of the arch-enemy, Napoleon. Clausewitz does not deny the correctness and necessity of Jomini's mathematical and tactical findings or his equations of comparison of forces – he merely adds an additional, completely new intellectual dimension to war, its political-strategic relevance, the factor of friction or chance, the clash of independent opposing wills, and a military understanding of command that encompasses all the personality forces and talents. The main reason for the dispute between Clausewitz and Jomini is probably that the former vehemently denies that a set of pragmatic theorems on warfare, which lacks these constitutive elements of the intellectual dimension, can be considered a high-brow theory at all. Although little read at first, Clausewitz is later celebrated as the spiritual father of Prussian military success in the wars of unification. Strictly speaking, however, it was precisely the latter, the Schlieffen Plan respectively its implementation, and a long series of major battles extending into the Second World War, that showed that the general staffs had barely absorbed any content past Jomini, i.e. the strategic dimension of Clausewitz's thinking. One might be forgiven for thinking that they would have been happy to be able to finally apply the familiar Jomini as patriotically correct, marked *made in Prussia*. Moltke the Elder, who had begun to push back the dwindling influence of politics down to the operational command level, to limit the former to the determination and specification of the beginning and end of the war, reduced Clausewitz to his operational calculation, misjudged the intellectual-strategic dimension of his theory and thus did not follow the implicit requirement to advise policymakers on content while respecting their strategic decision-making primacy. This assessment is also shared by Jehuda Wallach, who, in his work *Dogma der Vernichtungsschlacht*, concludes that the Prussian general staff did not recognise the actual message of Clausewitz's theory and deliberately withdrew to operational-tactical contexts – obviously not, however, as is often claimed by the military for self-protection, under

---

"Military science has always a narrow, limited, and technical connotation and is considered to be a subset of the larger body of knowledge known as the military art" (Piehler & Johnson 2013, p. 881).[13] Regarding this subchapter, cf.: Peischel 2017a p. 12-30 and cf.: Peischel 2020, pp. 46-48;

pressure from politics, but rather of its own free will. This voluntary self-limitation may have been justified by the Prussian equestrian spirit mentioned earlier, by the classification of thought in political dimensions as an activity incompatible with the code of honour of an upright officer, by the lack of the humanistic educational substructure which would have been necessary to follow Clausewitz's conclusions, but ultimately also by the unwillingness to face the challenging task of strategic thought. The latter motive is likely to have had a decisive influence on the relationship between strategy and the military up to the present day.

5. Functional principles of strategy/strategic thought

Since, as we have seen above, each of the different understandings of strategy is legitimate and has its specific use in the area of application in question, this study will not seek to evaluate which of the *existing* definitions of strategy is the more appropriate.

Rather, from the point of view of military science, it is necessary to ask how the content of strategic thought must be shaped and defined in order to be able to provide advice on state survival across all policy areas. It is necessary to generate a logical and functional concept for strategic thought and to prove its actual effectiveness. Thus, it is not simply a matter of repeating what the different schools of thought understand by the term strategy – but rather of developing a sketch for the design of a model of strategic thought which allows military science in today's Western pluralistic states to provide a security-relevant benefit for society. To this end, the core requirements that constitute such strategic thought are to be derived and a definition synthesised from them, regardless of whether these common definitions of strategy (which may originate from other ends, cultural regions or developmental historical foundations) follow or differ from them.

This strategic thought in military science should not be of a superficially 'military' character, but rather arise from a logic of assessment abstracted from military command principles – in the end (that would be the actual intention behind abstraction) it should be understandable and applicable to every civilian policy area (including private industry, public administration, police, etc.) without its military authorship/handwriting necessarily being recognisable in the language used. The decisive quality feature of such an abstraction is precisely that only the compelling derivation justifies the validity of the result, regardless of whether authorship is military in origin.

The justification for the idea that strategic thought for the benefit of state security should arise from a logic of assessment abstracted from *military* command principles (and thus for the fact that the relationship between strategy/state leadership and the military is a key factor in determining state security) can be found above all in the fact that

- the military already had to practise, master and develop cross-policy thought in view of its command capability based on the principle of staff work;
- in the escalation chain of possible defence measures against threats, it is not only necessary to continuously assess the security-political relevance of the civilian departments, but also to cover the military component of security in actual operations in cooperation with other ministries;
- as the only resource of the state, it is capable of mastering the highest intensity level of an escalating threat and thus represents the *ultima ratio* of the political leadership when it comes to ensuring survival against existential threats;
- it is capable of rapidly and autonomously/independently creating makeshift structures that enable the political leadership to regain strategic command effectiveness, even in situations where order in the state is impaired or temporarily suspended by external threats.

Examples of such a specifically military logic of assessment, from which abstractions must be made, can be found in the fact that economic strategy think tanks tend to start from the best case, whereas military assessments always have to consider the worst case, or in the fact that civilian entrepreneurial thought can also take the probability of threats into account, which is impossible for the (*ultima ratio*) instrument responsible for the state's survival, if only because of its constitutional mandate. Similarly, the attempt to limit the scope to certain scenarios that could be answered by defensive measures seems permissible from a security policy point of view, whereas the military assessment logic has to meet all threats covered by the constitutional mandate, or, in the case of an ordered departure from this mandate, to communicate the associated risk to political decision-makers in an undistorted way. It is precisely this dialectical difference between security policy and military assessment logic that suggests that the latter is the more reliable and effective basis for strategic thought in situations where the long-term survival of the state against existential threats is the identified ends.

The following key points could be identified in the course of the investigation as functional principles constitutive for a model of strategic thought[13]:

---

[13] Regarding this subchapter, cf.: Peischel 2017a p. 12-30 and cf.: Peischel 2020, pp. 46-48;

- Strategy (strategic thought) refers to a category of skills that is closer to the sphere of *thought* than that of *action*. Accordingly, it focuses more on finding the purpose (ends-led) than on planning and implementation (ways-led).
- It represents the original initiative of the strategic decision-making process and is long-term proactive/prophylactic rather than reactive/symptomatic. In systems of hierarchical strategic instances (e.g. National Interest-Grand Strategy, Grand Strategy-National Strategy, Comprehensive Strategy-Sub-Strategy), it regularly represents the higher echelon, i.e. the only echelon which truly identifies the ends.
- The range of options available to it allows it to draw upon creative and visionary approaches, freeing it from the need to resort to confrontational, without any alternative *physically forceful* conflict resolution.
- Nevertheless, it does not embody the win-win principle and is therefore fundamentally confrontational, i.e. it recognises only winners and losers. It is driven by interests and is de-moralised with regard to the means of force used against the competitor. With the help of creative/visionary approaches, it is possible – if not in all cases, then at least in many – to avoid a physical, forceful resolution of conflicts of interests. The opponent can also be strategically outmanoeuvred, for example through superior training measures, technological advantage, economic concepts or alliances, without having to endure an actual confrontation with military force – nevertheless, strategy remains fundamentally confrontational.
- Strategy is characterised by the long-term nature of the identified ends, which is also expressed, among other things, in the fact that the successes or failures of strategic ends are only felt after the end of the term of office of those who set the strategic direction. As a result, responsible strategists are often misjudged during their terms in office and those who are tempted to set ends which later turn out to be less conducive to security are often held in higher esteem at the time. Setting strategic ends thus places high demands on the moral and ethical integrity of the representatives of the strategic decision-making echelon.
- In line with Weber's ethics of responsibility, strategy is committed to the welfare of the state and its citizens. The axiomatic assumption that the sovereign acts in any case in the interests of the well-being of the citizens, and that it is therefore only a matter of ensuring that he asserts his power (as Machiavelli, Gracián and, for long stretches of his work, Sun Tzu do) is not enough, because strategy then gives up the opportunity of democratic control of the state's ends, thus paving the way for authoritarian regimes. Clausewitz names two core abilities of an officer – military expertise and qualities of character (here not in a moral-ethical sense, but in

the understanding of the classical virtues of masculinity). If the former were overemphasised in training, this could lead to technical experts/anoraks who lack the ability to transcend thinking in terms of services/branches. An overemphasis on the importance of the latter, on the other hand, could all too easily be instrumentalised and misused for an ideologization of future military commanders. He therefore sees a third pillar of requirements for officers as the necessary corrective to counteract both possible undesirable developments and thus creates the basis for responsible command. This third pillar is based on the broadest possible humanistic general education in the Humboldt sense, rolled out across all hierarchical echelons. It results in the right and duty to resist orders that violate human rights, the democratic reliability of armed forces and the ability to use and fill out the room for manoeuvre given by the superior command level (mission-type leadership/Auftragstaktik). Clausewitz thus describes a functional principle that is timelessly valid under almost all strategic concepts.

- If strategy is committed to the well-being of citizens, this means that it must also reflect the set of values of the society in question. This means that strategy is specific to a cultural region, i.e. it is also determined to a large extent by the set of values which lies at the core of the cultural region. In their World Values Survey (Inglehart & Welzel 2020), Inglehart and Welzel argue that the canon of values of Western pluralistic states is moving further in the direction of two dimensions (secularisation, self-development) and away from the more religiously and group cohesion oriented values of the less developed states. This would lessen the willingness to act in the interests of the community and the common good. Compared with authoritarian systems in which elites develop ambitious long-term strategies, the implementation of which rests on the shoulders of the people who are hardly involved in the political decision-making process, the enlightened Western democracies could find themselves affected by a `systemic strategy inhibition´.
- The strategic idea represents the first step of a decision-making process or one of its iterations. It equates ends projected into the future, which initially have no mathematical/computational link with the starting point of the planning or with the necessary resources. In order to prevent the strategic ends from turning into pipe dream, however, resource-related feasibility planning is carried out at a later stage and dialectically contrasted with the visionary purpose as a critical-rational counterpart.
- Strategy aims to ensure the long-term survival of a community, for the guarantee of which restrictions in the here and now have to be imposed on the citizen (the necessity of this barter between long-term survival and

immediate restriction in the now is rarely understood because the threatening consequences of wrong strategic aims lie outside a timescale which is tangible to the public).

- Strategic decision-making and strategic thought require a horizontal, cross-policy assessment capability (comprehensiveness). This probably corresponds to the more accurate meaning of στρατός ἄγειν, which, in contrast to leading the army, may also have meant leading the layer of strategists (strategists' collegium) who were called upon to carry out the political business of the polis, i.e. the ancient city-states.

- Strategy in the sense of this publication deliberately distinguishes itself from military strategy, i.e. the implementation of a sub-task assigned to the armed forces from the overall strategic decision-making level. In contrast to this, it represents the sum of the principles of general strategic, cross-policy area thought that can be abstracted from military command theory and which are also suitable for application beyond the military sector. The word strategy in the term military strategy is justified in that it is used in campaigns in which armed forces are deployed simultaneously in more than one major theatre of war. In this case – to put it simply – it can become the task of the military leadership to balance strategic resources and risks between the two theatres of war. This would give the military command level a dimension of strategic action – albeit only with regard to the balance *between the two theatres of war* – which is the exclusive preserve of political decision-makers *with regard to the entire campaign*. This process could be understood as a delegation of a strategic dimension of action to the military command level which is limited to the balance between two theatres of war, but which must at all times remain within the ends and the allocation of resources and risks for the entire campaign as determined by politics.

- Strategy and strategic thought should be understood as aiming at the ends dimension of the ends-ways-means metaphor, which is often stylised to be a triptych of command theory – i.e. at the contribution of military assessment logic to the national strategy development process ahead of decision-making. In contrast to the commonly held view that ends and means are determined by political decision-makers without substantial military advice first, and that the military leadership is to be limited to the operational implementation (ways), i.e. to the task of achieving the politically defined ends with the granted means, an understanding of strategy is assumed here which is more closely based on Clausewitz's theoretical approach. This shows that today's predominant interpretation of the ends-ways-means approach only seemingly corresponds to his Zweck-

Ziel-Mittel[14] relationship. In fact, Clausewitz understands strategy as bordering on politics and statecraft or rather becoming both itself – whereby the phrase bordering on politics clearly expresses that the interface between the military and the state must be meant here. Clausewitz suggests that if the statesman and the commander are not the same person, the commander should become a member of the cabinet "so that [the commander] would take part in the key aspects of actions" (Wallach 1970, p. 33) and in order to be able to inform the political leadership without delay about unexpected changes in the situation and about time-critical opportunities that arise[15]. Clausewitz thus speaks out unequivocally in favour of the contribution of the senior military leadership to strategic assessment ahead of the actual political decisions. This involvement cannot violate the primacy of politics because, if the statesman and commander are not one and the same person, it can only achieve a level of quality that serves in the preparation of decisions, whereas the actual strategic decision-making competence is unquestionably reserved for the sovereign body (continuation of politics by other means). Since the second edition of *On War* in 1853, passages have appeared in which the commander in the cabinet is called upon to have more far-reaching powers and which would actually go beyond the primacy of politics (this is because the purpose of the commander's right to speak to the cabinet is stated as follows: "so that he can participate in the decision-making process" (Wallach 1970, p.33). Hahlweg was subsequently able to expose these amended passages as forgeries. On the basis of this analysis, the current relationship between strategy and the military could be defined by the following assignment of tasks to the components of the ends-ways-means relationship, which would anyway leave the primacy of politics untouched in the case of decision-preparatory and advisory contribution of the senior military leadership:

„11. The political *object* comes to the fore again" (von Clausewitz 1989, pp. 80), and "Strategy is the use of the engagement for the *purpose* of war" (ibid., p. 177);

[15] „The first, the supreme, the most far-reaching act of judgment that the statesman and commander have to make …" (von Clausewitz 1989, p. 88) - Even if this wording does not make it clear beyond doubt whether Clausewitz assumes that the statesman and commander are the same person, it is clear that the functional `role´ of the commander (thus in the figurative sense, the military leadership) is obliged to make a substantive contribution to strategic assessment (in making preparation ahead of decision-making) in any case. In the event that the statesman and commander are not the same person, the strategic decision is of course reserved for the sovereign body, which means that the accusation that the involvement of the commander in the cabinet violates the primacy of politics is unfounded.

- o Task of the senior military leadership: to provide policymakers with advice on the strategic ends and in decision preparation, including expert feedback on the resources required and on the level of risk which can ultimately only be legitimised politically.
- o Task of the democratically legitimised political leadership: the actual decision on the strategic ends, the resources to be made available and the residual risk to be accepted (this task falls within the sole competence of the political decision-makers, enshrined within the constitution).
- As an academic subject, strategy/strategic thought (in the simultaneous conditionality of both directions: strategy at the interface with political decision-making and strategy as a starting point for operational implementation) would have the task of a content-related steering-instance over the core and subsidiary subjects of an organically structured military science and its interfaces to the security-relevant research of civilian disciplines. It is only by exercising this guidance function that military science can be made capable of providing a unique benefit for the long-term security of the state and of creating a substantial basis for strategic policy advice that cannot be provided by other scientific disciplines.

The functional principles derived here as constituting a model of strategic thought are not intended to create a semantically better definition of strategy. Rather, the aim is to use these functional principles as a basis for understanding the cultural area-specific dimension of strategy, to define its components (military scientific research, strategic assessment procedures, decision-making processes, training of strategic leaders, selection of future strategic leaders, etc.) in such a way that they generate a unique added value of military science for society and thus establish a mutually beneficial relationship between the strategic decision-making and military command levels. In other words, the understanding of strategy or strategic thought derived from the functional principles mentioned above determines the internal structure, the effectiveness and the unique added value of military science, its usefulness for the security of the state and, thus, the relationship between strategy and the military.

6. References

Angstrom, J. & Widen, J.J. (2015). *Contemporary Military Theory – The Dynamics of War*. London: Routledge.

Von Clausewitz, C. (1980). *Hinterlassenes Werk Vom Kriege*, Neunzehnte Auflage, Jubiläumsausgabe mit erneut erweiterter historisch-kritischer Würdigung von Professor Dr. Werner Hahlweg. Bonn: Dümmler Verlag.

Von Clausewitz, C. (1989). *On War*. Indexed Edition, Edited and Translated by Michael Howard and Peter Paret, with a Commentary by Bernard Brodie. Princeton University Press.

Van Creveld, M. (1982). *Fighting Power. German and U.S. Army Performance, 1939-1945*. Westport, Connecticut: Greenwood Press.

Demeter, K. (1965). *Das Deutsche Offizierkorps in Gesellschaft und Staat 1650-1945*. Frankfurt/M.

Gompert, D. C., Cevallos, A. S., & Garafola, C. L. (2016). *War with China: Thinking Through the unthinkable*. Santa Monica, California: RAND Corporation, RR-1140-A. Retrieved from https://www.rand.org/pubs/research_reports/RR1140.html (09.09.2020)

Hartmann, U. (1998). *Carl von Clausewitz, Erkenntnis – Bildung – Generalstabsausbildung*. Munich: Olzog.

Inglehart, R. & Welzel, C. (2020). World Values Survey. Retrieved from http://www.worldvaluessurvey.org/wvs.jsp (10/09/2020)

Peischel, W. (2017a). Militärische Fachmedien als Instrumente der strategischen Kommunikation und als Träger des militärwissenschaftlichen Diskurses – Einführung in Zielsetzung und Struktur der „Wiener Strategiekonferenz". In Wolfgang Peischel [Ed.]. *Wiener Strategie-Konferenz 2016. Strategie neu denken* (pp. 12-30). Norderstedt: Carola Hartmann Miles-Verlag.

Peischel, W. (2017b). Grundprinzipien militärischen, strategischen Denkens an der Schnittstelle zur politischen Entscheidungsfindung Fassung des Strategiebegriffes – Strategie und militärwissenschaftliche Bildung – der militärische Beitrag zur Gesamtstrategie des Staates . In Wolfgang Peischel [Ed.]. *Wiener Strategie-Konferenz 2016. Strategie neu denken* (pp. 138-170). Norderstedt: Carola Hartmann Miles-Verlag.

Peischel, W. (2020). The Essence and Core of Military Science: An Attempt at a Definition by Means of Applying Two Dialectically Opposed Approaches. In W. Peischel & C. Bilban [Eds.]: *Building Military Science for the Benefit of Society, International Society of Military Sciences* (pp. 17-52). Norderstedt: Carola Hartmann Miles-Verlag.

Piehler, G. K. & Johnson, M. H., V. (Ed., Associate Ed.). (2013). *Encyclopedia of Military Science*. Los Angeles: Sage Publications, Inc.

Sookermany, A. McD. (2020). Military Science – Missing in Action? In W. Peischel & C. Bilban [Eds.]: *Building Military Science for the Benefit of Society, International Society of Military Sciences* (pp. 53-73). Norderstedt: Carola Hartmann Miles-Verlag.

Stahel, A.A. (1996). *Klassiker der Strategie – eine Bewertung*. 2nd revised edition. Zürich: Vdf Hochschulverlag.

Wallach, J. L. (1970). *Das Dogma der Vernichtungsschlacht. Die Lehren von Clausewitz und Schlieffen und ihre Wirkung in zwei Weltkriegen*. Stuttgart: Arbeitskreis für Wehrforschung.

7. Further Reading

Ångström, J. & Widén, J. (2014). Contemporary Military Theory: The Dynamics of War. New York: Routledge

Brodie, B. (1959). Strategy in the Missile Age. New Jersey: Princetown University Press.

Buzan, B. & Waever, O. & De Wilde, J. (1998). Security: A new Framework for Analysis. Boulder: Lynne Rienner Publishers.

Clausewitz von, C. (1973). Vom Kriege. Bonn: Ferd. Dümmler Verlag.

Heuser, B. (2010). Die Entwicklung der Strategie seit der Antike. Paderborn: Ferdinand Schöningh.

Hinterhuber, H. (2010). Die 5 Gebote für exzellente Führung: Wie Ihr Unternehmen in guten und in schlechten Zeiten zu den Gewinnern zählt. Frankfurt: Frankfurter Allgemeine Buch.

Hobbes, T. (1986). Leviathan. Ditzingen: Reclams Universal-Bibliothek.

Jackson, R. & Sørensen, G. (2019). Introduction to International Relations: Theories and Approaches. Oxford: Oxford University Press.

Keohane, R. (1984). After Hegemony: Cooperation and Discord in the World Political Economy. New Jersey: Princetown University Press.

Machiavelli, N. (2011). Der Fürst. Berlin: Insel Taschenbuch.

Machiavelli, N. (2000). Discorsi: Vom Staate. Berlin: Insel Taschenbuch.

Maier, G. (2015). Das vergessene Vokabular der Strategie: Handbuch der Strategischen Prinzipien. Books on Demand.

Mearsheimer, J. (2001). The Tragedy of Great Power Politics. New York: Norton.

Morgenthau, H. (1989). Macht und Frieden. Grundlegung einer Theorie der internationalen Politik. Gütersloh: Bertelsmann.

Nye, J. (1990). Bound to Lead: The Changing Nature of American Power. New York: Basic Books.

Paret, P. (1986). Makers of Modern Strategy from Machiavelli to the Nuclear Age. New Jersey: Princetown University Press.

Peischel, W. (Ed.) (2017). Wiener Strategie-Konferenz 2016: Strategie neu denken. Norderstedt: Carola Hartmann Miles-Verlag.

Peischel, W. (Ed.) (2018). Wiener Strategie-Konferenz 2017: Strategie neu denken. Norderstedt: Carola-Hartmann-Miles-Verlag.

Peischel, W. (Ed.) (2019). Wiener Strategie-Konferenz 2018: Strategie neu denken. Norderstedt: Carola-Hartmann Miles-Verlag.

Souchon, L. (2012). Carl von Clausewitz: Strategie im 21. Jahrhundert. Hamburg: Mittler.

Stahel, A. (1996). Klassiker der Strategie. Zürich: Vdf Hochschulverlag.

Waltz, K. (1979). Theory of International Politics. Boston: Addison-Wesley.

Chapter 2: Strategy, Politics, and the Use of Force in Europe

Prof. Dr. Janne Haaland Matlary

Keywords: NATO; Hybrid Strategy; Design Strategy; Foreign Policy Prerogative; Military spending; Military Interventions;

> *"the warlike dealings of national leaders and governments with one another are subject to exactly the same logic of strategy as are the interactions of the fighting forces. But it is far more difficult for national leaders to understand that logic beneath all the complications of the multiple levels of an entire war. Besides, national leaders can rarely apply whatever strategic insights they may have. To preserve their power and authority within their own societies, democratic leaders must obey the linear logic of consensual politics. That means, for example, that they cannot act paradoxically to surprise external enemies, because they must inform and prepare their public before acting. ...a conscious understanding of the phenomena of strategy is a great rarity among political leaders"*
> Luttwak, Edward (2001) *Strategy: The Logic of War and Peace,* The Belknap Press of Harvard Univ. Press, p. 50

When Western states use military force, they often do so without a clear strategy. Emile Simpson wrote a book that reflects on this, aptly named *War from the Ground Up: 21ˢᵗ Century Combat as Politics* (Simpson, 2018). His military experience was mainly from the ISAF operation in Afghanistan, but he also analyses the European use of force in more general terms. He argues that 'the tail wags the dog', viz. that tactical military moves on the ground 'direct' politics, not *vice versa*. This he calls 'armed politics' – political implications of whatever is done at the operational level and below amount to 'strategy', in induction-like fashion. There political consequences of war are what they are, not planned for, simply effects of whatever happens in theatre. This is the very opposite of strategy guiding the use of force in order to realize desired political effects of the latter.

There is no *initial* strategy for the use of force that guides it, Simpson argues. An operation happens because there is too much violence or trouble somewhere, and 'something has to be done' about it. So one throws in some military force in order to stabilize the situation, like a fire-brigade that is sent in to quell a fire. But once quelled, what then?

Simpson is deeply disturbed by this state of affairs because strategy is supposed to direct the use of force, the most serious tool of the state, and not vice versa.

Is this a fair criticism? Is the use of force without strategy? Is the operational level of war the only that matters, strategy having been abdicated by governments and the 'strategic corporal' a reality?

In this chapter I ask whether the use of force in NATO-states in Europe – all liberal democracies – is characterized by a lack of strategy. I do not purport to exhaust the issue or provide a complete answer; but to provide some suggestions about how to analyze and evaluate this question. What are the empirical indicators of strategy being at work? How does strategy relate to types of threat and risk? It seems obvious that a humanitarian intervention does not need strategy to the same extent as deterrence or coercion. Yet the former needs strategic consideration of the post-conflict situation. Thus, there is a clear need for strategic planning also in the case of humanitarian intervention. During the 1990-2010 period in Europe the lack of strategy was perhaps understandable, as interventions wars were 'optional', but in the present situation of great power rivalry and state-to-state confrontation strategy is again a must (Johnsen and Matlary, 2020).

As a point of departure, let's assume that the use of force in Europe is like Simpson's 'fire-brigade'. This may be so because few European states have a strategic/military culture with the ability to make decisions that are strategically relevant. Also, postmodern politics and the long, deep peace in the 1990-2010 period in Europe have meant that the state's security interests have been thought of as a bygone concern, and domestic politics replace strategy as liberal democracies are prone to pay much attention to public opinion, hence a tendency to risk-aversion in using force. Finally, the present political class has only known peaceful international politics in their own part of the world and mostly unfamiliar with the use of military force (Coker, 2013).

1. Military strategy for state-to-state threat and risk

Is there military strategy in Europe? This is the question posed in *Military Strategy for the 21st century: the Challenge for NATO* (Johnson and Matlary, 2020). 23 authors try to answer this question, and they find that there is little systematic strategic thinking in the political class – with some exceptions, like France – and also that the officer concentrates on the so-called 'operational level of war. There is a clear need for strategic thinking, the various authors write – for nuclear strategy (Michaels, 2020), for conventional and for hybrid strategy (Johnson, 2020.). However, NATO adopted a military strategy in 2018, classified, but adapted to state-to-state competition (Dyndal and Hilde, 2020.)

The authors agree that there is little serious strategy-making in Europe today, despite the surge in threats and risks. Perhaps this is because the long period of 'deep peace' did not demand strategy. Now, however, the need is very obvious indeed: China and Russia stress the importance of military power in foreign and security policy and terrorism and other non-state violence is rampant in Europe. In addition there are cyber attacks across a range of targets.

What are the strategic needs for the various types of threat and risk? Johnson (Johnson, 2020) presents a useful matrix of types of use of force: in *competition*, military base structures matter, trade 'wars' take place, cyber attacks, intelligence gathering. This is all familiar in Western states as well as in authoritarian states, and strategic planning certainly goes into it. *Confrontation* is marked by more risk-taking, and can take the form of deployments, active measures, hacking, legal pressure military signaling, false flag operations, threats and signaling. Here military force matters more than before. If we move to *coercion*, sabotage, psy-war, blockade, covert operations, occupation of islands, political interference and manipulation, etc, become the order of the day. And finally, in *armed conflict*, we see traditional uses of force in war-fighting.

The point here is that the use of force is not only confined to clear warfighting modes or to humanitarian and stabilization operations. On the contrary, there is a spectrum of possible uses of force, some clearly military; others where military force is used along with other tools. All this makes the use of force today 'more political' in the sense that the use of force must be closely calibrated to political intentions and its use must be flexible, prone to change. If the political goal is to secure the freedom of navigation, armed escort to a supertanker may accomplish the goal, but should the situation escalate so that the escort is not enough, frigates may have to be deployed quickly – and perhaps frigates are able to deter escalation in the first place? If so, they should be deployed early.

Likewise, deterrence in general is back and needs risk-willingness but also careful consideration of the danger of escalation. This requires political-strategic ability of the first order, combined with a keen understanding of the military tool – how it achieves goals.

Coercion and deterrence are the two main military strategies. Deterrence is more 'passive', but rests on political credibility of taking risk (Gerson, 2009). If the adversary does not think that one will fight, one will not be able to deter. Coercion is more risky, being a specific action to put pressure on someone or some state, often in the form of an ultimatum. Coercion often fails when European states are behind it, argues Rob de Wijk, simply because the threat is not credible (de Wijk, 2005). Milosevic was threatened over Kosovo in

NATO's Actord, but did not believe in the threat until it was too late. Jakobsen has studied the minimum requirements for successful coercion and finds that massive threat of military attack is the key one, and one that Europe is not wont to make credibly (Jakobsen, 2016).

In sum, the risk and threat that Europe faces requires political strategy that is fine-tuned, risk-willingness, and versatility in the sense that situations change quickly. There is little indication that the Europeans are engaged to this end and that they will succeed, with the exception of states like France and Britain.

2. Strategy – what is it?

Before we can analyse this issue we need to *define* strategy and to *delineate the main empirical indicators* of strategic thinking in order to determine whether strategy obtains. This is perhaps the most salient part of this chapter, as the term strategy is used in a variety of ways, both regarding non-militaryaffairs and regarding general policy or general plans. Thus, what strategy means is by no means clear. Strategy is a term that is positive; connoting rational planning and control of a situation, so politicians are apt to talk about strategy for whatever policy they envisage. The same goes for business people who devise strategies for their activity when what they talk about is rather a business plan.

After defining the term we need to discuss which empirical indicators are fruitful in order to determine whether policy is strategic or not. I will argue that the presence of strategic culture in a country is a *necessary but not sufficient* condition for strategic action. Strategic culture is fairly well studied in the literature on defence and security policy (Britz, M; 2018, Matlary, J.H. 2018, Petersson and Matlary, 2010; Meijer and Wyss, 2018), and has been a central variable in the scholarship since Glenn Snyder wrote his study about Soviet strategic culture (Snyder, 1977).

After having discussed strategy and empirical indicators I continue to examine some recent cases of European use of force, applying these indicators. The value of this is to provide some preliminary conclusions on the presence of strategy in European use of force, albeit tentative ones. The empirical cases warrant much more in-depth study than I can provide in this short chapter and they should therefore be regarded as empirical illustrations rather than as proof of any hypothesis.

Strategy is a term that originates in Greek, 'strategia' and its historic meaning is tied to the use of force. However, it was not commonly used until the 18th century, and prior to that tactics was often used instead, something we find also in Clausewitz who rarely speaks about strategy. Yet wars have been directed politically at all times, so strategic activity has happened, even if not called so, a point made by Luttwak when discusses Roman strategy (Luttwak, 1976). That something is called strategy does not make it so; and strategic activity may happen even if called tactics, as was the custom for many centuries. Beatrice Heuser has written a very useful history of strategic thinking, and notes that the term is of fairly recent usage (Heuser, 2010).

Another major work on strategy is Lawrence Freedman's *Strategy. A History* (Freedman, 2013) which shows how widely used the term has become and how elusive it is in terms of precise definition. Baylis and Wirtz list no less than nine definitions of strategy in their introduction to *Strategy in the Contemporary World* (Baylis and Wirtz, 2016) where some are broad – strategy seen as a plan and the means to fulfilling it, and others defining it more narrowly, emphasizing the interaction with enemies. Cleary strategy simply means a plan for some, and the term 'grand strategy' refers to a country's overall foreign policy with all its means of power included.

Thus, strategy may be very general in scope – seen as a plan, and valid for also non-military domains. Yet this wide definition is not useful for our purposes. The use of force is very serious and requires knowledge of the likely interaction with enemies.

Duyvesteyn and Angstrom call for strategic thinking in Europe, arguing that it has been largely lost after the cold war, (Duyvesteyn and Angstrom 2005) and Sir Hew Strachan entitles his book on strategy *The Direction of War* (Strachan, 2013), in the tradition of Clausewitz, thus underlining that strategy's original purpose is exactly that – guiding the use of force, proving the rationale for using force – or not. Also he laments the lack of strategic guidance for Europe's us of force.

Let us define strategy as the political and military conduct of warfare. We should distinguish between the political and the military level; what is my concern here is the political steering or guiding of the military instrument of the state; not the military design of the operation itself. We are here speaking of military strategy in the sense of political-military interaction.

I would also add that interaction with hostile or competing actors captures the essence of strategy – the strategic *interaction* is what makes strategy special and different from mere planning, which is linear. Risk-taking is logically implicit in strategy because it involves hostile actors, in war, enemies. Strategy is therefore much more difficult than linear thinking and it requires unity of action and the ability to make decisions quickly, depending on the adversary's moves. Importantly, it involves risk to oneself, perhaps to one's life. It follows from this that strategy is a serious business, much more so than normal policy-making.

But strategy is more than the interactive part; it also requires the specification of political goals. What is the intention of the use of force; how does it further the state's interests? This is the role that the government plays, whereas the officer's task is to tell the government whether the political goals can be reached with the use of force. The officer 'translates' the political goal into military strategy, but the government must know enough about its military instrument in order to have a rough idea about its utility. Also, because the military instrument is so much more than an instrument, involving losing lives and taking lives, it is a serious decision to use it. The responsibility for its use rests with the government alone. The ethics of using force demands that its use is strategic; a government must weigh the importance of the political aim to be reached against the risk involved, and that risk is one of own soldiers' lives.

In sum, the politician's role in strategy is to specify the political goal for the use of force and to be able to decide on strategy in an unfolding interaction with adversaries, implying risk-taking.

The definition of strategy that is relevant is therefore cognizant of the element of risk, logically implied in the interactive character of dealing with an enemy. Clausewitz defined strategy as the direction of war, confining it to the military instrument. Like Sir Hew, I think this makes sense at a time when strategy is used for almost any activity, often in order to give an impression of highly rational, serious activity in fields that are very trivial indeed. But in addition to defining strategy as proper to military affairs, I strongly stress the interaction with foes that render strategic activity so difficult and so challenging. Here Sir Lawrence Freeman has a good definition:

"The realm of strategy is one of bargaining and persuasion as well as threats and pressure, psychological as well as physical effects, and words as well as deeds. This is why strategy is the central political art. It is about getting more out of a situation than the starting balance of power would suggest. It is the art of creating power" (cited in Baylis and Wirth, op.cit, p. 4)

Here strategy is defined by its interactive character and the possibilities and the risks inherent in this interaction, but it is not confined to the direction of military force alone, but embraces the totality of political engagement. Strategy is a 'bridge' between politics and the military, but the political element of strategy is the master of the military element.

Strategy assumes that goals – the end state desired – as well as the means and the ways can be defined. The ends, ways, means formula is traditionally a staple of strategic thinking, and also embraced by NATO (Dyndal and Hilde, 2020). However, the ability to define an end state in today's chaotic and shifting political landscape and the fact that some threats are not possible to eliminate makes some scholars and civil servants interested in so-caleld 'design strategy' which tries to navigate change in a dynamic fashion (Ellery and Saunders, 2020; Slensvik, 2020).

In short, a government takes risk when it engages in strategy, but it must do so if it uses force, also for ethical reasons. Is the risk taken acceptable, given the political importance of the operation/war? Can the war be won? Is the timing right? Are the reasons right? These and other questions must be answered by the political masters before using force.

3. Is alliance dependence strategy?

This immediately raises the question of alliance dependence as a strategy. We know a lot about how NATO's European states are guided by alliance dependence when they use force. For instance, Norway's 'strategy' is to be close to the US, UK, and other allies – first of all, the US. NATO's purpose, as Lord Ismay said, is to 'keep the Americans in, the Germans down, and the Russians out. 'Keeping the Americans in' is essential to NATO, and to individual NATO members. We know that alliance dependence is the key explanation for Norwegian, Danish, and Polish – as well as British – use of force (Jakobsen, 2020, Heier, 2020, Benbow, 2020, Kaminski and Smolny, 2020).

But is alliance dependence strategy? Should we count it as strategy? It is certainly an indirect strategy where a dependent state contributes to the hegemonic state's operations and wars as a good ally, assuming that the former will repay the solidarity in times of own crisis. Yet few states admit to this rationale for their deployments; they will usually justify their contribution in terms of general goals for the operation that are commensurate with their public's view of what is legitimate. Thus, ISAF was justified by general aims like democracy and improving the lot of Afghan civilians, especially women and children, but the rationales given for the use of force varied with circumstances, suggesting that governments lacked a strategy apart from that of alliance dependence. Norwegian politicians cited nation-building, democracy promotion, improving the lot for women and children, fighting terrorism, and stabilizing the country as the reasons for military deployment to Afghanistan, but there was no clear strategy and military commanders asked in vain for the latter (Stai and Saxi, 2020).

Although alliance dependence is an indirect strategy for a state in seeking security, it is not a strategy for the direction of force. It is thus not a military strategy, but should rather count as security policy. When alliance dependence motives a state's use of force, there may of course be 'overlap' with real security interests in theatre – if NATO deploys, we may assume that also smaller states in NATO share a common security interest with the leading states behind the action. But often there is little real interest on the part of the states that deploy for solidarity reasons; they go where the US, the UK etc go. One example of this is the findings of the Norwegian commission that studied Norway's role in ISAF. As said, officers serving in it asked in vain for a clear strategy for the use of force, and then only strategy the commission could find, was Norway being *'En god alliert'* (A good ally), as the title of the report in fact came to be.

In such cases, it is likely that states will rationally look for the 'Pareto frontier' in their deployment in terms of risk-taking and size, as Jakobsen argues is the case with Denmark (Jakobsen, 2020). He concludes that closeness to the US is the criterion for most Danish use of force and that governments seek to save money while satisfying America expectations. The point where the cost is the least while satisfying US expectations is the Pareto optimum. The Danes do not seek to minimize risk in this 'equation', but other states probably do. In ISAF there were many 'caveats' from many states that sought to reduce risk; Germany stood out, but there were few states that did the dangerous war-fighting in Helmand.

All this tells us that when alliance dependence is the prime motivation for the use of force, strategy proper suffers. There is no need to consider the political goals of the operation, what level of risk is acceptable, whether the political goals can be reached with the use of force planned, etc.

4. Decision-Making and Strategy

Historically the ruler (king, prince) was also the highest military commander and led forces in war. He or she took personal risk and knew the military instrument. This is why the King or Queen is commander-in-chief even today. We speak of the FPP (Foreign Policy Prerogative) which gives the power to deploy troops to the government, not parliament. The PM or the president decides on the use of force. In the US and France, the president is the commander-in-chief and parliament has little say in the decision to go to war, in Britain and Norway, the government. This is the opposite e.g. Germany were parliament can micro-manage far down at the tactical level.

The more power of decision is concentrated in one actor, the more strategic decisions can be. *Thus, states with the FPP have a great advantage in strategic terms.*

These states usually have a national council at the government's disposal, and there the political leaders can be discuss with the top military officers about the possible use of force to meet political goals. The US has the most famous

"National Security Council", but also France and Britain have such. This ensures the political-military dialogue and allows for close and classified discussions about military means and operations. *Thus, states with a national security council can undertake strategic analysis.*

Further, in such states there is usually a so-called strategic and military culture:

5. Strategic Culture

There are various definitions also of the term strategic culture (Lantis and Howlett, 2016). Snyder defined it as "a set of general beliefs, attitudes, and behaviour patterns with regard to nuclear strategy" (ibid. p. 92) and also others define it as attitudes to the use of military force that are rather permanent, a 'culture', rooted in national history. There is no space here to discuss what kind of variable 'strategic culture' is – this is as difficult as defining culture itself – but the point is that we can observe very different attitudes towards the use of force in different countries. The Russians use force in a traditional way, in pursuit of national interests, and this is also true of France, Britain, Poland, and the US. Some smaller states in Europe are also in this category – the Dutch, the Danes, and the Norwegians. The scholarship agrees on calling these states 'willing and able' to use military force, implying the taking of risk and contributing to sharp operations. The major states typically take the lead and can initiate operations, and they have a global reach. These include the US, France, and Britain among the democracies. Smaller states follow with contributions, often on the strategic logic of alliance dependence.

Germany is the most important state that does not have a strategic culture.

Analyses of various countries in this regard can *inter alia* be found in Part One in Meijer and Wyss, 2010, Britz et al., 2018, Petersson and Matlary, 2010; Matlary, 2018; and in Johnson and Matlary, 2020. These studies agree that France has perhaps the strongest strategic culture in Europe, followed by Britain. Germany is at the other end of the spectrum with its clear choice of not wanting to lead militarily, not wanting sharp contributions in Afghanistan or Africa, etc. In sum, there are major differences between states that are proud of their military and of its work and states like Germany where civilian terms replace military culture as a rule.

But how important is strategic culture for strategy itself? I have suggested that the former is a necessary but not sufficient variable for strategic use of force. *By that I mean that states without a strategic culture will not be engaged in deterrence, coercion, and operations in any risky and leading position.* Their public opinion will have a much greater say in the use of force than any strategic elite around the executive. Such public opinion may call for the use of force in a humanitarian crisis – as happened with Germany in Kosovo in 1999, but public opinion will not direct strategic action. In sum, only states with a strategic culture for the use of force, including the professional military risk inherent in it, are able to take the risk of deterring, coercing, and war-fighting on the ground. The risk is not only tactical, but also strategic: the adversary may attack your state; coercion may require brinkman-ship, especially if nuclear weapons are involved.

In sum, the strategic use of military force presumes a strategic culture which includes risk-willingness. In addition, states with an FPP and a national security council are able to act in a unitary manner, use surprise or paradoxical logic, and sustain long campaigns with own losses. In addition, great powers are the leading ones, smaller states are followers. The smaller ones, but also a great power like the Uk, look to the US and cement their 'special relationship'. Hence, alliance dependence as a strategy is important.

6. The Necessity of Risk-Taking in Strategy

A government is responsible for the risk taken with own troops and for making the decision that their use is so vital that this risk is warranted, but today few politicians are willing to assume this responsibility. The ultimate sacrifice requires a correspondence between the seriousness of the political purpose of the use of force and the risk taken. In short, the more important the goal, the more risk can be taken. It is unethical to send soldiers to die for a development project; it is ethical to risk their lives in existential danger.

For example, if the goal of ISAF were to improve living conditions and develop democracy in Afghanistan, I would argue that this is not important enough to risk soldiers' lives for. But if Norway is invaded, we expect all Norwegians, soldiers and not, to resist. Yet in contemporary wars there is rarely this stark difference. Usually the political goal of the use of force is unspecified and the it is also the case that politicians refuse to discuss the goals in detail as this entails taking responsibility. Regarding ISAF Norwegian politicians offered various reasons for the Norwegian participation, in peaceful periods related to the plight of women and children; in times of Norwegian losses and injured related to security and defence reasoning (Andersen and Sookermany, 2020). Then it was not appropriate to fall for a development goal.

This cognitive dissonance is deeply unethical and betrays a lack of strategy. This is particularly a problem in so-called humanitarian interventions where risk is reduced if the operation is an 'optional war'. On one level it makes sense that states do not risk their own soldiers' lives in ground fighting unless the political goal of the use of force is extremely important, but on a professional military level it is not, as using e.g. only air power implies that the effectiveness of the military tool is reduced as well. In both Kosovo in 1999 and in Libya in 2011 the choice was for air power only, and this reduced risk. But in Kosovo it is clear that the lack of ground troops prolonger the operation as there was no need to consider land forces coming in from Albania. Serb tanks could easily be concealed, and were when there were no ground troops involved. In Libya NATO had to rely on ground forces from the Benghazi opposition over which it had no control. Clearly this is very unfortunate from a military-strategic point of view. It follows from this that one type of use of force, viz. humanitarian intervention, often suffers from a lack of military strategy, and that this is unfortunate. Soldiers can expect that the military tool will be used professionally in the sense that the complementarity of the military branches will be respected. They can also expect that politicians do not meddle in purely military decisions that belong to the operational level.

But such operations are typified by the 'fire-brigade' type of intervention mode, as we mentioned at the outset of this chapter. Yet urgency of action does not preclude strategic thinking about political end-states. In both Kosovo and Libya there was – and is – a glaring lack of political strategy. In Kosovo no-one had any idea of the end-state and it took eight years of being a UN 'protectorate' before the US and allies actually created a new state, and this was done with military force. This violation of one of the central norms of European state-craft, viz. that new states are not made by war anymore, least of all in Europe, is often repeated by president Putin, and it had led Kosovo to lead the life of a quasi-state, recognized diplomatically by some, not by others. The saga is not yet over.

In similar manner, Libya was intervened into without any plan beyond the 'protection of civilians', a goal never defined – which civilians? The ones on Ghadaffi's side as well? Moreover, after seven months of warfighting the end state was that NATO withdrew and the UN never came. The so-called Libyan government, and even governments, were encircled by various guerrillas and lead a most precarious existence today. Russia and Turkey are heavily involved in Libya; NATO and Europe having no say at all. Paradoxically, wth all the war-fighting going on now, there is even more need for protecting civilians than before.

In sum, there is a need for strategy in so-called humanitarian interventions, and the fact that they are of less importance to the contributing states does not allieviate politicians of the need to specify ends, ways, and means. The fact that states may be less 'interested' in these cases does not imply that military strategy should be modified with risk-reduction measures and that polit-ical-level strategy should be ignored. Once the use of force is planned, both political and military strategy must be taken seriously.

7. Empirical indicators of strategy at work

Empirical indicators of strategic mind-set would *inter alia* be European inter-est in nuclear deterrence now that the INF treaty has been declared null and void. Intermediate range missiles affect Europe; not the US; yet where is the alarm over this in Europe? The French urge the Germans to take an interest and perhaps promote a common European nuclear deterrent based on French and British missiles – something that is stone-walled in Germany. One does not want to discuss the need for nuclear deterrence, not discuss a Euro-pean role in acquiring it, and not discuss how Russia can be deterred. It is as of the task of nuclear deterrence is America's even when we speak about in-termediate range missiles and not strategic ones.

The lack of European interest in Europe's own deterrence is striking, and a clear indicator of a near-to total lack of strategic sense. Here France and the UK are the expections.

Further, another indicator of lack of strategy is the underfunding of defence, even if the 2% of GDP goal is self-imposed. Again it is the Americans that demand more spending in Europe and Europe that refuses. Germany even breaks ranks and proposed 1,5% GDP spending for itself – the richest coun-try in Europe. The many quarrels between the Americans and the Europeans over this issue is another clear indicator of a lack of strategic sense in Europe. With the high US spending on defence, how 'cheap' is not the 2% to keep the US satisfied?

A third indicator is the aforementioned risk aversion in operations. If alliance dependence is so key, why allow for caveats that will be displeasing to Wash-ington? Why not develop a proper strategic culture in states that have none in order to eliminate risk-aversion?

A fourth indicator is the paradoxical results of gallups that ask about art 5 in NATO, is there willingness to defend allies that may be attacked? A Pew poll found that many more said no to own contributions to an art 5 situations than said yes to American assistance to themselves and others.

NATO publics more likely to believe U.S. would defend them from Russian attack than to say their own country should

% who say if Russia got into a serious military conflict with one of its neighboring countries that is our NATO ally, ___ to defend that country

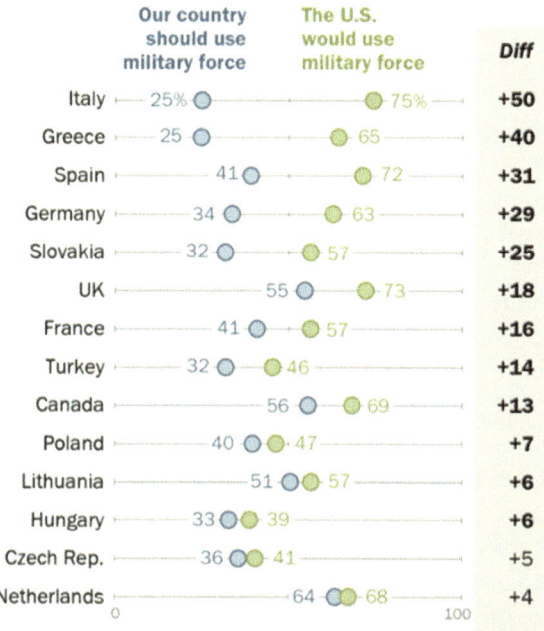

	Our country should use military force	The U.S. would use military force	Diff
Italy	25%	75%	**+50**
Greece	25	65	**+40**
Spain	41	72	**+31**
Germany	34	63	**+29**
Slovakia	32	57	**+25**
UK	55	73	**+18**
France	41	57	**+16**
Turkey	32	46	**+14**
Canada	56	69	**+13**
Poland	40	47	**+7**
Lithuania	51	57	**+6**
Hungary	33	39	**+6**
Czech Rep.	36	41	**+5**
Netherlands	64	68	**+4**

Note: Statistically significant differences in **bold**. The U.S., Russia and Ukraine were not asked both questions. Bulgaria not included due to a translation error.
Source: Spring 2019 Global Attitudes Survey. Q24 & Q25.
"NATO Seen Favorably Across Member States"

PEW RESEARCH CENTER

8. Conclusion

It is clear that few states in Europe are 'willing and able' with regard to military strategy and strategy in general. This has been the case for a long time, but this situation is the more grave today with state-to-state risk and threat from revisionist states like Russia and China and a weakened and inward-turning USA.

9. References

Anderson, M. and Sookermany, A. (2020). The Making of Military Strategy. The Gravity of an Unequal Dialogue. In R. Johnsen & J. H. Matlary (eds.). *Military Strategy for the 21st Century: The Challenge for NATO* (pp. 131-150). London: Hurst.

Arrequin-Toft, I. (2005). *How the Weak Win Wars. A Theory of Asymmetric Conflict.* Cambridge Studies in International Relations.

Baylis, J. et al. (eds.). (2016). *Strategy in the Contemporary World.* Oxford: Oxford University Press.

Benbow, T. (2020) UK Military Strategy: The Maritime Pivot, Rob Johnsen and Janne Haaland Matlary (eds.). *Military Strategy for the 21st Century: The Challenge for NATO,* pp. 349-368. London: Hurst.

Britz, M. et al (eds.). (2018). *European Participation in International Operations. The Role of Strategic Culture.* UK: Palgrave Macmillan.

Coker, C. (2018). A Farewell to Arms: Europe's Meritocracy and the Demilitarization of Europe. In J.H. Matlary & M. Petersson (eds.). *NATO's European Allies: Military Capability and Political Will* (pp. 25-37). UK: Palgrave Macmillan.

Duyvestyn, I. and Angstrom, J. (2005). *Rethinking the Nature of War.* London: Routledge.

Dyndal, G. L. & Hilde, P.S. (2020). Strategic Thinking in NATO and the New Military Strategy. In R. Johnsen & J. H. Matlary (eds.). *Military Strategy for the 21st Century: The Challenge for NATO* (pp. 303-328). London: Hurst.

Ellery, D. and Saunders, L. (2020). The Making of Military Strategy. Time for an Adaptive Approach?. In R. Johnsen & J. H. Matlary (eds.). *Military Strategy for the 21st Century: The Challenge for NATO* (pp. 85-110). London: Hurst.

Gerson, M. S. (2009). Conventional Deterrence in the Second Nuclear Age. *Parameters,* Autumn, 32-48.

Heier, T. (2020). Norway's Military Strategy after the Cold War: Between Demise and Revival. In R. Johnsen & J. H. Matlary (eds.). *Military Strategy for the 21st Century: The Challenge for NATO* (pp. 433-452). London: Hurst.

Heuser, B. (2010). *The Evolution of Strategy. Thinking War from Antiquity to the Present.* Cambridge: Cambridge University Press.

Kaminski, S. and Smolny, D. (2020). Polish Military Strategy: Watching the Suwalki Gap. In R. Johnsen & J. H. Matlary (eds.). *Military Strategy for the 21st Century: The Challenge for NATO* (pp. 405-414). London: Hurst.

Jakobsen, P.V. (2020). Military Strategy in Denmark. Retaining 'best ally' status with minimum spending. In R. Johnsen & J. H. Matlary (eds.). *Military Strategy for the 21ˢᵗ Century: The Challenge for NATO* (pp. 414-432). London: Hurst.

Ibid., "Coercive Diplomacy: Countering War-Threatening Crises and Armed Conflicts", in Collins, A. (ed.) (2019) *Contemporary Security Studies*, (pp. 285-299)Oxford: Oxford University Press

Johnsen, R. (2020). Military Strategy for Hybrid Confrontation and Coercion. In R. Johnsen & J. H. Matlary (eds.). *Military Strategy for the 21ˢᵗ Century: The Challenge for NATO* (pp. 227-250). London: Hurst.

Freedman, L. (2013). *Strategy: A History*. Oxford: Oxford University Press.

Lantis, J. and Howlett, D. (2016). Strategic Culture. In Baylis, J. et al. (eds.). *Strategy in the Contemporary World* (pp. 89-107). Oxford: Oxford University Press.

Luttwak, E. (1976). *The Grand Strategy of the Roman Empire: From the First Century AD to the Third*. London: Weidenfeld and Nicholsen.

Matlary, J.H. (2018). *Hard Power in Hard Times. Can Europe Act Strategically?* London: Palgrave Macmillan.

Mejer, H. and Wyss, M. (2018). *The Handbook of European Defence Policies and Armed Forces*. Oxford: Oxford University Press.

Michaels, J. (2020). Nuclear Strategy: The Politics of NATO's Nuclear Use. In R. Johnsen & J. H. Matlary (eds.). *Military Strategy for the 21ˢᵗ Century: The Challenge for NATO* (pp. 191-206). London: Hurst.

Pew Research Center. (2019). *Global Attitudes Survey*, qus. 24 and 25.

Simpson, E. (2018). *War from the Ground Up: 21ˢᵗ Century Combat as Politics*. Oxford: Oxford University Press.

Snyder, G. (1977). *The Soviet Strategic Culture: Implications for Nuclear Options*. Santa Monica: Rand Corporation.

Stai, A. and Saxi, H. (2020). Why Small European States Need Military Strategy: Theory and Practice. In R. Johnsen & J. H. Matlary (eds.). *Military Strategy for the 21ˢᵗ Century: The Challenge for NATO* (pp. 153-172). London: Hurst.

Slensvik, T. (2020). An Adaptive Approach to Military Strategy. In R. Johnsen and J. H. Matlary (eds.). *Military Strategy for the 21ˢᵗ Century: The Challenge for NATO* (pp. 11-130). London: Hurst.

Strachan, H. (2013). *The Direction of War*. Cambridge: Cambridge University Press.

De Wijk, R. (2004). *The Art of Military Coercion: Why the West's Military Superiority Scarcely Matters*. Amsterdam: Mets & Schilt.

10. Further Reading

Nye, Joseph (1990). *Bound to Lead: The Changing Nature of American Power*. New York: Basic Books.

Paret, Peter (1986). *Makers of Modern Strategy from Machiavelli to the Nuclear Age*. New Jersey: Princetown University Press.

Peischel, Wolfgang (Ed.) (2017). *Wiener Strategie-Konferenz 2016: Strategie neu denken*. Norderstedt: Carola Hartmann Miles-Verlag.

Peischel, Wolfgang (Ed.) (2018). *Wiener Strategie-Konferenz 2017: Strategie neu denken*. Norderstedt: Carola-Hartmann-Miles-Verlag.

Peischel, Wolfang (Ed.) (2019). *Wiener Strategie-Konferenz 2018: Strategie neu denken*. Norderstedt: Carola-Hartmann Miles-Verlag.

Waltz, Kenneth (1979). *Theory of International Politics*. Boston: Addison-Wesley.

Chapter 3: Strategy and Philosophy, War Theory

ao. Univ.-Prof. MMag. DDr. Christian Stadler, BG Mag. Mag. Franz Hollerer, Dr. Mauro Mantovani

Keywords: Theory of War; Strategic Thinkers; Polemos; Polemology; Understanding War; Purpose, Aims, Means; Ethics; Responsibility;

> *"Everything in strategy is very simple, but that does not mean everything is very easy."*
>
> Carl von Clausewitz, On War, III, 1

0. Introduction
Franz Hollerer

Surprisingly rapid and dynamic developments and changes in the recent past, in particular also in the economic sphere, have made and are increasingly making it necessary to examine the full breadth of what constitutes strategy: it is a term that has been the subject of great thought in relation to leading armies since ancient times and has correspondingly evolved in this area. Clearly an obvious first step is to look at classic strategic thinkers; this is all the more true because examining theories that have evolved in this field in some depth enables one to broach relevant questions of fact with intellectual rigour.

The following deliberations focus on the question of what has been deduced from classic strategic thinking for strategic thinking that embraces the strategic challenges of the future.

The **first article** will therefore set out basic principles of philosophy and the theory of war. If one examines these basic principles, one finds valuable ideas in classic works by strategic thinkers. The names Sun Tzu, Machiavelli and Clausewitz are just a few examples of many thinkers who in the past have focused primarily on strategy in the context of military thinking. This article focuses on THE "philosopher of war", Carl von Clausewitz (1780-1831), whose name will almost always feature in any writing or discussion of classic strategy: he was a soldier of great experience, a historically minded philosopher, an historian and a political theorist. To this day, his work "On War" (written from 1818 to 1830, published posthumously in 1832) still elicits responses from soldiers, theorists and practitioners examining economic affairs, as well as politicians. It seeks to apply orderly thinking to a completely disorderly world – a parallel with today as we experience a period of change marked by great instability. The experiences, thoughts and actions of Clausewitz are essentially based on the same facts that we are faced with today. Clausewitz deserves great credit for creating long-lasting strategies for operating in an unstable environment.

Furthermore a focus on the innovative concept of the relationship between purpose, aims and means which Clausewitz developed is provided. The concept as such should be understood to be dynamic: a change in one parameter changes the other elements too. It is stated that it is particularly important for the aims to be based on the concept of how the war is waged. In each case, it is crucial to achieve one's aim, which generally means forcing the enemy to do what you want.

Last but not least, this article shows that "On War" should be seen as a product of its age, which was influenced by military conflicts and epoch-defining changes. With his comprehensive analysis, Clausewitz – in whom two worlds, the worlds of theory and of practice, are combined – not only provides theory but also delivers practical conclusions that still attract attention today, particularly in politics, business and the military.

The **second article** presents, from a historical perspective, scarce resources as the essential foundation of "Polemos" – in the meaning of "conflict" and "confrontation". Polemology as the "philosophy of war" has the essential task of understanding war, conflict and confrontation – as a prerequisite for being able to safeguard peace. The "economic", "political" and "cultural" dimensions at the root of any conflict or war must be identified. This makes it possible to formulate a precise strategic objective (according to Clausewitz).

The **third article** addresses the conflicting tension between strategy and responsibility, which is derived in particular from the dimension of time – whereas "strategy" looks to the future, "responsibility" conceptually refers to the past. It highlights the dilemma that leaders in liberal-republican polities face between the need for "strategic thinking" on the one hand and on the other hand the challenge that this thinking often only delivers results in distant parliamentary terms. However, it is made clear in this context that ultimately institutionalisation of the moral imperative is the real task and condition for the success of strategy.

1. Clausewitz: Philosophical Characterization and Methodology of Thought

Mauro Mantovani

The article on which the now revised and expanded contribution by Mauro Mantovani is based, was first published under the title 'Clausewitz: Philosophische Prägung und Denkmethodik' in Band 17/Jahrbuch 2021 der Clausewitz-Gesellschaft, ISBN: 978-3-9816962-7-1, Chapter III, pp. 126-135 and is published here with the kind permission of the president of the Clausewitz Society, Lieutenant General Carsten Jacobson.

For more than a century, the research debate on Carl von Clausewitz's legacy has revolved around the questions of how far his theory of war was influenced by philosophical concepts of his time and, in particular, the significance of the methods of thought of dialectics and the relation between purpose, ends (goals) and means.

This article attempts to summarize the original passages in this regard as well as the judgement of scholars.

The fact that Clausewitz does not mention a single philosopher by name in his magnum opus *On War (Vom Kriege)* may have driven curiosity about "hidden sources". Clausewitz hardly considered himself a philosopher, even if certain formulations (e.g. *On War* VI, 6; VI, 30) have been interpreted as expressions of such ambitions.[1] However, the Prussian war theorist used the terms philosophy/philosophical – quite in keeping with the linguistic usage of his time – synonymously with theory/theoretical, science/scientific or logic/logical.[2] And Clausewitz was explicitly skeptical about the usefulness of "philosophical" reflections in many places in his work (see below).

We do not have full knowledge of Clausewitz's reading of philosophical texts, let alone of the social contacts that inspired his work. However, it is well documented that Clausewitz first came into contact with philosophy when he attended the Prussian War Academy in Berlin from 1801 to 1804. There, Johann Gottfried Carl Christian Kiesewetter, himself a disciple of Immanuel Kant's teachings, taught philosophy to the cadets. Clausewitz may thus have gained indirect knowledge of Kant's distinction between pure and empirical

---

[1] See e.g. Stumpf, Reinhard (Hg.), *Kriegstheorie und Kriegsgeschichte. Carl von Clausewitz, Helmuth von Moltke*, Frankfurt am Main (Deutscher Klassiker Verlag) 1993, pp. 707, 845f.

[2] Aron, Raymond, *Clausewitz. Den Krieg denken*, Frankfurt a. M. (Propyläen) 1980, pp. 155, 330; Kondylis, Panajotis, *Theorie des Krieges. Clausewitz – Marx – Engels – Lenin*, Stuttgart (Klett-Cotta) 1988, p. 100; Müller, Christian Th., *Clausewitz verstehen. Wirken, Werk und Wirkung*, Leiden (Brill, Ferdinand Schöningh), 2021, p. 43; Stumpf, pp. 743, 857.

concepts, as well as of general logic and of the dialectical consideration of proposition and counter-proposition[3] via Kiesewetter's treatises. Although Clausewitz did not share Kant's view of war as a phenomenon to be overcome, he was in complete agreement with the principle of rational analysis generally advocated by the Enlightenment and central to Kant's logic.[4] Namely, Clausewitz strove to have his thinking guided by "logic" and "reason", as evidenced by dozens of remarks in his work. To what extent Clausewitz actually succeeded in applying Kantian-style logical thinking to his work remains a debatable question, partly because *On War* is known to have remained unfinished and fraught with inconsistencies. It has been suggested that Clausewitz borrowed certain terms such as "interaction" from Kant or that he alluded to Kant's table of categories (Kategorientafel) with his famous model of the trinity of war (Dreifaltigkeit des Kieges).[5] The findings on Kant's influence on Clausewitz thus remain somewhat ambivalent.

Alongside this is the assertion that Clausewitz applied Georg Wilhelm Friedrich Hegel's dialectical method.[6] However, it is just as unlikely that Clausewitz would have read original texts by Hegel as in the case of Kant. However, there is indeed a large number of concepts of binary opposition in his work that have been used as evidence that Clausewitz attempted to argue dialectically: War vs. politics, absolute vs. "real" war, escalating vs. de-escalating factors ("interactions" or "modifications"), attack vs. defence, art vs. science, dogmatism vs. pedagogy, theory vs. reality, intention vs. execution, material vs. moral factors, or the general vs. the particular.[7] Clausewitz thus undoubtedly used a form of dialectical thinking that operated with pairs of opposites and attempted to determine their nature and dynamic interaction.[8] He was

---

[3] Müller, p. 43.

[4] Aron, *Clausewitz. Den Krieg denken*, p. 658ff., Aron, Raymond, "Clausewitz – Stratege und Patriot", in: *Historische Zeitschrift*, Band 234 (1982), pp. 295–316; Gat, Azar, *A History of Military Thought: From the Enlightenment to the Cold War*, Oxford (OUP), 2001, p. 177f.; Paret, Peter, *Carl von Clausewitz and the State: The Man, His Theories, and His Times*, New Jersey (Princeton UP) 1985, p. 200ff.; Stumpf, p. 702ff.

[5] Aron, *Clausewitz. Den Krieg denken*, p. 327ff.

[6] See Gat, p. 233; Cormier, Youri, "Hegel and Clausewitz: Convergence on Method, Divergence on Ethics", *The International History Review*, 2014, Vol. 36, No. 3, pp. 419–442; Müller, p. 43ff.

[7] See Aron, *Clausewitz. Den Krieg denken*, p. 321f.; Gat, p. 234–238; Hartmann, Uwe, *Carl von Clausewitz and the Making of Modern Strategy*, Potsdam (Miles) 2002, p. 11; Waldman, Thomas, "Clausewitz and the Study of War", *Defence Studies*, Vol. 12, No. 3 (2012), pp. 345–374, in particular pp. 355–368.

[8] Howard, Michael and Peter Paret (ed. and transl.), *Carl von Clausewitz, On War*, Princeton (UP), 1976, p. 15f.; Strachan, Hew, *Clausewitz's On War: A Biography*, New York (Atlantic Monthly Press), 2007, p. 19; Waldman, p. 355.

obviously influenced by the dialectical method, which was, certainly wide-spread among German Enlightenment thinkers – including, for example, Friedrich Schleiermacher, whom Clausewitz knew personally.[9] But Clause-witz did not apply the method with the same consistency as Hegel.[10] A single passage reveals the Hegelian three-step from thesis to antithesis to synthesis:

> *"Up to now we have considered the incompatibility between war and every other human interest, individual or social – a difference that derives from human nature, and that therefore no philosophy can resolve. We have examined this incompatibility from various angles so that none of its conflicting elements should be missed. Now we must seek out the unity into which these contradictory elements combine in real life, which they do by partly neutralizing one another. We might have posited that unity to begin with, if it had not been necessary to emphasize the contradictions with all possible clarity and to consider the different elements separately. This unity lies in the concept that war is only a branch of political activity; that it is in no sense autonomous."* (On War VIII, 8, 6B; transl. by Howard/Paret, see fn. 8)

But even from this passage one will not be able to deduce more than a "convergence" of methodological thought between the two "fathers of the 'dialectic war theory'".[11]

Other philosophical influences on Clausewitz have been suspected, for example on the part of the idealist Johann Gottlieb Fichte. The starting point is a reference in Clausewitz's letters of 1808, which shows that he shared Fichte's views on human destiny and on religion.[12] Clausewitz also makes mention of the philosopher of the state, Montesquieu, supporting the thesis that the latter's works had served as a general model for him and that he had seen the community of European states in a similar way to Montesquieu – or Voltaire, for example.[13]

The question as to the influence of great philosophers or state theorists on the Prussian war theorist can of course be carried on almost indefinitely: For example, the similarity of Clausewitz's and Plato's thoughts on the martial virtues has been noted, or an "interesting commonality" between Thomas Hobbes and Clausewitz has been seen in the fact that both regarded war as a

---

[9] Gat, p. 193f.; Stumpf, p. 705.
[10] Howard/Paret, p. 15f.; Strachan, p. 69; Waldman, p. 355.
[11] Cormier, p. 423.
[12] Stumpf, p. 683; Strachan, p. 70f.
[13] Aron, *Clausewitz. Den Krieg denken*, pp. 157f., 323; Gat, p. 196, Howard/Paret, pp. 15-19; Stumpf, p. 707.

means of politics and not as a political entity itself.[14] And so there is ample room, also for future research, to identify argumentative parallels between Clausewitz and other thinkers.

On the whole, then, only borrowings from methods of contemporary philosophy that serve the purpose of "intellectual disciplining"[15] can be identified in Clausewitz. As shown, Clausewitz essentially borrowed from philosophy a modified form of the dialectical method employed by Enlightenment thinkers and made some allusions to Kantian concepts, which, however, are all likely to have been taken from Kiesewetter's teaching. Ultimately, they simply attest to Clausewitz's broad interest in the intellectual life of his time. Basically, however, Clausewitz was convinced that the army commander – the central addressee of his work – should stay away from philosophy and rely instead on historical knowledge:

> *"No theorist, and no commander, should bother himself with psychological and philosophical sophistries." And: "Historical examples clarify everything and also provide the best kind of proof in the empirical sciences. This is particularly true of the art of war." (On War* II, 2; transl. by Howard/Paret, see fn. 8)

Clausewitz was inspired primarily by historical generals, campaigns and military publicists of his time, above all by Napoleon and his new type of warfare and by Scharnhorst, his highly esteemed teacher and rector at the War Academy.[16]

In terms of his political convictions, Clausewitz, who had read the writings of the state philosopher Niccolò Machiavelli from an early age, was close to the tradition of European thought known as realpolitik. In his profound endeavour to grasp the nature and mutability of the phenomenon of war, however, he also made use of philosophical methods. If one understands philosophy as the search for answers to fundamental questions about the world, man and his actions, then one will thus consider the designation of Clausewitz – widespread since the end of the 19th century – as the "philosopher of war" or "philosopher in battle dress" to be quite appropriate, even if he was not interested in the containment of wars under international law or the question of their meaning from a historical-philosophical perspective.[17]

---

[14] Kleemeier, Ulrike, *Grundfragen einer philosophischen Theorie des Krieges. Platon – Hobbes – Clausewitz*, in: *Politische Ideen* 16, Berlin (de Gruyter) 2002, pp. 312–316.

[15] Kondylis, p. 100.

[16] Gat, p. 168f.; Stumpf, p. 700f.; Waldman, p. 352.

[17] Müller, pp. 43–45. On the "weaknesses" of Clausewitz' concepts see also Heuser, Beatrice, *Clausewitz lesen! – eine Einführung*, München (Oldenbourg) 2005, pp. 232–239.

A second central method of thinking in Clausewitz's works is, as is well known, the "ends-ways-means relation" in modern wording. This is not only more original than his dialectical mode of argumentation, but also of greater impact. The connection between purpose, ends (goals) and means can already be grasped in his "Strategy of 1804" and is developed at the very beginning of the work *On War*, where Clausewitz reflects on the nature of war, which he compares to an extended duel:

> "Each [wrestler] tries through physical force to compel the other to do his will; his immediate aim is to throw his opponent in order to make him incapable of further resistance. War is thus an act of force to compel our enemy to do our will."

This thought continues:

> "Force-that is, physical force [...] is thus the means of war; to impose our will on the enemy is its object. To secure that object we must render the enemy powerless; and that, in theory, is the true aim of warfare. That aim takes the place of the object, discarding it as something not actually part of war itself." (On War I, 1, 2; transl. by Howard/Paret, see fn. 8)

In other words: By "means" of the use of force or the warlike action, the enemy is to be rendered defenceless ("goal") and thus the ultimate political "end" lying outside of war or the art of war is to be pursued, namely that of imposing one's own will on the enemy or making him incapable of continuing to resist this will. The state of powerlessness of the enemy is thus, to a certain extent, the generalized precondition for achieving the purpose of a war. This purpose is to be sealed with a conclusion of peace, the concrete form of which Clausewitz, however, does not wish to commit himself to:

> "This object of course is usually remote, and only rarely lies very near at hand. A series of secondary objectives may serve as means to the attainment of the ultimate goal; these intermediate ends, which are means to higher ends, may in practice be of various types. Even the ultimate object, the purpose of the entire war, differs in almost every case." (On War III, 3, 8; transl. by Howard/Paret, see fn. 8)

Incidentally, these sentences also testify to a linguistic problem that was to give translators such as Howard and Paret a headache: Clausewitz used the two terms "aim/goals" (Ziel) and "purpose" (Zweck) essentially synonymously throughout much of his work. In the early version of his work *On War*, Clausewitz still distinguished between the "purpose of war" (Zweck des Krieges) and the "purpose in war" (Zweck im Kriege). It was only during the revision of the work that he began to replace the term "purpose in war" with the term "aim/goal", without consistently carrying this project through to its conclusion.[18]

Clausewitz makes more concrete statements about the means (or ways or also aims in war). A wide range of things and actions come into question for this purpose:

> *"We can now see that in war many roads lead to success, and that they do not all involve the opponent's outright defeat. They range from the destruction of the enemy's forces, the conquest of his territory, to a temporary occupation or invasion, to projects with an immediate political purpose, and finally to passively awaiting the enemy's attacks. Any one of these may be used to overcome the enemy's will: the choice depends on circumstances."*

He concludes this thought with these words:

> *"... questions of personality and personal relations raise the number of possible ways of achieving the goal of policy to infinity."* (On War I, 2, transl. by Howard/Paret, see fn. 8)

The variety of means on offer is expanded even more elsewhere in *On War*, ranging from physical entities such as one's armed forces (II, 2; IV, 4) and their "creation and training" (I, 2) or superiority (VII, 7), cognitive states such as intelligence (I, 1) and actions such as physical violence (see above) to operational behaviours such as (war) leadership (I, 1; III, 7), (main) combat (I, 2; IV, 11; VI, 26), engagement (1, 2; II, 2; VII, 6; VIII, 1), eliminating/destroying the enemy and his armed/fighting forces (I, 2; IV, 3 and 4; IV, 12; VII, 3A; VII, 6, 6), from people's war (VI, 8), concentric or lateral attack (VI, 28; VIII, 11), defence (in the mountains) (VI, 15), retreat (VIII, 9) to money (VIII, 8), mere threat (VIII, 6A) or mere armed observation (I, 1, 11)!

Central to our understanding now is that in Clausewitzian thought a means (path or goal in war) can transform itself into a means for a more distant goal, even for a (political) end:

> *"One can go on tracing the effects that a cause produces so long as it seems worthwhile. In the same way, a means may be evaluated, not merely with respect to its immediate end: that end itself should be appraised as a means for the next and highest one; and thus we can follow*

---

[18] Herberg-Rothe, Andreas, "Clausewitz's Concept of Strategy – Balancing Purpose, Aims and Means", *Journal of Strategic Studies* 2014, Vol. 37, Issue 6-7, p. 905f.; Strachan, p. 77.

a chain of sequential objectives until we reach one that requires no jus-
tification, because its necessity is self-evident. In many cases, particularly
those involving great and decisive actions, the analysis must extend to
the ultimate objective, which is to bring about peace." (*On War* II, 5)

Overall, despite all the linguistic difficulties, there is a broad consensus within the Clausewitz research community that the "ends-ways-means relationship" is characterised by a number of features: First, the concept is to be understood instrumentally: The means are to serve the military ends, and these in turn the political ends. Secondly, the concept is to be understood as hierarchical: Political ends take precedence over military ends. A political community (be it a state or a non-state actor) determines the (end) purpose of the war as well as the means required to achieve it, and exerts influence in various ways on the (intermediate) goals of the military leadership waging the war. Third, the concept reflects sequential thinking: The political leadership determines the (end) purpose of the war, uses the military instrument to do so and allows its leadership to define (intermediate) objectives at its level to support the (end) purpose. Fourth, the concept is dynamic in nature and this in a double sense: on the one hand, what is the end in the context of war becomes the means in the context of politics. On the other hand, the political end not only determines the military objectives, but also has to be measured according to these and according to the means available and employed:

> *"That [...] does not imply that the political aim is a tyrant. It must*
> *adapt itself to its chosen means, a process which can radically change it;*
> *yet the political aim remains the first consideration. Policy, then, will*
> *permeate all military operations, and, in so far as their violent nature*
> *will admit, it will have a continuous influence on them."* (On War I,
> 1, 23)

Fifth, the concept is inherently pragmatic in the sense that its components are to be understood as rational: Political ends are "value-rational" (in the sense of Max Weber), i.e. the best option in each case should be chosen; military ends, in turn, are "procedural-rational", i.e. the given means should be used optimally; and finally, the means are "purpose-rational", i.e. they are suitable and sufficient to achieve the ends sought.[19]

In short, Clausewitz developed a "conception of war as a whole structured by the hierarchy of means and ends", whereby one and the same phenomenon

---

[19] Herberg-Rothe, Andreas, *Clausewitz's Puzzle: The Political Theory of War*, Oxford (OUP), 2007, p. 129ff.; ders., "Clausewitz's Concept of Strategy", pp. 913–915.

can be either a purpose or an end or a means, depending on the level of action – politics, war, strategy and tactics.[20] The "ends-ways-means relation" is thus, on the one hand, the second characteristic of Clausewitzian thought and hence constitutes a guide to and provides structure for the reader[21]; on the other hand, Clausewitz is thus truly creative in introducing this relation into military thought. Moreover, the creation of this intellectual triad is groundbreaking in that it has become the basis of the modern understanding of strategy as the linking of ends, ways and means.

2. Polemology – On the Hermeneutics of War and Peace
Christian Stadler

The "polemos" is as old as humankind itself. Back in the age of hunters and gatherers, a time when humanity was not sedentary, there was a culture of cooperation in a big family unit – a joint effort to jointly conquer the natural environment and the dangers, as well as the opportunities, it presented. When man began to settle into a sedentary existence, the moment of common endeavour was replaced with the moment of competition for scarce resources: from the Bible (conflict between Cain the farmer and Abel the shepherd) to the philosophy of Rousseau ("homme sauvage") there are countless references to the fact that in the "modern society" of a property-based agricultural economy, competition is the defining moment of culture. This in turn gives rise to the basis of the "polemos" – scarce resources. We know from Immanuel Kant that space and time not only represent the forms of "apperception", but therefore also represent the parameters of our sensory consciousness. Anything that we can think of as "real" must exist somewhere in space and somewhere in time.

The "polemos" is already referred to by the forefather of Western philosophy, Heraclitus (approx. 500 BC, Ephesus), as the "father of all things". Polemos means not only – indeed not even primarily – "war", but essentially "conflict", "confrontation". This addresses the basic principle of dialectics (Hegel), negation, which is intrinsic as a principle of "opposition" to any "settlement". Polemos is essentially dynamic (Heraclitus: "No man steps in the same river twice"), i.e. the only thing that is reliable or constant is change, transition; true being therefore means "doing", but not the "act" (see in this regard Johann Gottlieb Fichte's Science of Knowledge). The essence of things is not derived

---

[20] Aron, *Clausewitz. Den Krieg denken*, p. 150, bzw. Müller, p. 109ff.
[21] Müller, p. 108ff.

from the "understanding" which for pragmatic reasons must bring the river of existence to a standstill ("under-stand"), but rather merely from the "reason" from which the principles, values and notions on which the river of existence and its flow are based are derived. For their part, they exist and their discernment gives rise to any "understanding", any solid existential pause in the flow of the existence of things. The philosophical discipline that is essentially dedicated to "understanding" is hermeneutics – and polemology is thus the hermeneutics of the polemos.

The notion of polemology as the "philosophy of war" originates from the Dutch sociologist Sebald Rudolf Steinmetz (1862-1940) and was picked up and developed further by the French sociologist Gaston Bouthoul (1896-1980). The task of polemology is to understand war, conflict and confrontation. Whereas the classic sentence uttered by Vegetius states that one must prepare – oneself? – for war, the intention was to secure peace, Bouthoul, in expanding this sentence hermeneutically, says: If you want to secure peace, you need to understand war. The central question now is: how can one adequately "understand" war, conflict and confrontation? An analogy from the legal sciences can be used here: the phenomenon of law can only really be "understood" – and therefore grasped – if one is aware of and understands the conflicts of interest on which the normalisation is founded. Law seeks to bring about peace, and the prerequisite for this is that one knows the truth about the constellation of the conflict in the background; otherwise, any normative action remains superficial and has no lasting effect on peace whatsoever.

The first step to understanding conflict and war is to recognise that by nature (modern) human beings are intrinsically prone to conflict (see Thomas Hobbes) and, with this in mind, peace represents the central cultural product of human civilisation. Just as "war" certainly requires a basic understanding, by the same token "peace" also needs to be comprehensively grasped. It concerns harmony and thus interaction between possibly divergent forces, trends and interests, it is about – and this is where we must agree with Rousseau – the cultural-political reconstruction of the peace that defined human beings in their pre-civilisational, and thus truly "natural", period. At any rate, one should not assume that culture, politics or civilisation are the root cause of situations of conflict, but rather the scarcity of "resources for survival".

In this context, a significant Western European philosopher is Plato (400 BC; Athens). In his early idealistic concept, he assumed that the true purpose of human life was ensuring that society is "just" and therefore that people live together "harmoniously". He also already envisaged "modern" society with a division of labour whose philosophical principles he analyses: he sees human society as being akin to the human body. The body has a soul consisting of three parts: *logistikon* – *thymoeides* – *epithymetikon*; the soul of reason – the soul of courage – the soul of desire. Broadly conceived, the life of a human being is happy or successful whenever these three souls are each in harmony in their own right and with each other. The head is the thinking part, the chest is the place of battle, and the lower abdomen is the place of basic survival. The "virtues" of these three parts of the soul are "wisdom", "courage" and "temperance". It is the harmonious accord between these different parts that then creates "justice". By analogy, in his *"Politeia"* Plato also views society (of the ancient polis) as having three elements, distinguishing between the philosophers, the guardians and the producers: the philosophers are noted for wisdom, the guardians for courage and the producers for temperance. In society, the virtues are also analogous to a human being: wisdom, courage and temperance, whose harmonious accord ultimately leads to justice. What is pertinent about Plato's conceptual insights is that they display a certain timelessness, which makes their structural relevance insightful for the present day.

In light of this conception, polemological hermeneutics can also address the understanding of conflicts, crises and ultimately wars: the Platonic triad is also astonishingly adept in providing explanations for this central area of interaction between people and societies: there is at any rate always an "economic", a "political" and a "cultural" dimension to every conflict, every crisis, indeed every war. In short, one can refer to these three levels as: oikos – polis – logos. The crucial thing is to view these three levels hermeneutically and not directly in instrumental terms.

Re. the oikos level: When the producing soul, the producer, is spoken about on this level, what this means for analysing wars and conflicts in the 21st century is that one must look at the essential resources needed for a society to survive: this level therefore relates to natural resources (oil, gas, water, climate, soil, minerals and rocks, but also biodiversity). Besides the question of natural resources, the question of human resources must also be addressed in this field (demography, health, training, commercial-administrative qualifications, skilled technological qualifications, patents, research capabilities, etc.). Furthermore, the availability or accessibility of these resources are of crucial importance – this is where questions of access to natural resources, transport and distribution systems (pipelines, etc.), but also migration (competition to secure the brightest minds around the world), play an important role. Transport routes and lines of communication are also of relevance in this area to the question of the survival of societies.

Re. the polis level: This level of crisis and war hermeneutics is all about the political conceptions (for example of geopolitics) and also corresponding institutions which extend from the constitutional order on which state power rests, and bureaucracy through to the question of the administration of justice. Reference is merely made here to the modern phenomenon of "lawfare". The security agencies, in particular the military, provide essential momentum for these state institutions. Its task is to fight the existential battle to safeguard the constitutional order externally. "Externally" is likewise to be understood comprehensively (not just geographically) and to be interpreted from the perspective of the constitutional order: what is meant here is forces from outside the constitutional order which forcefully "attack" the constitutional polity as such – disregarding this constitutional system – in order, depending on the intensity of the attack, (a) to shake it up, (b) to destroy it or (c) to replace it with a different constitutional order. At this level, it is therefore about maintaining one's own sovereignty and self-determination of the political system – at the end of the day it is about power!

Re. the logos level: This, the "wisdom" level, speaks to the phenomena of culture, religion, education, worldview, ideology and values, but also of language as the basis of culture ("Language is the birthplace of the spirit"; Hegel). Which worldview is adopted by societies, their respective elites, the populations, the artists? Which traditions are maintained, which practised lifestyles shape the world in which the respective society lives? Which concepts, theories or ideas are systemic-normative in nature? Which normative narratives define a respective society? At this point, it should explicitly be pointed out that "understand" does not mean "excuse"! This is a basic prerequisite for any hermeneutics. It is not about affirming various narratives of different societies, it is about identifying them, analysing them and thus laying bare their relevance to conflict.

Polemology then attempts always to record conflicts by measuring their economic, cultural and therefore ultimately (power-) political dimension. From a hermeneutic point of view, the following "formula of understanding" is crucial: *Oikos x logos => polis*. This formula should mean that, in the event of tension, pressure, problems or shortages in the area of the oikos (shortages are generally key here), it is essentially the logos level that matters in determining the way in which the polis level will respond. If for example there is a massive loss of wealth in a society, it is essentially up to the cultural level how the polis level – which is actually relevant for the polemology – responds; is the culture a "performance culture with a Calvinist character" or more of a "suffering culture with an Orthodox character"? Against which narrative background can the political leadership respond to the oikos developments?

Only when one has ascertained these underlying structures and correlations of conflicts, crises and wars ("polemological perspective") is one truly able to formulate a precise strategic objective (according to Clausewitz). Analogously to the methodology of the jurisprudence of interests, in the area of polemology there is also the tool of looking behind the purely "political-strategic" scenes of a polemos in order to understand where a conflict has truly arisen from and where – according to its internal logic – it is, in all probability, heading. And it is only those who have gained these insights into the basic dynamics and structure of a conflict that are able to take the steps to secure peace – *if you want to secure peace, you need to understand the war/conflict ...*

3. Strategy and Responsibility – On the Ethos of Strategic Thinking
Christian Stadler

To establish the relationship between strategy and responsibility, the terms themselves should first be considered more closely. It is striking that strategy is intrinsically associated with the "future", whereas "responsibility" conceptually refers to the past. However, both terms describe dimensions of "actions"; the area of strategy involves actions to be carried out in the future while responsibility focuses on actions that have been performed and for which one must now answer. In both terms, there is also a central link to freedom, because an action is freedom embodied – freedom that on the one hand requires careful future analysis and planning, but also throws up the question of responsibility in the event that the action should go wrong.

In a first approach, the notion of ethics should be briefly outlined: Ethics is one of the philosophical disciplines (such as metaphysics, rationale, aesthetics, etc.) which pursues its subject matter – the moral behaviour of people and societies – in a scientifically systematic way, and examines this behaviour to determine whether it is justified. Ethics examines the (Kantian) question: "What should I do?" – the question of individual and social morality. Morality is the setting of moral standards, while ethics is the systematic science of morality in practice.

Ethos in turn is an established set of rehearsed behaviours whose morality was negotiated by society generations ago. It is now traditionally stabilised and thus has a stabilising effect on behaviour, which essentially protects social coexistence from any structural friction and helps to maintain stability and peaceableness on all sides. Ethos is therefore related to normativity, stability and thus principally to any state polity whose strategic potential is to be focused on here. A distinction must be made between two dimensions, which will each be addressed separately below: first, ethical responsibility, which means actually thinking "strategically" when you perform a leadership role in a liberal-republican polity. The second dimension would be determining what type of strategic thinking is ethically commendable and therefore strictly "responsible".

On the morality of strategic thinking and actions

If you perform a leadership role as part of a liberal-republican polity (according to Kant), you are not only obliged to handle the status quo, but you must also help to shape the future today. The problem with the future is that it cannot really be concisely visualised within the generally very short parliamentary terms of a democracy. In fact, it always relates at least to the next-but-one parliamentary term which is not currently the focus of the operational interest in retaining power, and it may in fact be true that – looking purely at the calculus of power – it is actually not advisable to make decisions for the future now and bear the negative political costs, if the benefits of this endeavour will only become apparent in 5-10 years and "fall into the lap" of one's political rival, who may in fact secure power in the very parliamentary period in which the rewards from the future-facing decisions will be reaped as a result of criticising the current measure.

For this (structural) reason, it is not surprising that there is no particular interest in "strategic thinking" among modern liberal-republican political elites because, in terms of power politics, this may even become "dangerous" for the parties involved because the costs are immediately apparent, but the benefit does not manifest itself for many years. In view of the political reality in Western democracies, the call for classic "statesmen" (or "stateswomen") who would have thought and acted across the generations evokes a phrase that Nietzsche once uttered about Goethe's Faust: a lovely waste of time.

But this structural fact does not undermine the need for "strategic thinking" as part of liberal-republican polities – safeguarding human dignity and the basic human rights of freedom and security is such an ambitious undertaking that the representatives of this political concept will not be able to afford in the long run to withstand the corresponding resistance that builds up without "strategic thinking". However, the "instrumental" nature of the strategic choice must not be overlooked. In light of Carl von Clausewitz's triad – politics / strategy / tactics – a clear distinction must be made between the strategic aim and the – overriding – political objective.

Political objectives must be legitimised as such, examined for their moral quality; they can be "good" or "bad". In a democracy, the people are materially involved in setting the political objectives that are pursued by each polity. This is also the origin of the notion of "political responsibility", which should not just be reduced down to the criminal responsibility of officials exercising their office. It is also about a higher moral responsibility which a political objective must satisfy if one does not just want to accept, as per Augustine, that a political system is not really any different from a band of robbers. According to Augustine, justice is the crucial difference, the moral substance that political steps imply.

By contrast, in light of the political objective which they serve, strategic aims are either expedient or they are not. A strategy may "work out – or it may not. The "value" of strategic aims as such is their usefulness, their capacity for serving, of implementing the political objective. They are therefore critiqued according to their usefulness, not their morality. It thus seems that a strategy, strategic thinking, is "responsible" whenever it realises the political objective that was or is intended – at a political level – as precisely as possible. However, it is not that simple, because in this context the "strategy of morality" – which is not prima facie insightful – must also be considered.

On the strategy of morality

To demonstrate this correlation, the extent to which "morality" is linked to "prudence" should briefly be outlined. Generally, – following Kant – morality (*understood to mean behaviour derived from the categorical imperative 'you ought'!*) is contrasted with prudence as being not of normative, but of strategic quality: which steps need to be taken – in due consideration of the environmental conditions – to achieve a desired aim? It is often claimed that there is an irreconcilable contradiction between moral and prudent behaviour: either you behave morally, but as a result "imprudently", or you behave strategically prudently, but in most cases this is then not especially "moral" behaviour.

However, if one examines the teachings of German idealism in greater depth, you find with Hegel for example the famous claim: *What is rational is real and what is real is rational...* If one views this sentence from an "Aristotelian" viewpoint, meaning as an empirical statement, you may at first glance doubt that it is correct. However, if one understands this sentence "platonically", then it means: what is rational SHOULD be real and what is real SHOULD be rational! Hegel is well known for having reconciled Platonic and Aristotelian thinking.

We therefore have a statement that points us to the rational underlying structure of reality which primarily needs to be "set" (Fichte). We are thus presented with a hermeneutic task which – assuming morality to be rational – leads us to the formula: *Morality × time = prudence*. Moral behaviour is only "imprudent", i.e. not promising, under the immediate condition of the present. However, if one manages to rescue the moral stance over time so that its fruits become visible, then moral behaviour regularly leads to prudent, successful results... why is this so? Because fundamentally reality is indeed rational – and morality is indeed an expression of rationality. So it is clear: time is the factor that dictates whether or not morality and therefore rationality can become real.

The moral importance of time has therefore been (indicatively) highlighted; if human behaviour wishes to be successful, it needs to be rational (i.e. moral) and have a lasting effect over time – into the future – because, if moral behaviour has no future, then it also has no reality in the present... with this in mind it is possible to surmise the ethical dimension of strategy; without strategy, human behaviour cannot break out of the present and break into the future – and can therefore never be truly successful. Without addressing the implied problem of time in greater depth, it should be pointed out that institutionalisation of the moral imperative is the real task and also the condition for the success of strategy... any strategic interest that has a moral dimension must therefore at least be based on the necessary institutional structure.

4. References

Aron, R. (1980). *Clausewitz. Den Krieg denken*. Frankfurt a. M.

Aron, R. (1982). Clausewitz – Stratege und Patriot. *Historische Zeitschrift*, 234, 295-316.

Bouthoul, G. (1953). *La guerre*. Paris.

Bouthoul, G. (1970). Traité de polémologie. Paris.

Bouthoul, G. (1976).: Essais de polémologie. Paris.

Gat, A. (2001). *A History of Military Thought: From the Enlightenment to the Cold War*. Oxford (UP).

Hahlweg, W. (1979). *Carl von Clausewitz. Verstreute kleine Schriften*. Osnabrück.

Handel, M. I. (ed.). (2005). *Clausewitz and Modern Strategy*. Abingdon: Routledge.

Hartmann, N. (1962). *Ethik*. Berlin.

Heuser, B. (2005). *Clausewitz lesen! – eine Einführung*. E ST 831.

Herberg-Rothe, A. (2007). *Clausewitz in the Twenty-First Century*. Oxford: Oxford University Press.

Herberg-Rothe, A. (2014). Clausewitz's Concept of Strategy – Balancing Purpose, Aims and Means. *Journal of Strategic Studies, 37/6-7*, 903-925.

Höffe, O. (2018). *Ethik*. München.

Howard, M. (1970). *Studies in War and Peace*. London: Temple Smith

Howard, M. (2002). *Clausewitz. A Very Short Introduction*, Oxford (UP).

Jäger, T. & Beckmann, R., Carl von Clausewitz' Theorie des Krieges. In: *Handbuch Kriegstheorien*, 214-226.

Kant, I. (2000). *Kritik der praktischen Vernunft*. Frankfurt/M.

Kant, I. (2000). *Grundlegung zur Metaphysik der Sitten*. Frankfurt/M.

Kleemeier, U. (2002). Grundfragen einer philosophischen Theorie des Krieges. Platon - Hobbes – Clausewitz. *Politische Ideen* 16, de Gruyter.

Klinger, M. (2007). *Héritage et actualité de la polémologie*. Paris 2007

Molina Cano, J. (2019). *Gaston Bouthoul, inventor de la polemología. Demografía, guerra y complejos belígenos*. Madrid.

Münkler, H. (2003). Clausewitz' Theorie des Krieges. In: *Würzburger Vorträge zur Rechtsphilosophie, Rechtstheorie und Rechtssoziologie*. Baden-Baden: Nomos.

Lütsch, K. (2011/2017). *Der Geist des Krieges. Ein Neuansatz in der geistesgeschichtlichen Betrachtung der Theorie des Krieges bei Carl von Clausewitz*.

Paret, P. (1993). *Clausewitz und der Staat. Der Mensch, seine Theorien und seine Zeit*. Bonn. (Translation of *Carl von Clausewitz and the State: The Man, His Theories, and His Times*, Princeton UP 1985.)

Paret, P. (1993). *Understanding War: Essays on Clausewitz and the History of Military Power*. New Jersey: Princeton UP.

Plato. (1989). Der Staat. Über das Gerechte. Hamburg.

Reil, H. (2015). *Ethik als Strategie*. Frankfurt/M.

Rothfels, H. (1920). *Carl von Clausewitz, Politik und Krieg*. Berlin (Reprint 1980).

Schering, W. M. (1935). *Die Kriegsphilosophie von Clausewitz. Eine Untersuchung über ihren systematischen Aufbau*. Hamburg: Hanseatische Verlags Anstalt.

Schmidt, A. (2007). Carl von Clausewitz, Kriegstheoretische Konzeption und geschichtsphilosophische Hintergründe. *Internationales Clausewitz-Zentrum, Clausewitz – Information, 1/2007*. Hamburg.

Schössler, D. (1989). Das Wechselverhältnis von Theorie und Praxis bei Carl von Clausewitz. *Archiv für Geschichte der Philosophie, vol. 71 (1)*, 39-62.

Sehested von Gyldenfeldt, C. (2002). *Von Alfred Vierkandt zu Carl v. Clausewitz. Walther Malmsten Schering und die Quellen gemeinschaftlichen Handelns in Frieden und Krieg*, Reihe: Beiträge zur Geschichte der Soziologie, Band 12. Münster: LIT-Verlag.

Souchon, L. (2012). *Carl von Clausewitz. Strategie im 21. Jahrhundert.* Hamburg.

Spinoza. (2012). *Ethik.* Hamburg.

Stadler, C. (1996). *Fichtes Grundlegung des ethischen Idealismus.* Cuxhaven-Dartford.

Stadler, C. (2009). *Krieg.* Wien.

Stadler, C. (2001). Philosophie et Stratégie. *AGIR Journal de la Société de Stratégie.* Paris.

Stadler, C. & Stupka, A. (2000). Vom Wesen und Wert des Militärischen überhaupt. Militärwissenschaft im Zeichen der Polemologie. *Österreichische Militärische Zeitschrift, 2000/6.* Wien.

Steinmetz, S. R. (1907). *Die Philosophie des Krieges.* Leipzig.

Steinmetz, S. R. (1929). *Die Soziologie des Krieges.* Leipzig.

Stone, J. (2017). Beyond Clausewitz: Better ways of thinking strategically. *Comparative Strategy, Vol. 36, No. 5,* 468-478.

Strachan, H. (2007). *Über Carl von Clausewitz. Vom Kriege.* München.

Strachan, H. (1993). Clausewitz and the Dialectics of War. In: Strachan H. & Stumpf, R. (Eds.), *Kriegstheorie und Kriegsgeschichte. Carl von Clausewitz, Helmuth von Moltke.* Frankfurt am Main.

Tugendhat, E. (1993). Vorlesungen über Ethik. Frankfurt/M.

van Creveld, M. (2005) *The Art of War. War and Military Thought.* New York: Smithsonian Books.

Waldman, T. (2012). Clausewitz and the Study of War. *Defence Studies,* vol. 12, no. 3, 345-374.

5. Further Reading:

Bouthoul, G. (1953). *La guerre.* Paris .

Bouthoul, G. (1970). Traité de polémologie. Paris

Gat, A. (2001). *A History of Military Thought: From the Enlightenment to the Cold War.* Oxford (UP).

Handel, M. I. (ed.). (2005). *Clausewitz and Modern Strategy.* Abingdon: Routledge.

Heuser, B. (2002). *Reading Clausewitz.* London: Pimlico.

Heuser, B. (2010a) *The Strategy Makers: Thoughts on War and Society from Machiavelli to Clausewitz.* Santa Barbara, CA: Praeger.

Heuser, B. (2010b). *The Evolution of Strategy: Thinking War from Antiquity to the Present.* Cambridge: Cambridge University Press.

Herberg-Rothe, A. (2007). *Clausewitz in the Twenty-First Century.* Oxford: Oxford University Press.

Howard, M. (1970). *Studies in War and Peace*. London: Temple Smith

Howard, M. (2002). *Clausewitz. A Very Short Introduction*, Oxford (UP).

Klinger, M. (2007). *Héritage et actualité de la polémologie*. Paris 2007

Molina Cano, J. (2019). *Gaston Bouthoul, inventor de la polemología. Demografía, guerra y complejos belígenos*. Madrid.

Paret, P. (1993). *Clausewitz und der Staat. Der Mensch, seine Theorien und seine Zeit*. Bonn. (Translation of *Carl von Clausewitz and the State: The Man, His Theories, and His Times*, Princeton UP 1985.)

Paret, P. (1993). *Understanding War: Essays on Clausewitz and the History of Military Power*. New Jersey: Princeton UP.

Spinoza. (2012). *Ethik*. Hamburg.

Stadler, C. (1996). *Fichtes Grundlegung des ethischen Idealismus*. Cuxhaven-Dartford.

Stadler, C. (2009). *Krieg*. Wien.

Stadler, C. (2001). Philosophie et Stratégie. *AGIR Journal de la Société de Stratégie*. Paris.

Stone, J. (2017). Beyond Clausewitz: Better ways of thinking strategically. *Comparative Strategy, Vol. 36, No. 5*, 468-478.

Strachan, H. (1993). Clausewitz and the Dialectics of War. In: Strachan H. & Stumpf, R. (Eds.), *Kriegstheorie und Kriegsgeschichte. Carl von Clausewitz, Helmuth von Moltke*. Frankfurt am Main.

van Creveld, M. (2005) *The Art of War. War and Military Thought*. New York: Smithsonian Books.

Chapter 4: Military Strategy

BG Mag. Philipp Eder, BG Mag. Andreas Rotheneder

Key Words: Military Strategy; NATO; Operations; National Defence; Military Strategic Command; Operational Level Command; European Union; Commons; Cyber Force;

0. Abstract

Military strategy has only come into being over time and is thus not satisfactorily described in most classic texts on the matter, and its tasks often listed as part of the traditional command echelons, mostly strategy.

However, especially since the concept of strategy has begun to move from the purely military to the whole-of-nation echelon, it has taken on an important role in the long-term orientation, operations planning and operations preparation of armed forces, as well as the conduct of operations.

The procedures and tasks to be mastered by the individual services are of great importance in this context, as they are the main instruments available to the military-strategic echelon in the achievement of strategic goals, also in today's hybrid conflicts.

In order to really grasp the role the military-strategic echelon plays, it is necessary to be aware of its embedding in the strategic echelon on the one hand as well as its processes and responsibilities *vis-à-vis* the operational and tactical command level on the other.

In any case, the military-strategic level is part of strategic command with all the dependencies, responsibilities and requirements associated with it. This determines the demands made of the higher officer training, continuation training and further training.

1. Introduction

This chapter shows how long-term armed forces planning, operations planning, operations preparation as well as conduct of operations are implemented at the military-strategic echelon.

The former's framework conditions result from the directives defined by the superordinate echelon, in particular by the strategic concept, the military doctrine, and the allocation of resources.

Given the role of the North Atlantic Treaty Organization (NATO) as Europe's most important military alliance and as the pace-setter of interoperability for the European states, some of its documents and processes are reproduced to illustrate the theoretical content.

The services' procedures and tasks are awarded great importance in this paper, as they are essential instruments of the military-strategic echelon for the achievement of strategic goals. It is also possible to derive very good practical examples of military-strategic action from the armed forces profiles, capabilities and joint or individual procedures of the land forces, naval forces, air forces, space forces, special operations forces, cyber forces and information forces.

2. Hierarchical Integration of Military Strategy

NATO defines military strategy as follows:

> *that component of national or multinational strategy, presenting the manner in which military power should be developed and applied to achieve national objectives or those of a group of nations* (cf. NATO 2017, p. 3-1).

Given the fact that military strategy is part of strategy, the following (Austrian) definition also applies:

> *Strategy is the coordinated application and exploitation of all means and possibilities of the state to achieve its goals* (Militärlexikon 2020).

Strategy is the task of the political leadership of a state or an alliance.

Military strategy is exercised at the level of a Federal Ministry of Defence, the military headquarters of an alliance or a general staff. The implementation of military strategy is carried out at the operational or, subsequently, tactical echelon.

Three examples:

In NATO, the strategic level is the North Atlantic Council. The military-strategic level of NATO includes the Military Committee, the International Military Staff and the two commands, Allied Command Operations (ACO) and Allied Command Transformation (ACT).

The Council of the European Union (EU), in conjunction with the EU Commission and the European Parliament, represents the strategic level. The EU Military Staff or the EU Military Committee can be described as the military-strategic level. As there is no collective defence, the EU boasts no commander-in-chief.

The strategic level in the United States of America (USA) is the President together with Congress. The President is also the sole commander-in-chief of the armed forces. The military-strategic level of the USA is made up of the Department of Defense and the Joint Chiefs of Staff.

States or political alliances have a wide range of means and possibilities at their disposal to achieve their goals. This chapter will focus on these through the prism of security policy. This is where the concept of hybrid conflict has manifested itself in recent years. Knowledge of this concept makes it easier to understand the role of the military-strategic level in whole-of-nation actions.

3. Military Strategy and Hybrid Conflicts Allied Joint Publication-01 (AJP-01), dated February 2017

For European armed forces, the erstwhile concept of war, clearly standardised under international law, has been replaced by a wide range of often unpredictable uses of force in the grey area between war and peace. The term *hybrid conflict* has become known to a wider public at the latest since Russia's intervention in the Crimea or the conflict in eastern Ukraine.

In hybrid conflicts, several if not all available instruments of power-politics (below the threshold of armed conflict) are made use of to achieve strategic goals, with the military not necessarily employed.

This can unfold simultaneously or consecutively, with the aggressor's covertness regarding the identification and the intention of the use of force a further important characteristic.

Conflicts use the following spheres of power:

- foreign policy, e.g. by using diplomacy to isolate, blackmail, influence allies/coalitions;
- the economy, e.g. by exploiting the monopoly position as an energy supplier, exerting influence on the capital market and/or on capital flows and monetary policy, etc;
- the civil field, e.g. by using corruption and blackmail in state structures, such as the police and the judiciary;
- information, e.g. by controlling the media, use of propaganda, such as the dissemination of false information;
- the military, e.g. through attacks and terror by irregular forces or by regular state forces acting covertly, intimidating measures, exercises (close to the

border), deployment of conventional troops and, if goals cannot be achieved any other way, attack by regular forces;

In most cases, these spheres of power are applied, if not comprehensively, in a coordinated manner and combined flexibly.

The main players in these conflicts are states or state-like actors, which have the various instruments of power at their disposal and can employ them. State-like actors can be organisations which are not regarded as states pursuant to international law, but which boast numerous instruments of power traditionally attributed to states only. Such actors include, for example, extremist organisations with a political agenda, such as the Islamic State (IS) during its most successful phase, or formerly the Palestine Liberation Organisation (PLO), which have the appropriate resources available through their networks.

Without any advance warning, every action of an attacker can have a direct effect on the opponent's weak points (vulnerabilities) or create such weak points for a subsequent effect by exploiting environmental conditions.

The direct use of physical force can – separately or in combination – include conventional and sub-conventional warfare, terrorism, as well as violent actions of population groups, including organised crime.

In this, existing national and international law reaches its limits – not only in cyberspace.

A characteristic feature of hybrid conflicts is that actions are highly cloaked and thus not attributable, which also includes the exercise of different escalation levels in the use of force, and, if necessary, long phases without any recognisable activities. The escalation levels do not have to be ascending, but can alternate with de-escalation phases or include preparations for the use of force, which do not materialise. A detectable and mostly concurrent phase formation cannot be identified.

From the aggressor's point of view, destabilising the attacked party is a decisive prerequisite to strategic goal achievement, as it makes it much easier to impose the former's interests. A final end to the conflict does not necessarily have to be aimed for; achieving a situation which permanently restricts the attacked party's freedom of action can also produce goal achievement (frozen conflict).

For the defence against hybrid opponents, military national defence is seen as the deployment of the military within the framework of *comprehensive national defence*, often also called *total defence* or *complete defence*. Crucial in this context is not the type of opponents and their possible identification with foreign armed forces, but only the established necessity to use military assets of defending against threats in order to prevent a loss of sovereignty.

The responsibilities, resources and role of military strategy within a state or an alliance are determined by the strategic echelon.

4. Strategic Parameters for Military Strategy

The strategic level uses laws and strategies to specify how the security policy (security strategy) and especially the military defence of the state is to be set up (military doctrine). It thus defines purpose, resources and the risks to be accepted. This is the task of the heads of state and government or parliaments; three examples from NATO, the EU and the USA should serve as illustrations:

4.1 NATO

In Europe, the majority of states are members of NATO, whose directive for military-strategic planning is the *NATO Strategic Concept*.

The *Strategic Concept 2010* (cf. NATO 2010a) defines the following core NATO tasks:

- collective defence,
- crisis management, and
- cooperative security.

4.1 European Union

The EU is not a military alliance in the sense of a collective defence capability like NATO. The EU, like NATO, does not have its own armed forces. Instead, the EU has recourse to the member states' armed forces, which decide autonomously on the deployment in individual cases.

The EU Global Strategy defines the EU's strategic ambition in five priority fields of action (cf. EU 2016):

- Security and defence: reinforcing joint action in the areas of defence, cyber security, the fight against terrorism, energy security and strategic communications; strengthened cooperation with international partners, in particular NATO;
- Resilience: strengthening the resilience of states and civil society in the southern and eastern neighbourhood, with particular reference to the accession prospects of the Western Balkans;
- Integrated crisis management: Peacebuilding and sustainable crisis management through the integration of all available EU policies (foreign policy, development policy, CSDP, etc.), active involvement at all levels of the conflict cycle and cooperation with partners;

- Regional order: taking into account regional dynamics in EU external action and support for regional cooperation initiatives;
- Global governance: commitment to the principles of international law; promotion of human rights, sustainable development and effective multilateralism, hence continuous cooperation with international partners at both state and non-state level;

4.2 United States of America

The USA is the only country in the world with a conventional global offensive capability. Pursuant to the US National Security Strategy (cf. White House, 2017), the four national vital interests are

- Protect the homeland, the American people, and the American way of life
- Promote American prosperity
- Preserve peace through strength
- Advance American influence

4.3 Military Doctrines and Defence Strategies

Neutral or non-aligned states define their military doctrine without being embedded in an alliance.

In Europe, military doctrines are currently more defensive in nature. Therefore NATO, its allies, neutral and non-aligned countries, Russia and its partners, as well as China do not have conventional offensive capabilities which would go beyond regionally limited offensives. In accordance with their military doctrines, all states with nuclear capabilities only keep these ready for a possible counter-attack (second strike against first strike).

At the defence policy level, i.e. in the ministries of defence, assessments are derived from the strategic guidelines, which lead to armed forces profile variants. These represent alternative strategic thrusts regarding the defence-political orientation, based on various ways of perceiving the strategic tasks portfolio. In this context, the military-strategic echelon must play a key advisory role with regard to the general capabilities portfolio and performance potential of the armed forces.

After a thorough assessment, the minister of defence, parliament, or the commander-in-chief of the armed forces (in many countries this is the head of state, who is at least closely involved) selects a force profile, usually in combination with an ambition.

The specification of how this force profile can be achieved is laid down in one (defence strategy) or several documents produced by the defence-political echelon. This guarantees civilian control over the planning and command of the military.

This can be illustrated quite well by the example of the EU, whose current defence strategy is formed of the military Headline Goals. The military 2003 Headline Goals defined at the 2003 Helsinki Summit set out that 50,000 – 60,000 soldiers (= ambition) should be deployable within 60 days for a period of up to one year for the entire range of Petersberg Tasks as an EU Rapid Reaction Force (= force profile).

There is a similar process in NATO, which, however, is focused on the above-mentioned core tasks pursuant to the 2010 Strategic Concept. Multi-nationality plays a key role here. In order to enable the armed forces of different nations to work together, standardisation and interoperability in operational procedures, tactics and technology are promoted at the strategic level.

In the USA, the National Defense Strategy (cf. Department of Defense, 2018) sets out, *inter alia*, the following ambitions:

- During normal day-to-day operations: the Joint Force will sustainably compete to deter conflicts by degrading terrorist or WMD threats, and defend U.S. interests from challenges below the level armed conflict in the three key regions Indo-Pacific, Europe, and the Middle East.
- In wartime: the fully mobilized Joint Force will be capable of defeating aggression by a major power, deterring opportunistic aggression elsewhere, and disrupting imminent terrorist and WMD threats.
- During peace or in war: the Joint Force will deter nuclear and non-nuclear strategic attacks and defend the homeland.

5. Military-Strategic Planning and Command

Derived from the strategic guidelines, the military-strategic echelon has the task of defining goals, framework conditions as well as resource requirements/resource availability for armed forces planning and for immediate armed forces deployment, thus, on the one hand, creating the prerequisites for implementation, and, on the other hand, for the operational command echelon.

The military-strategic level, usually a general staff or similar institution, assumes responsibility for the implementation of the force profile and the ambition. In this, a distinction must be made between

- military-strategic armed forces planning,
- military-strategic operations planning and operations preparation, as well as

- military-strategic conduct of operations.

5.1 Military-Strategic Armed Forces Planning

The main task of military-strategic armed forces planning is to close identified capability gaps. This can be done in the long term (approx. 10 years) or in the short term (as quickly as possible).

In the long term, the systematic closing of identified capability gaps must be brought into line with the available resources. This requires long-term military-strategic trend analyses which reflect the future character of military conflicts.

Military-strategic concepts are often the main document resulting from this process with a long-term planning horizon of more than 10 years. They contain an overview of the security and defence-political framework and, as derivations, the military-strategic objectives, tasks, procedures, dischargers of tasks, principles and policies, as well as guidelines for armed forces development. Military-strategic armed forces planning comprises the further development of all services, including nuclear forces where necessary.

The military-strategic capability requirements can be determined from this. They are then compared with the current status of the armed forces, which produces the capability gaps.

Once the necessary financial requirements have been determined, long-term budgetary programme planning can be used to determine the investment requirements. In this case, a stable, long-term investment framework is helpful to develop the armed forces further on the basis of corresponding strategic priority setting along all lines of development in a military-strategically synchronised manner.

The lines of development differ slightly in most countries, but typically include

- personnel,
- organisation including structure,
- equipment including allowances,
- infrastructure,
- regulations, and
- training.

Procurement processes are used to invest in defence products to close capability gaps, whereby here, too, all lines of development must be systematically considered. Defence products are provided, operated and phased out from the armed forces at the end of their life cycles.

In the short term, the urgent need to fill capability gaps may arise from operational requirements. According to Clausewitz, the character of military conflicts changes like a chameleon, despite all professional advance planning. This fact will never change. In ongoing operations, therefore, armed forces planning must act expeditiously in order to be able to make suddenly required capabilities available to the forces as quickly as possible along the above-mentioned lines of development.

Military-strategic armed forces planning, including the procurement of defence products, is the responsibility of the nation states. Depending on their membership in NATO or the EU, they act more or less in coordination with the respective organisation. In both NATO and the EU military-strategic armed forces planning is the purview of the competent staffs of the organisation.

In NATO, the Military Committee, on the basis of the above-mentioned Strategic Concept, additional strategic guidelines derived therefrom, and additional military-strategic concepts, sets planning objectives for the member states so that they meet the identified capability requirements for the collective defence of the Alliance. With countries which are linked with NATO in the Partnership for Peace, Partnership Goals are agreed upon on a voluntary basis so that joint peace support operations can be carried out. On the basis of these objectives, units and formations are made available to NATO. Planning objectives and partnership objectives both include requirements to achieve interoperability through standardisation requirements pertaining to all lines of development.

The Member States voluntarily notify the EU of all or parts of the units made available to NATO. Troop requirements are defined on the basis of an assessment of the EU Global Strategy and the Military Headline Goals. These are compared with the units made available by the Member States and corresponding future requirements are formulated (Requirements Catalogue). This produces capability gaps, which are continuously reviewed to ensure that they can be closed jointly (Progress Catalogue).

Units and formations are available for military-strategic operations planning, derived from these NATO and EU processes and based on additional national requirements.

5.2 Military-Strategic Operations Planning and Preparation

These range from measures of general operations preparation such as training and exercise planning to capability requirements for the forces, military-strategic contingency planning and concrete operations planning based thereon.

Capability requirements for the forces are military-strategic directives which define the concrete implementation of the military procedures the forces need to master.

Military-strategic contingency planning is the elaboration of plans in the context of an assessment regarding the generic feasibility of force provision on the basis of the operational procedures and other requirements laid down in military-strategic concepts. They serve as a basis for the rapid elaboration, if necessary, of military-strategic options in the context of the planning of an imminent concrete operation. The option selected by the strategic echelon is subsequently made concrete in military-strategic plans of operation.

In NATO, military-strategic contingency planning and military-strategic courses of action are developed by the Military Committee with the involvement of the Supreme Allied Commander Europe (SACEUR, Commander of Allied Command Operations – ACO). In the event of an operation, a course of action is approved by the North Atlantic Council. This is the basis for the concrete military-strategic operations planning of the SACEUR.

The following military-strategic fields of action are applied in NATO (cf. 2017a, pp. 2-19f), for example:

- wage war
- provide security
- support peace
- military activities in peace

Military strategic operations planning must be able to assess up to two levels of command more deeply in order to be able to draw up operationally achievable military strategic contingency plans. These include the operational actions (often involving several services) and the tactical procedures of the branches. This requires understanding – and ideally experience – of operations planning and command and control and use at the upper tactical command level of the Component Commands.

Types of operations in e.g. NATO (cf. ibid., 2-21ff) are:

- combat
- crisis response
- counter irregular activities
    - counter-insurgency
    - counterterrorism
    - counter-criminality
- military contribution to peace support
- military contribution to humanitarian assistance

102

- military contribution to stabilisation and reconstruction
- non-combatant evacuation
- extraction
- sanctions and embargoes
- freedom of navigation and overflight

Military-strategic operations planning takes all available services into account. Depending on the nation, these can be, for example:

- land forces
- naval forces
- air forces
- space forces
- special operations forces
- cyber forces
- information forces

Until the First World War, the interaction of services was an exception. Since then, cross-service cooperation, i.e. *jointness*s, has become an indispensable part of successful warfare worldwide. If necessary and expedient, however, the individual services are still able to achieve strategic objectives independently by applying military-strategic procedures.

5.2.1 Land Forces

In recent decades, Western and Russian land forces have not been charged with the task of achieving military strategic objectives by attack, defence or delay without the cooperation with other services. It should be noted that many land forces are organically equipped with army aviation to support their land forces.

With regard to conventional warfare as well as counterinsurgency operations, the tactical procedures (cf. NATO 2018, chapter 2, 4, 5, 7) of land forces have remained unchanged in recent years, i.e. attack, defence, delay and protection being available for assessment by military-strategic planners.

- Attack has the purpose of disrupting or destroying the opponent and/or gaining terrain. Attacks can be deliberate attacks, hasty attacks, counter attacks, hasty counter attacks, or pursuits.
- In defence, a defined space is to be held against enemy attacks, and enemy elements are to be destroyed. This can be done from positions or by means of mobile defence.
- The purpose of delaying operations is to slow down enemy forces while maintaining combat strength or to bring enemy forces to a halt

for a limited period of time, thereby achieving attrition and gaining time. Its operational forms are time-limited defence or delaying operations.

- Protection means safeguarding important objects, traffic routes, areas and persons from surprise attacks by open or covert enemy forces or civil disruption. This can involve the protection of areas, objects, transports, traffic routes, borders, persons as well as organisations or counterpursuits as well as the inspection and searching of spaces and objects. Protection is the tactical procedure which is mainly used by land forces as part of the military strategic field of action known as *peace support*.

- The procedures required to ensure the operation are reconnaissance of the enemy and the terrain, security, march, and surveillance.

- There are also other special procedures, such as meeting engagement, disengagement, bypassing, rearward passage of lines, channelling, relief in place, negotiating and/or breaching of obstacles, raid and ambush.

5.2.2 Air Forces

Air forces can also be deployed autonomously to project power, gain air dominance or air superiority, or to prevent or restrict enemy air movements, while at the same time remaining an important military-strategic instrument to support other services.

- The purpose of strategic air strikes is to combat specially selected military, political or economic targets by means of strategic air warfare assets in order to pursue military-strategic objectives (cf. NATO 2016a, pp. 1-10).

In recent decades, there have been a number of examples of strategic air strikes based on prepared contingency plans, such as NATO's Operation Allied Force in 1999 against the then Federal Republic of Yugoslavia.

Key procedures (cf. NATO 2010b, chapters 4, 5) of air forces are:

- In offensive combat against enemy air forces, the enemy air potential on the ground, in the air, at sea, and in space is neutralised. This can be done by means of fighter assaults, fighter escorts, air attacks against enemy land-based air warfare assets, or by suppressing or destroying land-based enemy air defence assets.

- Defensive combat against enemy air forces aims to protect friendly air warfare assets and installations against aerial threats and comprises all active and passive measures to prevent or mitigate the effect of enemy air warfare assets, preferably before weapons are employed. These include interception, armed air patrol, air escort, and object or area protection by land-based air defence.

In their contingency plans for conventional warfare, both NATO and Russia have always taken defensive and/or offensive action against enemy air forces into account.

Defensive combat against enemy air forces is already an essential task in the context of military activities in peacetime.

- Due to the different capability requirements created by different distances, air transport can be differentiated into strategic, operational-level or tactical air transport. The basic purpose is to use aircraft for the transport of people, animals and/or material. This can be logistic air support, air insertion, or medical evacuation (cf. NATO 2016a, pp. 1-12ff).
- The support of land forces (including special operations forces) by air forces by means of air interdiction and close air support destroys, paralyses or neutralises enemy land forces, assets and installations before they can act against friendly forces (cf. NATO 2009, pp. 1-1f).
- Air support for naval forces is provided against the enemy naval force potential by means of airborne naval target engagement, conduct of operations against submarines, as well as mine laying (cf. NATO 2016b, 61f).
- Additional air force-specific procedures to render the operation possible include airspace observation, air-to-air refuelling, air traffic coordination, meteorological or geographical support, navigation and positioning, as well as armed and unarmed search and rescue services (cf. NATO 2016a, pp. 1-14ff).

5.2.3 Space Operations

Operations in space can be carried out by air forces or by specially designated space forces. Their purpose is to deny the opponent the use of space and to ensure friendly use.

A differentiation is made between

- offensive operations and
- defensive operations in space (cf. ibid., p. 5-7).

5.2.4 Naval Forces

Naval forces have a long tradition of acting autonomously in all four of the above-mentioned military-strategic fields of action through maritime power projection, the gaining of maritime dominance or maritime superiority, or the prevention/restriction of enemy maritime operations. But their procedures also continue to play an important role in the cooperation with other services (cf. NATO 2016b, pp. 14-18ff, 59-61f).

- Coastal defence has the purpose of protecting ports and sea accesses from attacks.
- In the protection of shipping, the freedom of movement of shipping is protected against attacks within a defined area. For this purpose, close and distant escorts, and naval co-operation and guidance for shipping (or ship convoys) are employed.
- By gaining maritime superiority, a section or a maritime marching movement is to be monitored and controlled, or the use of a section is to be prevented by means of maritime exclusionary action, maritime zone defence or the establishment of a maritime exclusion zone.
- Maritime blockade is intended to prevent the import or export of certain civil and military goods in a defined maritime area by maritime blockade of enemy maritime and air forces, maritime blockade of commercial shipping, enforcement of embargoes or quarantine, or sea blockade.
- By means of maritime power projection, targets on land are to be engaged from sea by using naval aircraft, sea-based cruise missiles, sea-based artillery, amphibious forces or special operations forces. This is done through maritime air strikes, amphibious operations, maritime special operations and sea-based fire support.
- Maritime support for integrated air defence of other branches of the armed forces is provided by maritime airspace surveillance, airborne early warning, electronic airborne combat, sea-based command and control infrastructure, sea-based air defence and missile defence.

5.2.5 Special Operations Forces

Given the counter-terrorism measures of the past decades against irregular activities, special operations forces have become increasingly important in the achievement of strategic and thus military-strategic goals.

They fight against subversive, conventional or sub-conventional regular and irregular forces, train friendly security forces, advise and support them, or free hostages, prisoners, and evacuate persons.

The following tactical procedures (cf. NATO 2019a, pp. 7-9f, 24ff) employed by special operations forces have to be considered in operations planning.

- Special reconnaissance such as long-range reconnaissance, close target reconnaissance, personnel reconnaissance, reconnaissance of the parties to the conflict, reconnaissance of the theatre environment, target and effect reconnaissance, reconnaissance in coastal areas as well as sector reconnaissance with the purpose of obtaining or verifying key information for the military-strategic and/or operational command echelon and to prepare for special operations.

- Commando operations, such as raid, ambush, disruptive action, prisoner and hostage liberation, target designation, retrieval or recovery, precision attack, or the capture and searching of ships, have the purpose of destroying enemy strategic or operational targets, locating and/or capturing or retrieving target objects, and liberating personnel or protecting protected personnel from hard-to-reach or enemy territory.

  Special reconnaissance and commando operations made it possible for the USA to track down Osama Bin Laden on 2 May 2011 in Operation *Neptune Spear.*

- Special Operations Forces provide military support through training, advice or assistance/cooperation for specific military assistance at the request of partners or friendly nations in potentially hostile environments.

- Additional procedures, specific to special operations forces are transport, recovery, infiltration, exfiltraton, survival, bypass, resistance or escape.

5.2.6 Cyber Forces

Cyber forces have become indispensable combat assets at all command echelons. With their tactical procedures (cf. NATO 2019b, pp. 30-31, 36-37), they can be employed, either independently or in cooperation with other services, in all four military-strategic fields of action, waging war, creating security, supporting peace, or be employed already in military actions in peacetime.

- In the defence of computer networks, harmful activities in cyberspace are identified and analysed by means of various measures, and attacks on computer networks repelled by means of pre-approved, offensive reactions in the sense of active defence before any damage is inflicted.

- The exploitation of computer networks follows the purpose, by means of gathering information from open sources or through the monitoring of cyberspace, of collecting information about information and communication systems and services by combining various measures in cyberspace.

- An attack on computer networks by means of a single attack or a concerted attack involves actions in the sense of a counterattack in cyberspace to interrupt, deny or reduce the flow of information in information and communication systems and services or to destroy data.

- In the defence of information and communication systems and services, all measures to prevent, react to and recover after a cyber attack are applied to information and communication systems and services.

5.2.7 Information Forces

The fight for and with information has always played an important role in military-strategic planning. The following procedures (cf. NATO 2019c, pp. 67, 103) are used in this context:

- By means of information, will is strengthened through targeted internal and external communication work.
- Selected target groups in the area of operations are influenced by targeted measures to change their attitude, behaviour or understanding of measures.

5.3 Military-Strategic Command

At the level of military-strategic command, the employment of all the available military forces and assets is coordinated in such a manner that a military contribution geared towards the political goals can be guaranteed. In doing so, it translates political goals into military objectives.

In most states, the military-strategic command is incumbent on a chief of general staff or chief of defence staff. In NATO it is the responsibility of the SACEUR, in the USA of the Chairman of the Joint Chiefs of Staff.

A classic historical example of successful military-strategic command is George C. Marshall, U.S. Army Chief of Staff (the predecessor role to what the Chairman of the Joint Chiefs is today) from 1939 to 1945. His main task was, as can be seen in the above definition, to coordinate the employment of the available military forces and assets. Despite the fact that it was Japan's attack on Pearl Harbor which finally led the USA to enter World War II, the decision was taken during the Arcadia Conference in early 1942 to defeat Germany, regarded as the most dangerous enemy, first (Germany first). This meant that the European theatre of war under General Dwight D. Eisenhower, the operational-level commander in today's understanding, took priority in resource allocation over the Asian theatre of war under General Douglas McArthur. Churchill praised Marshall as the organiser of victory.

This historical example proves the importance of military-strategic command in large conventional wars with several operational-level commands. Military-strategic command remains critical also in modern hybrid conflicts and especially if there is pressure on resources, especially its role of providing highest-level military advice to the strategic command, and above all for setting of priorities in the conduct of operations.

Military-strategic command must primarily ensure its own command effectiveness. By taking the necessary measures, commanders and their staffs are enabled to fulfil command tasks with the given personnel, technical, and organisational conditions.

A major military-strategic goal is the achievement of command superiority. On the basis of information and decision superiority decision-making processes are accelerated and protected, as well as enemy decision-making processes at least temporarily undermined and/or impaired.

Two essential tasks of military-strategic command are ISTAR (Intelligence, Surveillance, Target Acquisition and Reconnaissance) and Targeting. ISTAR (cf. NATO 2013) is a general military task in operations, in which the decision-making and effect process of ongoing and future military operations is supported by the sum total of all measures regarding the planning, controlling and conduct of reconnaissance, processing of intelligence, as well as the documentation and provision of intelligence products, basically independent of command echelon and in a targeted manner.

In all the fields of action described above, a corresponding role is played by the intelligence products of military intelligence services, which are usually led by the military-strategic level. In targeting (cf. NATO 2019c, p.127), targets are selected and prioritised by a support procedure derived from the strategic and military-strategic decision making process, and all lethal or non-lethal assets synchronised. Derived from this, targeting also takes place at the operational and tactical echelon.

6. The Relationship Between Military-Strategic Command and Operational-Level Command

When considering the work at the operational echelon, a distinction has to be made between operations preparation and operations command. In operations preparation, the military-strategic contingency plans are used for the individual operational command's operational-level planning . In alliances, but also in some states, these commands often do not have forces subordinated to them in times of routine duty so as to be able to prepare for operational tasks without having to carry out day-to-day business. In the event of an operation and on the basis of the selected military-strategic option, the military-strategic echelon assigns them forces of the service assessed as required or of all services. This may also require a multinational planning process at the military-strategic level as soon as several nations take part in an operation.

NATO currently has three commands at the operational command level: the Joint Force Command Brunssum in the Netherlands, the Joint Force Command Naples in Italy, and the Joint Force Command Norfolk in the USA. During operations, the operational command translates military-strategic directives into orders issued to the tactical command level and is the link between strategy and tactics. This means that in operational matters the operational commander is directly led by the strategic commander-in-chief. In this, the military-strategic command plays a role in resource allocation and in supporting the operational command or in advising the strategic command. This can be a very difficult task, especially if resources are allocated to several operational commands in several areas of operations, as the above-mentioned example from World War II clearly illustrates. This all the more so as these are usually multinational operations.

The operational command defines tactical goals and generates concepts of operations, operation plans and operation orders. It plans, commands and controls operations of the forces and assets released for this purpose by the military-strategic level in a defined area of operations and coordinates and synchronises the entirety of the tactical and logistical measures required for this purpose, also with non-military actors. It determines the command to be supported at the higher tactical echelon. Here, too, it is necessary to plan two echelons lower. This means that at the operational level not only the orders to the component commands must be assessed, but also the operational readiness of the formations operating below them.

7. The Relationship between the Military-Strategic Command and Other Spheres of Power

The relationship between military-strategic and operational-level command described in the previous chapter is, on the one hand, relatively clear as regards the delimitation of responsibilities, and, on the other hand, homogeneous at the level of interaction between decision-takers and persons in charge, as almost all of them are soldiers who have undergone similar training and have experienced a similar structure of employment within the military hierarchies. It is also almost exclusively military questions which will have to be dealt with between these two echelons. Even if the military-strategic level should be multinational, this assertion remains valid.

The situation is different in the relationship between military-strategic command as part of strategic command to the other spheres of power listed in Chapter 3, whose personnel usually boast a completely different character and socialisation from those of soldiers: foreign policy is dominated by diplomats, who, like soldiers, have undergone special training, have experienced a special structure of employment, and have their own professional culture which transcends national borders. These characteristics, however, can vary considerably between diplomacy and the military, and it is no secret that the foreign and defence ministries of most countries, although both active in the field of foreign and security policy, do not always have the best relations. It can be assumed, however, that both spheres pursue the same goals (to a large extent at least).

Especially in the economic sphere this need not necessarily be the case. Due to globalisation and the concomitant creation of globally networked conglomerates, their goals usually cannot be brought into line with the goals of national economic policy, and a state's national economic goals do not necessarily have to be in line with its foreign and security political ambitions. In many cases, it will even be the case that foreign and defence policy measures are used to pursue economic goals. This can range from national armament to military action to safeguard economic interests.

It is similar in the areas of civil authority and information. The personnel working in these fields as well as the respective decision-takers and persons in charge will have developed a similar culture due to their training and the character of their jobs, which will not necessarily coincide with the cultures of the other spheres.

Above the respective apparatuses of the various spheres of power is the political echelon in the shape of the ministers, who represent the government and the parliaments. The goals of politicians, regardless of their professional careers and party affiliations, do not necessarily coincide with the goals of the apparatuses described above. In any case, politicians, whether as parliamentarians in the course of legislation or as ministers in the course of implementation, are in the forefront of strategy. The Clausewitz ideal that a political leader should know the instrument s/he is to use should not always be assumed, especially in the military sphere. Also, the condition defined at the time of Thucydides that a *strategos* must have knowledge in the field of strategy in order to be able to reach this position may no longer be fully valid in modern democracies.

The challenge for the military-strategic level is now, in this predominantly non-military area of strategy, to contribute to strategic decision preparation and decision-making through expertise and advice on the one hand, and to translate the strategic goals and objectives into military action on the other.

The difficulties are obvious: As discussed in Chapter 5.1, military-strategic planners usually work with a planning horizon of at least 10 years. Politicians are usually elected for a legislative period of 4-5 years, and from the experience of various countries it can be assumed that their planning horizon often does not go beyond that, which can have an impact especially on armament and procurement which fall within the military strategic area of responsibility.

Another aspect is that if a state has an arms industry of some significance and the political leadership is concerned about jobs in that sector, pressure could be brought to bear on the military-strategic leadership to procure goods from these corporations, which, in their type, number or priority, may not be on the military's shopping list. In addition, the defence industry has an even longer planning horizon than the military for certain weapon systems and this horizon can be up to thirty years or more for aircraft, ships and even tanks.

Another problem area can be peacekeeping or humanitarian operations, especially in a multinational setting. In his book *Strategy*, the Romanian-American military strategist and political scientist Edward Luttwak is severely critical of UN missions (cf. Luttwak 2003, p. 87) Political guidelines often restrict the military's room for manoeuvre to such an extent that meaningful military action is impossible, or the deployment violates military principles. The military should do what it cannot do (e.g. police tasks) and may not do what it can do, or only do very little, namely fight.

The military-strategic leadership is particularly challenged In these two problem areas, not only in the sense of the military, but especially in the sense of strategy, to contribute its advisory services in such a manner that a solution acceptable to the state or the alliance can be achieved. Although strategic thinking, planning and action are particularly and traditionally strongly developed in the military, it will depend on the strategic culture of the respective countries how strongly the military-strategic level can contribute to the overall strategy.

8. Requirements for Personnel at the Military-Strategic Command Echelon

Which requirements, especially for decision-takers and persons in charge at the military strategic level, can be derived especially from chapters 6 and 7? Regarding the operational command echelon, it seems quite clear: Military qualification for the military-strategic level of command, based on appropriate training and practical experience through a versatile range of employments, which must include postings at the upper tactical and operational level and should include employments in the military-diplomatic field and in training.

It must therefore be experienced soldiers who are used in the decisive positions at the military-strategic level, otherwise they will be met with only limited acceptance at the operational command echelon (cf. Gray 2018, p. 52ff).

This applies only to a limited extent to the desk officers in the various specialist areas. Above all, they must be experts in their fields of activity, such as force planning, armament, procurement and training, in order to be able to make a contribution. However, a reasonably up-to-date military background and the ability to think strategically are required.

In addition, further requirements which go beyond purely military expertise can be derived from the interaction with other spheres of state power. The ability to think and act in terms of overall strategy is of particular importance. The main focus will be on understanding the idiosyncrasies, strengths and weaknesses as well as the culture of other spheres of power, of potential or current opponents and coalition partners – in short, of the international and national environments (cf. ibid., p.44ff). In decisive positions, personnel will be required who, despite all the required specialisation, can keep abreast of the big picture, as unrealistic strategies would otherwise be the product of a mechanised strategy process (cf. Maier 2015, p. 37).

Harry R. Yarger, a professor at several military universities has described the ideal type of strategist as follows:

...a student of the contemporary who

- is aware of the past,
- is sensitive to the possibilities of the future,
- is aware of the danger of bias,
- is wary of ambiguity and uncertainty,
- perseveres in chaos,
- is willing to think through the consequences of various courses of action, and then
- is able to articulate all this with sufficient precision for those who have to implement these directives (Freedman 2013, p. 238).

Just like overall strategists, military strategists must also be well versed in the present, i.e., they must have a candid and realistic view not only of the military, but also of the environments described above. They must be aware of the past in so far as strategies do not develop out of nothing, but can be seen as a bridge from the past via the present to the future. They must therefore be able to anticipate the future, as described in Chapter 5.1, especially in scenarios.

Strategy is never a linear process, but always has to be seen in interaction with possible opponents, with allies and the environment. Especially in the course of the implementation of strategy, i.e. strategic action, it is necessary to proceed along developed scenarios. Bias, ambiguity and uncertainty are enemies of every and any strategic plan and action. This environment therefore requires rational, detached people (cf. Gray 2018, p. 73ff). Empathy may have become *en vogue*, but it has just as little place in the strategic environment as exaggerated emotions or feelings have. Strategy is also fundamentally free of ethics and morals, they limit strategists in their actions. In an immoral environment, moral actions cannot be taken without jeopardising success.

Persevering in chaos is derived from Clausewitz's awareness of friction and Moltke's insight that the best plan does not survive first contact with the enemy. Thinking through the consequences of various courses of action is closely linked to the scenarios of the future described above. Strategy is always interactive, therefore not only one's own courses of action have to be considered, but also those of all actors. The precise formulation of guidelines for the operational command echelon is of decisive importance for their task of being able to translate the (military-) strategic directives into military action.

We can therefore see that the general requirements for a strategist also fully apply to a military strategist. Above all – and this is expressed in Chapter 7 – it must be officers who are able to go beyond military expertise and acceptance, in order to interact with the other areas of strategy and, above all, with politicians in such a manner that they can, on the one hand, represent the interests of the military in the best possible way, and, on the other hand – and almost more importantly – make a contribution to the overall strategy and then correctly interpret the role of the military in it.

9.   Conclusion and Summary

The military-strategic echelon has only established itself over time and is therefore mostly not adequately described in classic texts on strategy, or its tasks are listed among the traditional echelons of command, usually strategy. It has, however, taken on an important role, especially since the concept of strategy has tended to move from the purely military to the whole-of-nation level.

In times of peace, i.e. in times of military-strategic force planning, operations planning and preparation for potential operations, such important issues as the recruitment system, personnel strength of the military, equipment and allowances, armament, organisation, structure and garrisoning, infrastructure, training, regulations on procedures and types of operations, cooperation with allies, command systems including command organisation, creation of the legal framework for operations preparation and employment, establishment of a logistics system, military intelligence, etc. are dealt with. In addition to these so-called hard topics, the military-strategic contribution to the development of an overall strategy or to emergent or event-driven strategies is of particular importance for the establishment of a state's or alliance's strategic capability.

In the military-strategic conduct of operations, it is the guidelines in the shape of a 'translation' of the strategic directives to the operational command echelon that come to the fore. These include, above all, the definition of military-strategic objectives, possibly military support for the creation of alliances, the military implementation of legal directives or restrictions on the conduct of operations in the shape of caveats, the participation in the political definition of the area of operations, the definition of operational areas of responsibility, designating an OHQ and in particular the operational commander, the definition of command and control relations, the regulation of transport to the area of operations or resupply, and much more.

In any case, the military-strategic echelon is part of the strategic command with all its dependencies, responsibilities and requirements. This determines the requirements made of the corresponding training goals, training contents and curricula of higher officer training, continuation training and further training.

10. References

Department of Defense. (2018). *2018 National Defense Strategy Summary.* https://dod.defense.gov/Portals/1/Documents/pubs/2018-National-Defense-Strategy-Summary.pdf (20 March 2020)

European Union. (2016). *The Global strategy for the foreign and security policy of the European Union.* Retrieved from: https://eeas.europa.eu/sites/eeas/files/language_versions_0.zip

Freedman, Lawrence. (2013). *Strategy: A History.* Oxford: Oxford University Press.

Gray, Colin (2018). *Theory of Strategy.* Oxford, England: Oxford University Press.

Luttwak, Edwars (2003). *Strategy: The Logic of War and Peace.* Cambridge, Massachusetts: Rev.Enlarged Edition.

Maier, Gunter (2015). *Das Vergessene Vokabular der Strategie: Handbuch der Strategischen Prinzipien.* Norderstedt: Books on Demand.

Militärlexikon des Österreichischen Bundesheeres. (2020). (16 March 2020).

NATO. (2009). *NATO Allied Joint Publication* -3.3.2 Edition A, September 2009.

NATO. (2010a). *Strategic Concept 2010.* Retrieved from https://www.nato.int/nato-welcome/index_de.html (19 March 2020)

NATO. (2010b). *NATO Allied Joint Publication* -3.3.1 Edition B, July 2010.

NATO. (2013). *NATO Allied Tactical Publication -77 NATO Guidance for ISTAR In Land Operations.*

NATO. (2016a). *NATO Allied Joint Publication-3.3.* Edition B Version 1, April 2016.

NATO. (2016b). *NATO Allied Joint Publication* -3.1 Edition A Version 1, December 2016.

NATO. (2017a). *NATO Allied Joint Publication-01 (AJP-01).* Edition E Version 1, February 2017.

NATO. (2017b). *NATO Allied Joint Publication-01 (AJP-01).* Dated February 2017. Retrieved from https://assets.publishing.service.gov.uk/government/uploads/system/uploads/attachment_data/file/860502/doctrine_nato_allied_joint_doctrine_ajp_01.pdf

NATO. (2018). *NATO Allied Tactical Publication* (ATP) 3.2.1 Edition B Version 1, August 2018.

NATO. (2019a). *NATO Allied Joint Publication* -3.5 Edition B Version 1, August 2019

NATO. (2019b). *NATO GLOSSARY OF TERMS AND DEFINITIONS AAP*-06 Edition 2019.

NATO. (2019c). *NATO Allied Administrative Publication*-06 Edition 2019.

White House. (2017). *US National Security Strategy*. Retrieved from https://www.whitehouse.gov/wp-content/uploads/2017/12/NSS-Final-12-18-2017-0905.pdf (20 March 2020)

11.   Further Reading

Brodie, Bernard (1959). *Strategy in the Missile Age*. New Jersey: Princetown University Press

Keohane, Robert (1984). *After Hegemony: Cooperation and Discord in the World Political Economy*. New Jersey: Princetown University Press

Mearsheimer, John (2001). *The Tragedy of Great Power Politics*. New York: Norton

Nye, Joseph (1990). *Bound to Lead: The Changing Nature of American Power*. New York: Basic Books

Paret, Peter (1986). *Makers of Modern Strategy from Machiavelli to the Nuclear Age*. New Jersey: Princetown University Press

Waltz, Kenneth (1979). *Theory of International Politics*. Boston: Addison-Wesley

Chapter 5: The Historical Evolution of Strategic Theory

Prof. Sir Hew Strachan, Lt Col (res.) Dr. Eberhard Birk, Prof. Dr. Wolfgang Etschmann

Keywords: Strategic Theory; Thinking War; Strategic Thinkers; Military History; Evolution of Strategy; Art of War;

1. Introduction

Some have argued that both the concept of strategy and related strategic thinking originate from Antiquity (**Beatrice Heuser, The Evolution of Strategy: Thinking War from Antiquity to the Present, Cambridge University Press, Cambridge 2010; Beatrice Heuser/Anja Hartmann (ed.), Thinking War, Peace and World Orders from Antiquity until the 20th century,** London 2001). Others, however, see their origins as lying either in the Renaissance (**Peter Paret/Gordon A. Craig, Felix Gilbert (ed.), Makers of Modern Strategy from Machiavelli to the Nuclear Age,** Oxford 1986) or in the late-eighteenth century Enlightenment (**Werner Hahlweg (ed.), *Klassiker der Kriegskunst*,** Darmstadt 1960; **Jehuda L. Wallach, *Kriegstheorien. Ihre Entwicklung im 19. und 20. Jahrhundert*,** Frankfurt am Main 1972; **Albert Stahel, *Klassiker der Strategie – eine Bewertung*,** Zurich 2004).

Since the emergence of the "history of strategy", it has been considered as being almost purely confined to the military sphere A standard definition of "strategy" nevertheless failed to truly materialise in any period of history and confusion often reigned as to how to distinguish it from other terms such as "policy", "operations" or "tactics". As a result, widely ranging approaches to strategy appeared and continue to appear, differing by virtue of what the authors deemed relevant to their theories. There are thus many factors and subjects that can potentially influence strategic theory, such as politics, diplomacy, international law, the military, geography, technology, the economy, culture, religion and society.

It is generally recognised that the authors' "function" also shaped the substance and scope of their arguments. As such, "pure theorists", who have written more or less abstract studies on strategy based on academic research, stood alongside "pure practitioners", whose insight was based on their professional experience, whether acquired as a politician, a diplomat or in the military. Between both camps were authors who are or were operating as advisors in the middle ground between academia and practical policy.

As demonstrated in military history, two concepts are fundamentally juxtaposed in strategy, even though they may have previously been labelled differently: (1.) the purely (military) historical approach, which analyses strategic operations and the underlying formative developmental steps of strategic theory from a research and academic perspective and which often warns against projecting different historical conditions onto present-day strategic challenges, and (2.) the political approach of strategic studies, which attempts to do precisely this by drawing immutable "certainties" from history in order to derive practical solutions. The term "strategic" is understood to mean the direct or indirect influence of power (including military potential) upon fundamental political pathmaking. The guiding principle of this approach is that: „There is an essential unity to all strategic experience in all periods of history because nothing vital to the nature and function of war and strategy changes" (Gray 1999 p. 1).

That is true on the one hand. Every state, every society and even every theorist of war or military strategy – whether aerial, naval or land-based strategy or founded on axiomatic philosophy or power politics shifting between unipolarity, bipolarity, multipolarity or apolarity – has tried to "recondition" the state, politics, the (arms) economy, sometimes even society, but especially the military so that, whether to avoid or instigate a war (understood to be the ultimate strategic or security-political challenge), the maximum level of success through one's own efforts was achievable, or at least appeared to be.

Strategies undertaken by political communities of all sizes should primarily guarantee that the community survives and, ultimately – as is the case in operational and tactical military affairs – must consider the equation of power/space/time and repeatedly address the fundamental questions of: "What do I want? What do I have? What can I do?"

Therefore, strategic matters were and still are always tied to security policy and should be understood as a comprehensive package at state level. The basis for this remains the answer to the questions: who wants to achieve something? What do they want to achieve? And how do they intend to achieve it? The (political) desire to achieve the objectives – generally maintaining or gradually improving the status quo or broadening a claim to power, whether directly or indirectly – together with the provision of the resources required for this and the generation of the necessary energy, remained, in some ways, "naturally" consistent as a fundamental question of strategy: decision-making predicated on assertiveness, in favour of a general strategic guiding principle, the definition of structures and the sustained generation of the necessary resources, to enable the objective to be met. This "conventionally" involves protection or pursuit of the – defensive or offensive – objectives of the state and/or alliance, primarily in the face of an "external" opponent.

On the other hand, it is clear that the underlying conditions, as well as the resources and methods for assertion, have undergone a sea change since the days of antiquity, including on the battlefield. "Strategy" therefore requires "retrospection". Ultimately, the familiar adage of "bad history, worse policy, wrong strategy" still holds true.

Whoever ignored or failed to react correctly to qualitative changes was doomed. History is littered with examples of failure to adapt to new underlying conditions. New approaches in the evolution of strategic theory were often the result of the direct experiences of the authors or active stakeholders who reacted to qualitative changes in the environment. Strategic theories that failed in practice subsequently required either revision or redevelopment from the ground up. However, certain failed theories managed to become topical once more when recontextualised. The military has always played an almost privileged role in this process, albeit in combination with the political sphere. This partly because it is professionally committed to the study of strategy as others are not, and partly because it embodies or can embody the final expression of political action in theory and practice. The use of armed force is the most established approach to strategy in history.

2.   Strategic theory
2.1   Antiquity

Strategy and strategic thinking may have been around since the dawn of human action and (systematic) planning, but the earliest recorded writing on the subject originated in Asia (**The Art of War**, **Sun Tzu**, believed to date from around 554-496 BCE) and Europe, particularly in Ancient Greece. The growing complexity of incipient societies and political communities rendered general (theoretical) and specific (practical) approaches necessary to overcome existential challenges. From a contemporary perspective, the concept of "strategy" in Antiquity was mainly confined to a military commander's skill, which primarily focused more on tactics and operations. **Onasander** (*Strategikos*, 1st century AD) believed that a strategist was someone with "experience of military command". The first methodical work – a treatise – was **"Strategik [How to Survive under Siege]"** written by **Aeneas Tacticus** as early as 357/56 BCE. Whether all politicians and commanders from that point onward were inspired by it, certainly needs no answer; Alexander the Great considered Homer's Iliad to be his "manual on the art of war". There is little evidence in the literature of the ancient world for 'strategic theory' as it would be understood today, either etymologically or conceptually. However, Greek and Roman thinking about war both theory and practice, with the latter being capable of validating or negating strategic planning in war. This line of thought formed a European tradition that filtered from Antiquity through to the present day.

Even though the treatises of Antiquity did not address national preventive security, as we understand it today, they do reveal many examples of strategic reasoning and action in practice. Consider, for example, the wars of Alexander the Great as well as the obvious example of the Romans, who would never have been able to establish and hold such a prestigious empire for centuries without having a "strategy" that adapted multiple times (cf. Luttwak 1976).

Around 900 AD, Byzantine ruler Leo VI the Wise built upon the fundamental theory expounded by the Greeks and Romans to develop the art of war through works on strategy and tactics in which he understood strategy to be "the art of military campaigns".

2.2   Renaissance

It is therefore unsurprising that the focus of later "strategists" during the Renaissance period reverted to Antiquity – after all, it was founded on learning, in particular, and through the heritage of that era in which myriad possibilities were introduced as direct examples of fundamental relevance.

Niccolò Machiavelli addressed gave shape to the concept of strategy at the point when the Middle Ages transitioned into the contemporary city or territorial state era. In his works, not only **"The Art of War"** (*Dell'arte della guerra*, Florence 1521), which is divided into a series of dialogues, Machiavelli highlighted the political nature of war. He rejected warfare with mercenaries as it was practised up to that point in history and demanded additional military accountability of all citizens for their (city) state.

However, in some cases, such as in Italy a few years later, the professional organised armies such as the lansquenets proved to be superior to the Swiss mercenaries (Reisläufer) and citizen militias.

Another element that was later developed even further originates from the international law expert, **Hugo Grotius** (*De jure belli ac pacis* [On the Law of War and Peace], 1625). He advocated that warfare be integrated with secular law and separated both the legal conditions of "jus ad bellum" and "jus in bello" from each other and these principles from the religious view of what had been seen as "just war". Against a backdrop of sweeping globalisation during the "Age of Discovery" and the growing significance of maritime trade, he also called for *Mare Liberum* [The Freedom of the

Seas], 1609), which represented a significant legal norm with respect to strategy.

However, the manner in which warfare was conducted failed to reflect all the innovations in strategic reasoning. On the contrary – sustained military campaigning lay beyond the resources of the state during the Thirty Years' War (1618-48) and so depended on military enterprisers who waged war for profit. The excessive violence of mercenaries literally "devastated" large expanses of Central Europe. **Thomas Hobbes**, in **Leviathan**, 1651, responded to the experience of civil war by calling for the state to monopolise the use of force in a bid to contain war

2.3   The modern period / absolute monarchy

The strategic theory of the 17th and 18th centuries was characterised by the streamlining of all areas in which state action was evident. This process culminated in the Age of Enlightenment, the influence of which also filtered through to the battlefield.

This required a radical "revolution": the "invention" of the modern state in which warfare became a national interest rather than a private one, as a result of which the monarchy's powers to tax citizens could permanently fund standing armies. In reality, the resources at the command of even a state as powerful as Louis XIV's France were limited, and so war was itself constrained. The objective was to use diplomacy to "win over" provinces or to use war if this political objective was not met. Such combat was subject to strict rules in theory and practice out of fear of repeating the trauma suffered during the Thirty Years' War. The desire to avoid bloodshed was also part of the balancing act between military functionality and political control. In his work "*Les Reveries Ou Memoires Sur L'Art De La Guerre*" (1756), **Maurice de Saxe**, a key French commander and theorist on war of the absolutist era, recognised that the hazards of combat could put at risk the gains to be achieved by strategy (a word which entered the French language from the 1770s but is not found in English until 1811), and even hypothesised that a skilled general could wage war his entire life without being compelled to fight a single battle. The idea that war was a game of chess, from its outbreak through to the operations and tactics, was followed throughout Europe for almost 150 years and led to the "tamed Bellona" period.

The alternative to battle was to avoid it by exhausting the enemy's armies through manoeuvre. In the late nineteenth century, the German historian Hans Delbrück, called this a "strategy of attrition", although the frequency with which it was used was contested by general staff historians. However, the deployment of regular and irregular troops in more forested and mountainous terrain on the Habsburg borders of eastern Europe and both American and British troops during the American Revolutionary War (1775-1783) was a clear indication that a new era was dawning.

2.4   The Napoleonic era

The "birth" of the French state in the aftermath of the 1789 revolution created – not least due to the introduction of a form of conscription, the "leveé en masse" – the foundation for a new form of warfare with neither restrictions nor any regard for soldiers in particular. At its heart was France's readiness to seek battle and to have the manpower to be able to do so repeatedly.

Minister of War Lazare Carnot and his representative Louis Antoine de Saint-Just initiated the total military and civil mobilisation of France beginning in 1793, which showed scant regard for the losses it incurred and, through Saint-Just, meted out extremely severe sanctions to punish deviant conduct in the military and civil sectors.

Napoleon, who became emperor in 1804, ruthlessly tapped into the ensuing potential of the military. Effective organisation of his armies, patriotism and an open approach to promotions remained a key part of the Napoleonic system until 1813. Beating the main enemy forces, advancing on the enemy capital quickly, and a comprehensive supply network for the French armies (although this failed in Spain and also later in Russia) were also characteristic for the Napoleonic conduct of war.

By establishing shrewd political structures (the Confederation of the Rhine in 1806 and the Franco-Russian alliance in 1807), Napoleon seized control of almost the entire European continent (excluding Iberia), which brought him closer to realising his dream of "Alexander's empire stretching to India" following the failed campaign of 1798/99 in Egypt. This was an empire founded on war and fed by sequential successes on the battlefield. Once victory turned to defeat in Russia in 1812, its foundations were rocked. Moreover, France lacked the seapower to continue overseas trade and to maintain its credit in the face of the British Empire ("the whale versus the elephant", i.e. France), especially after 1805.

Napoleon was nevertheless a "practitioner", rather than a "theorist". Not a single fundamental work documenting his thoughts on strategy survived him. He did, however, "inspire" two theorists and generals who were integral to the evolution of strategic theory: the Swiss Antoine-Henri Jomini and the Prussian Carl von Clausewitz.

The extent to which the opinions of **Jomini** (*Précis de l'Art de la Guerre: Des Principales Combinaisons de la Stratégie, de la Grande Tactique et de la Politique Militaire*, 1838) were shaped by the personal experience of the battle-leader Napoleon, including in the formulation of his strategic premises of his "art of war", also explains his concept of strategy. His was a guide on how to win, based on the establishment of 'principles of war', which he argued were of enduring validity, and an understanding of strategy which rested on the choice of lines of manoeuvre and "the art of directing the masses to the theatre of war".

Clausewitz was far more of a critical strategic thinker, posing questions through a dialectal approach and using both his own experience and recent military history to delve into all features of policy and war and their interdependencies in his main opus (**"Vom Kriege" [On War]**, 1832-34). Although Clausewitz shared that era's notion of strategy espoused by Jomini – "the use of combat for the purpose of war" – he also highlighted the political dimension of war: "Subordinating the political point of view to the military would be absurd, for it is policy that has created war. Policy is the guiding intelligence and war only the instrument." In order to understand the nature of war, which he referred to as "[more than] a true chameleon" and "a continuation of political intercourse, carried on with other means", it is necessary to analyse it in conjunction with the surrounding factors of politics, the economy, society and culture. He therefore also became the "general theorist" for the reception of his observations on the subject, almost philosophical in parts, which has carried through to the present day. Nevertheless, this did not lead to a straight "line of tradition" in strategic thinking. He initially shared the fate of many a strategy theorist: Jomini, not Clausewitz, was the dominant influence in professional military education until 1871, and in many respects since.

2.5   19th century

Strategic theory from the mid-1800s onwards was challenged by industrialisation. It permeated into all areas of life: politics, the military, technology, the economy, and society. The pace of industrial change led to a sector-specific division of labour and argued that war was being fundamentally altered from the bottom up, not – as strategic theory suggested – from the top down. This process carried on for over a century until the Second World War.

Material change also challenged the place of military history in strategic thinking, creating in it a form of duality from that point onwards. On the one hand, a purely military question was asked: How do you wage a war in order to be victorious in battle? On the other hand, these considerations had to be assessed against Clausewitz's broader and more basic postulate: What is war and what needs to be taken into consideration? These two basic positions still viewed history as a "teacher". Both Jomini and Clausewitz supported their arguments by basing their theories on the Seven Years' War (1756-63) as well as on their own experiences in the Napoleonic Wars.

The attempt to compare old and new was also a cornerstone in the formation of maritime strategy. Although slower to develop than the strategy of land warfare, its framework was much wider, embracing empire, economics and geographical position, as well as eroding the distinction between war and peace. The work of **Alfred Thayer Mahan (The Influence of Sea Power upon History, 1660-1783**, New York 1890) in particular is considered to be a definitive work for the substantiation of naval strategy. Mahan largely rejected the role of new technologies, steam, iron and steel, and looked to the age of sail. He focused on British history and examined how Great Britain had successfully established and strengthened its dominant global standing. He was labelled the "Clausewitz of the sea" and exerted major influence on US geopolitics and public opinion.

The French admiral Théophile Aube also attempted to enable relatively small navies to succeed in naval combat by advocating the "Jeune École" concept (small, heavily armoured and armed coastal defence ships, rapid torpedo boats to protect the coastline against stronger fleets and rapid cruisers for commerce raiding).

However, any debate from that point onward concerning land and naval strategy had to clarify how to integrate the technical innovations of steel, armour and enhanced firepower into a doctrine for future military success.

Since peace largely prevailed in Europe between 1815 and 1848, and even the wars thereafter were – until 1914 – short and contained, many theories were just that. The quick successes by Prussia in the wars of German unification (1864/1866/1870-71) elevated Prussia's influence in the forty years up until the First World War. Helmuth von Moltke the elder, the chief of the Prussian general staff (which itself became an institutional model of the generation of strategy), summarised strategy in the aftermath of the war against France as "a system of expedients; it is more than a mere scholarly discipline. It is the translation of knowledge to practical life, the improvement of the original leading thought in accordance with continually changing situations. It is the art of acting under pressure under the most difficult conditions."

Even though early signs of the significance of firepower, logistics and "trench warfare" were already evident from the Crimean War (1853-56), the American Civil War (1861-65), in which General William Tecumseh Sherman led an almost "total war" against the Confederate states in the south from 1864, and the Russo-Japanese War (1904-05), almost every "theorist" in Europe was focused on dynamism, speed and aggression with a view to bringing about a decisive battle in short order. The introduction of the railway seemed to have favoured the strategic offensive over the defence, minimising the constraints of logistics and enabling armies on 'external lines' to envelop their enemies by concentrating rapidly on the decisive point. However, railways built for national purposes also conferred these advantages to an even greater extent on the defence. Moreover, strategic thought made insufficient allowance for the effects of technology and mass production on tactics. The firepower revolution favoured the tactical defence. In 1914 the war plans of the great powers – themselves evidence of how strategy had become institutionalised in peace time – were shattered by these two realities. Germany's plan for the rapid defeat of France in 1914 was mirrored by the stunning success of its defence of East Prussia against Russia, and so provided an object lesson in both. The challenge that the belligerents now faced was how to convert what was in effect a system designed to generate campaign plans into a method to design strategies for protracted war, fought in three dimension, land, sea and air, on multiple fronts and with allies.

Strategic thinking was swamped by protracted positional warfare, especially on the Western Front, in which the mounting casualties caused by machine warfare came gradually to resemble an industrialised war of attrition, in which exhaustion was achieved not by manoeuvre but by killing more of the enemy in battle and by depleting his resources.

Although mobile warfare in Eastern Europe led to the Central Powers making major territorial gains, after losing many Austro-Hungarian soldiers during the initial months of the war and between 1915 and 1917, and led to the collapse of the Tsarist Empire and the subsequent Russian Revolution, they still failed to win the war. The coalition led by Germany had achieved its objectives in the east by March 1918, but Germany's allies had little interest in the war in the west. The pressures exerted in France and Belgium by the Entente, especially after it was joined by the Americans, meant that Germany no longer had the manpower from September 1918 to reinforce other fronts, especially in the Balkans.

Although the Entente powers focused on the war's principal theatres, they also conducted operations on so-called secondary battlefields such as the Middle East. These were motivated initially by a desire to contain the war in Europe and prevent it from spreading to their colonies. Germanys' alliance with the Ottoman Empire opened routes to Asia and Africa, which the British and French most conspicuously tried to halt with the amphibious campaign on the peninsula of Gallipoli in 1915. It failed to rapidly defeat the Ottoman Empire or to open the warm-water route to their ally, Russia. The campaigns in Iraq and on the Sinai peninsula, in Palestine and lastly in Syria were protracted, logistically complex operations that, while successful, could only be classed as decisive victories in 1917 and 1918. In this respect they contributed, as did the operations in the Balkans and Italy, to fracturing the Central Powers. Each member of the coalition sought an armistice at a time and in a theatre of its own choosing.

The First World War redefined strategy and the vocabulary associated war with fundamental consequences for how both were interpreted in the Second World War. First of all its scale gave rise to a new definition of strategy, which had its roots in maritime strategy and which embraced its economic and political dimensions, and was called 'grand strategy' **(J.F.C. Fuller, The Reformation of War**, London, 1923). Second, the need to mobilise nations, societies and national economies "logically" led directly to the concept of "total war" **(Erich Ludendorff, Der totale Krieg**, Munich 1935). Both democracies and totalitarian states were empowered to mobilise all their citizens for the purposes of war, although only the latter would also do so during peacetime.

2.6   From one world war to another

Deliberations on how to rethink warfare and to remove the image instilled by the First World War marked the 1920s and 1930s. Many army officers blamed the lack of mobility and manoeuvre on the mass army. In practice the mass army would survive until after 1945 and conscription would not decline significantly until after the end of te Cold War. But many countries endeavoured to mechanise infantry and to form elite armoured units of tanks, themselves newly created in the First World War.

Officers in European armies, such as the Austrian Ludwig Ritter von Eimannsberger ("Der Kampfwagenkrieg", 1934), the Frenchman Charles de Gaulle ("Vers l´armée de métier". 1934; in which he also called for a professional army), the Britons, J.F.C. Fuller and B. H. Liddell Hart ("When Britain goes to war", 1935) and the German Heinz Guderian ("Achtung – Panzer" 1937), provided an essential contribution to the mechanisation of war. However, their objective, more operational than strategic, still remained anchored to the "old way of thinking", particularly in Germany **(Jehuda Wallach, Clausewitz and Schlieffen**; *Das Dogma der Vernichtungsschlacht. Die Lehren von Clausewitz und Schlieffen und ihre Wirkungen in 2 Weltkriegen*, Frankfurt am Main 1967). As in 1914-18, so in 1939-41, Germany achieved major operational successes without winning the war. The Third Reich never developed the thinking or the institutions for the making of strategy appropriate to the scale of the conflict which confronted it.

The Italian general **Giulio Douhet** arrived at a completely different conclusion. He called for "strategic air forces" in his 1921 work, "**Il dominio dell'aria**" [**Command of the Air**]. Industrialised states would be able to bypass the drawn-out battles on land by dramatically upscaling their air forces and using them to launch a strategic aerial attack against the opposition to "disarm" them by destroying their strategic hubs – political and military control centres, airfields and aircraft on the ground, weapons caches, etc. – without warning. Douhet's influence in Italy was limited both by the production problems of creating bombers capable to carrying sufficient payloads and by doctrinal opposition. Amadeo Mecozzi advocated the operational deployment of strong, tactical air forces against enemy troops and frontline targets and, in his written doctrines "Aviazione d´assalto" and "Guerra contro inermi", called for greater tactical air forces and for the protection of civilians from aerial attack. This marked a clear rejection of the theories espoused by Douhet.

In 1918 Britain had created the world's first independent air force. Although it too confronted similar problems, it used its status to make the case for strategic bombing. In the Second World War, not least because of the practical difficulties of precision bombing, it would refine this approach to target cities and their inhabitants with a view to destroying civilian morale in area attacks conducted at night. After the United States entered the war in 1941 its Army Air Force mounted daylight raids which prioritised economic production but which over Japan similarly created massive firestorms in the cities of Japan. The dropping of the two atomic bombs in 1945 was the culmination of this approach. which gave effect to the promise of "total war".

On land the Soviet Union led the way in fusing mechanisation, mass warfare and economic mobilisation in the 1930s. Michael Tukhachevsky formulated the principles of the "Soviet Deep Battle", in which tanks, motorised infantry, cavalry, paratroop reinforcements and tactical air forces would convert the breakthrough into a breakout by deploying formations in depth and so would convert operational into strategic success.

Sharing the intention to avoid (confrontational) positional warfare, Basil H. **Liddell Hart** began to theorise on how to replace strategies that were previously based on "direct" success with an "indirect" strategy. The enemy should be weakened through a multitude of integrated political actions at state level and by distracting them via an "indirect approach". He first outlined this argument in **The Decisive Wars of History** in 1929, and after the Second World War he had developed it into **Strategy – the Indirect Approach, London 1954**. By then he had responded to both world wars by developing theories for limited war which proved to be effective responses to the dropping of the atomic bombs in 1945. Bridging a plethora of "conventional" strategists and the ultimate challenge posed by nuclear weapons, Liddell Hart therefore stands at a definitive turning point in terms of strategy.

In "Strategy", Liddell Hart not only emphasises the fundamental importance of an "indirect approach" inclusive of military action, but also refined "Grand Strategy", by widening the concept of strategy and elevating previous definitions to a new and more comprehensive plane. Although this "Grand Strategy" is practically synonymous with the concept of policy that governs warfare, it differs in that it sets out the objective, the purpose. "Grand Strategy" therefore refers to a type of "policy in execution", for its purpose is to manage and coordinate all sources of power within a nation or alliance in order to achieve the objective of war set by policy. Therefore, it also cannot be understood as a purely military concept: "Moreover, fighting power is but one of the instruments of grand strategy – which should take account of and apply the power of financial pressure, of diplomatic pressure, of commercial pressure, and, not least of ethical pressure, to weaken the opponent's will." Unlike purely military strategy, which is dependent upon military victory over the opposition and therefore finds its place within the war, Grand Strategy pursues a loftier ambition: to generate or create suitable conditions for subsequent peace. In order to achieve this, Grand Strategy should "not only combine the various instruments [of war], but so regulate their use as to avoid damage to the future state of peace – for its security and prosperity".

Naval battles in European theatres of war during the Second World War witnessed a return of the principle of blockades and counter-blockades, which had been applied during the Napoleonic Wars, the American Civil War and the First World War. The British Royal Navy's plan for long-distance blockade was undercut by Germany's rapid conquest of western Europe. Possessed of ports with direct access to the Atlantic, Germany could send its surface vessels on commerce raids and mount a counter-blockade by means of submarines with virtually no restrictions. Despite initial successes, it ultimately failed in 1943. The Allies' signals intelligence and ability to decode and direct German submarine radio communications, new positioning technology (SONAR, RADAR) and an increasingly effective convoy system consisting of escort vessels and air forces that provided a high level of protection all made it possible to secure supplies and to deliver stocks of food, raw materials and munitions to other allied forces and ultimately to open a second front in mainland Europe.

From late 1942, in the war against Japan, a modern naval strategy that aimed to gradually cut off Japanese bases and isolate the motherland and which was based on submarine warfare and the deployment of groups of modern and robust aircraft carriers matched the initial successes enjoyed by the Japanese and ultimately led to the collapse of their control throughout Eastern Asia and the Western Pacific.

2.7   Cold War

The atomic bomb dictated strategic theory during the Cold War. The first strategist of the burgeoning "age of the bomb" was Bernard Brodie (**The Absolute Weapon**, Yale Institute of International Studies, New Haven 1946; **Implications of Nuclear Weapons in Total War**, Rand Corporation, Santa Monica 1957; **Strategy in the Missile Age**, Princeton University Press, Princeton 1959).

The atomic bomb necessitated a complete U-turn in strategic thinking, even though a number of theorists still tried to adhere to the "conventional" ideals. Nevertheless: the planning undertaken prior to 1945 by Chiefs of Staff on all sides to triumph in military conflict changed radically by the end of Cold War. In the era of life under "the nuclear sword of Damocles", the desire to assert oneself, once so crucial during the bipolar confrontation between systems, hinged strongly on the credibility of deterrence.

Aside from "proxy wars" such as the Korean and Vietnam Wars, the idea of major powers engaging in conflict with one another was essentially only feasible in theory, which is why governments usually sought academics to act as advisors. Historians had to take a back seat as statistics provided a firmer foundation in the science-based nuclear age. From statistics came game theory, mathematical simulation models and hard economic data (**Thomas C. Schelling, The Strategy of Conflict**, Harvard University Press, Cambridge, Mass. 1960).

The central tenet nevertheless remained – that peace was the object, whether it was achieved by collaborative security policy adopted across various blocs or by deterring the enemy from a nuclear attack. This resulted in the field of "strategy" being expanded in several ways over the decades that followed.

New political science theories and models were developed: neoliberalism, interdependence, constructivism, realism and defensive and offensive neorealism (**Hans Joachim Morgenthau, Politics Among Nations. The Struggle for Power and Peace,** New York 1948; **Robert O. Keohane and Joseph S. Nye Jr., Power and Interdependence: World Politics in Transition,** Boston 1977).

Since the Cold War led to antagonistic political ideologies battling for supremacy around the world, an older strategic approach developed as early as the start of the century was also reconsidered, that of geopolitics. Geopolitics is a blend of geography, political science, history and social science. It developed into a guiding maxim, particularly within US foreign policy. Its core principles can be traced back to German geographer like Friedrich Ratzel and were developed in English by **Halford Mackinder** (**The Geographical Pivot of History**, 1904 and **Democratic Ideals and Reality: A study in the Politics of Reconstruction**, London 1919). His concept of the Heartland was based on permanent conflict between land and sea powers, writing: "Who rules East Europe commands the Heartland. Who rules the Heartland commands the World Island. Who rules the World Island commands the World." In **America's Strategy in World Politics: The United States and the Balance of Power** (New York 1942) and **The Geography of the Peace** (New York 1944), Mackinder's disciple, **Nicholas J. Spykman**, offered a different outlook. Spykman contended that the future need to contain the Soviet threat revolved around dominating the fringes of Asia in the "Heartland", i.e. the "Rimland", writing: "Who controls the Rimland rules Eurasia, who rules Eurasia controls the destiny of the World."

As was evident in these concepts, the "Heartland" was really Russia before 1917 and the Soviet Union thereafter. At the mid-point of the 20th century, the German Reich was no longer the main opposition to Anglo-American powers. They sought to rein in the Soviet Union with US-led alliances such as NATO and SEATO, which were formed precisely where preventing "Heartland" access to the "Rimland" was worthwhile because the Heartland's sheer population, natural resources and industrial development had massive consequences for the USA's future global role.

Raymond Aaron also reflected on Clausewitz the "philosopher" during the era of the atom bomb as a "political weapon" (***Penser la guerre, Clausewitz***, Paris 1976). However, strategic matters were also addressed by "contemporary philosophers", such as **André Glucksmann** (***Le discours de la guerre, théorie et stratégie*** (1967) and ***Philosophie der Abschreckung***, Frankfurt am Main 1986) or Leon Wieseltier (***Frieden durch Abschreckung. Strategische Überlegungen zur Verhinderung eines Atomkrieges*** [Nuclear War- Nuclear Peace], Munich 1984). Glucksmann postulated that deterrence is "the agreement of what cannot be agreed (...) The opponents agree (...) that suffering is negative (...) and consequently agree upon a legal principle that acts as a deterrent against (evil) actions." Wieseltier labelled deterrence as "the only public arrangement that is a total failure if it is successful 99.9 percent of the time".

Influenced by the national movements in south-eastern Asia and North Africa calling for liberation from French colonial rule, French general **André**

Beaufre (*Introduction à la stratégie*, Paris 1963 [**Introduction to Strategy**, New York: Praeger 1965]) attempted to blend "direct" and "indirect" strategies, believing that a combination of the two had the greatest chance of success. He defined the objective of strategy as: "[obtaining a decision] by creating and then exploiting a situation resulting in sufficient moral disintegration of the enemy to cause him to accept the conditions it is desired to impose upon him". Overall, he viewed strategy as "the art of the dialectic of two opposing wills using force to resolve their dispute". In terms of organisation, he put forward various specific strategies designed to effect a "total strategy" under the umbrella of a strategic pyramid. He thus elevated the concept of strategy (continuing the tradition of Clausewitz) to being a systematic way of thinking.

In doing so, he differed slightly from Henry Kissinger. Kissinger began his career in strategy as an academic (**Nuclear Weapons and Foreign Policy**, New York 1957) and later transformed himself into a policy "practitioner". In 1973, as the US Secretary of State, he summarised his understanding of (power-political) strategy as follows: "It is the task of strategic doctrine to translate power into policy."

Together with the numerous "academic" contributions to the debate on strategy, those that expressed political will in the military sphere, e.g. those that defined NATO within the framework of its strategies, have a special role. The strategies based on deterrence also had to be able to provide answers to what would happen "if deterrence fails."

Douhet's theories from decades before therefore played a role once more, which shows that a knowledge of older theories can help by providing the answers to subsequent challenges.

This was also reflected among US thinkers who, as their contemporary environment changed, opted for a model based on making comparisons using examples from history, no matter how far back they dated. In the aftermath of the US defeat in the Vietnam War, **Edward Luttwak (The Grand Strategy of the Roman Empire from the First Century A.D. to the Third**, Baltimore 1976) considered the USA to be in the same strategic position as that of the Roman Empire. From that point onward, he felt that "defensive imperialism" had to be practised.

While all Western strategists showed flexibility in their definitions of strategy and considered new systems, often shifting ever further from the purely military understanding of it, little appeared to change in the Soviet Union. The Soviet Military Encyclopaedia summarised it thus in 1967: "Strategy concerns the development of the principal maxims and recommendations for preparing the country and its forces for war in line with its nature and objectives".

However, ultimately, in the debate on strategy during the Cold War, nuclear weapons imposed an absolute limitation on the image of warfare, with respect to policy, in a way never before witnessed in military history or the history of warfare. They also had a second long-term effect: strategy in practice was overshadowed by strategy in theory, comparatively unfettered by practice. The significant exception, reflecting first the wars of colonial withdrawal and then 'proxy' wars outside Europe waged between the United States and the Soviet Union, was the study of revolutionary war, insurgency and counter-insurgency (**Robert Thompson, Defeating Communist Insurgency: experience from Malaya and Vietnam,** London, 1974; **Frank Kitson, Low Intensity Operations: Subversion, Insurgency and Peacekeeping,** London, 1971).

The interest in irregular warfare, even its use by states, surged especially after the 9/11 attacks on the United States in 2001 and the American readiness to use its military power while enjoying its 'unipolar moment' (**David Kilcullen, The Accidental Guerrilla: fighting small wars in the midst of a big one,** 2009). Following the end of the Cold War, the pace of change in the phenomenology of the forms of conflict matched that of the quest for the terms with which they can be described. It also led to more studies of quality on the topic of strategy. As a result, differing definitions of strategy were continuously produced. This is most evident in the continuous definitions of strategy across a very wide range of scientific disciplines, and also through the latter's ownership of those definitions – such as: international relations (**Colin S. Gray, War, Peace and International Relations: An Introduction to Strategic History,** London 2007), geopolitics (**Zbigniew Brzezinski, The Grand Chessboard: American Primacy and Its Geostrategic Imperatives,** New York 1997; and **Samuel P. Huntington, The Clash of Civilizations and the Remaking of World Order,** New York 1996) and almost all sub-areas of economics and finance. An additional consequence of this since the end of the Cold War is that in all national, European and North Atlantic strategy papers, the new and increasing complexity of the challenges has become a mantra which drives both codification and the search for "comprehensive approaches" which integrate both forms of strategy and the agencies responsible for their implementation. .

The current debate on strategy focuses on two "new" fields and two "old" ones: hybrid warfare and cyberspace address the "new" challenges posed: the "return" of the Cold War in Europe and of geopolitics established over a century ago, against the backdrop of climate change and the rise of China. Underpinning all four is the merging of the aims and methods of inter-state war with those of intra-state conflict. Since 1991, civil war and its offshoots, domestic revolts and terror attacks, have been the dominant form of armed conflict but has invited intervention by state actors and so become internationalised.

3. Conclusion

Strategy research continues to be plagued by the same fundamental problems: the nature and outward appearance of power politics, a key formative driving force in global policy, are forever changing and war, just like strategy, remains a chameleon, to use Clausewitz's metaphor. War is not universal. No two approaches to war are the same – whether by virtue of the reasons for initiating it or the way in which it is waged. It may be coloured entirely by patriotism, which in turn can only be explained by the history and culture of the country in question. Therefore, historical knowledge remains indispensable for strategic theory. After all, individual states have developed in completely different ways (monarchy, dictatorship, democracy) with ramifications for each state's strategy. Although democracies may be reluctant to go to war "if diplomacy fails", they are ready to fight if they are convinced of the cause. Democracy has been a powerful force for mass mobilisation since 1789, even if largely overlooked in contemporary theory. Theories should not exclude developments in society.

A significant grey area remains however – that of the role of responsible policy makers who must take fundamental strategic decisions, not least at the onset of a critical escalation of a situation. Their second and third order effects can detrimentally affect subsequent developments. Policy makers generally have very little idea of or interest in strategic issues relating to their states' foreign policy because they tend to arrive in office as a result of domestic politics and recognise emerging threats too late, if at all.

However, strategists hold the basic assumption that democratically elected "Heads of State" have a keen desire to deal with strategy and can formulate and implement it within practical policy. In reality, they rely on "learning by doing", which results in trial and error. This is the approach that has ultimately shaped the entire history of strategic theory.

4. References

Aeneas Tacticus. (357/356 BCE). Strategik [How to Survive under Siege].

Beaufre, A. (1963) *Introduction à la stratégie*, Paris. [(1965). Introduction to Strategy, New York: Praeger]

Beaufre, A. (1965) (*Introduction à la stratégie*, Paris 1963 [Introduction to Strategy, New York: Praeger 1965])

Brodie, B. (1946). *The Absolute Weapon*. New Haven: Yale Institute of International Studies.

Brodie, B. (1957). *Implications of Nuclear Weapons in Total War*. Santa Monica: Rand Corporation.

Brodie, B. (1959). *Strategy in the Missile Age*. Princeton: Princeton University Press.

Brzezinski, Z. (1997). *The Grand Chessboard: American Primacy and Its Geostrategic Imperatives*. New York.

von Clausewitz, C. (1832-1834). Vom Kriege [On War].

Douhet, G. (1921). *Il dominio dell'aria* [Command of the Air]

Fuller, J.F.C. (1923). *The Reformation of War*. London.

Glucksmann, A. (1967). *Le discours de la guerre, théorie et stratégie*.

Glucksmann, A. (1986). *Philosophie der Abschreckung*. Frankfurt am Main

Gray, C. S. (1999). *Modern Strategy*. Oxford: Oxford University Press.

Gray, C. S. (2007). *War, Peace and International Relations: An Introduction to Strategic History*. London.

Grotius H. (1609). *Mare Liberum* [The Freedom of the Seas].

Grotius H. (1625). *De jure belli ac pacis* [On the Law of War and Peace].

Hahlweg W. (Ed.). (1960). *Klassiker der Kriegskunst*, Darmstadt.

Hobbes, T. (1651). *Leviathan*.

Heuser, B. & Hartmann, A. (Eds.). (2001). *Thinking War, Peace and World Orders from Antiquity until the 20th century*. London.

Heuser, B. (2010). *The Evolution of Strategy: Thinking War from Antiquity to the Present*, Cambridge: Cambridge University Press.

Huntington, S. P. (1996). *The Clash of Civilizations and the Remaking of World Order*. New York.

Jomini, A. H. (1838). *Précis de l'Art de la Guerre: Des Principales Combinaisons de la Stratégie, de la Grande Tactique et de la Politique Militaire*.

Keohane, R. O., & Nye Jr., J. S. (1977). *Power and Interdependence: World Politics in Transition*. Boston.

Kilcullen, D. (2009). *The Accidental Guerrilla: fighting small wars in the midst of a big one.*

Kissinger, H. (1957). *Nuclear Weapons and Foreign Policy.* New York.

Kitson, F. (1971). Low Intensity Operations: Subversion, Insurgency and Peacekeeping. London.

Liddell Hart, B. H. (1929). *The Decisive Wars of History.*

Liddell Hart, B. H. (1954). *Strategy – the Indirect Approach.* London

Ludendorff, E. (1935). *Der totale Krieg.* Munich.

Luttwak, E. (1976). *The Grand Strategy of the Roman Empire from the First Century AD to the Third.* Baltimore.

Machiavelli, N. (1521). *Dell'arte della guerra.* Florence.

Mackinder, H. (1904). *The Geographical Pivot of History.*

Mackinder, H. (1919). *Democratic Ideals and Reality: A study in the Politics of Reconstruction.* London.

Mahan, A. T. (1890). *The Influence of Sea Power upon History*, 1660-1783.

Morgenthau, H. J. (1948). *Politics Among Nations. The Struggle for Power and Peace.* New York.

de Saxe, M. (1756). *Les Reveries Ou Memoires Sur L'Art De La Guerre.*

Onasander. (I. Century AD). *Strategikos.*

Paret, P., Craig, G. A., & Gilbert F. (Eds.), *Makers of Modern Strategy from Machiavelli to the Nuclear Age.* Oxford.

Schelling, T. C. (1960). *The Strategy of Conflict.* Cambridge: Harvard University Press.

Spykman, N. J. (1942). *America's Strategy in World Politics: The United States and the Balance of Power.* New York.

Spykman, N. J. (1944). The Geography of the Peace. New York.

Stahel, A.A. (2004). *Klassiker der Strategie – eine Bewertung.* Zürich.

Sun Tzu. (Vth Century BCE). *The Art of War.*

Thompson, R. (1974). *Defeating Communist Insurgency: experience from Malaya and Vietnam.* London.

Wallach, J. (1967). *Clausewitz and Schlieffen; Das Dogma der Vernichtungsschlacht. Die Lehren von Clausewitz und Schlieffen und ihre Wirkungen in 2 Weltkriegen.* Frankfurt am Main.

Wallach, J. L. (1972). *Kriegstheorien. Ihre Entwicklung im 19. und 20. Jahrhundert,* Frankfurt am Main.

Wieseltier, L. (1984). *Frieden durch Abschreckung. Strategische Überlegungen zur Verhinderung eines Atomkrieges* [Nuclear War- Nuclear Peace]. Munich.

5. Further Reading

Beaufre, A. (1963) *Introduction à la stratégie*, Paris. [(1965). Introduction to Strategy, New York: Praeger]

Bellamy, C., & Strachan, H. (2001). *The Oxford companion to military history*. Oxford University Press.

Douhet, G. (1921). *Il dominio dell'aria* [Command of the Air]

Dupuy, R. E., Dupuy, T. N. (1970).*The encyclopedia of military history: from 3500 BC to the present*. New York, NY: Harper & Row.

Heuser, B. (2010). *The Evolution of Strategy: Thinking War from Antiquity to the Present*, Cambridge: Cambridge University Press.

Keegan, J. (2011). *A history of warfare*. Random House.

Liddell Hart, B. H. (1929). *The Decisive Wars of History*.

Mackinder, H. (1904). *The Geographical Pivot of History*.

Mahan, A. T. (1890). *The Influence of Sea Power upon History*, 1660-1783.

Mearsheimer, J. J. (1988). Liddell Hart and the weight of history. Cornell University Press.

Paret, P., Craig, G. A., & Gilbert F. (Eds.), *Makers of Modern Strategy from Machiavelli to the Nuclear Age*. Oxford.

Strachan, H. (2008). *Clausewitz's On war: a biography*. Grove Press.

Wallach, J. (1967). *Clausewitz and Schlieffen; Das Dogma der Vernichtungsschlacht. Die Lehren von Clausewitz und Schlieffen und ihre Wirkungen in 2 Weltkriegen.* Frankfurt am Main.

Chapter 6: Strategic culture

Dr. Thomas Pankratz (†), BG (retd.) MMag. Wolfgang Peischel, PhD

Keywords: Strategic Culture; Constructivism; Grand Strategy; Security Policy; Game Theory; Behavioural Science;

> *"Thus, then, in strategy everything is very simple, but not on that account very easy."* Carl von Clausewitz, On War (Book III, p. 96)
>
> *"With his forces intact he will dispute the mastery of the Empire, and thus, without losing a man, his triumph will be complete. This is the method of attacking by stratagem."* Sun Tzu, The Art of War (p. 21)
>
> *"The tactics and strategy of Leninism are based on the fact that the transition from slow quantitative to sudden qualitative changes is a law of evolution and that the transition from capitalism to socialism can only take place by means of revolution."* Strategie und Taktik des Leninismus (Kommunist, 1953)

1. Strategy: military, economic, political

The terms culture and strategy are both commonly used in everyday language, although their etymological meanings are not always known by those who use them, and they are often used without any profound thought as to what they mean. The term strategy has military roots and goes back to the Greek term "stratos", equivalent to commander, a position in the upper leadership or political class, and "agein", which in turn means to lead, to take action or to act. The word "strategia" can be translated as "office of commander, art of command, generalship".[1]

With regard to military terminology, von Clausewitz stated that strategy is the "economy of forces" (von Clausewitz, Book III, p. 125). He also made the following general remark regarding strategy: "According to our classification, therefore, tactics is the theory of the use of military forces in combat. Strategy is the theory of the use of combats for the object of the war" (von Clausewitz, Book II, p. 50). Napoleon was convinced that strategy was the art of harnessing space and time. However, the Prussian field marshal Helmuth von Moltke

---

[1] Onasandros, from his treatise written in 49/59 AD "Strategikos": one experienced in the art of command (cf. Peters 1972).

held the following view: "Strategy is a system of expedients. It is more than a science, it is the transfer of knowledge to practical life, the further development of the original guiding thought in line with the constantly changing conditions, it is the art of acting under the pressure of difficult conditions" (Stahel 2003, p. 5). British military historian B. H. Liddell Hart, by contrast, ranks strategy as a form of intermediate plane between the two poles of tactics and grand strategy: "As tactics is an application of strategy on a lower plane, so strategy is an application on a lower plane of 'grand strategy'" (1956, p. 335). He defined the role of strategy in relation to grand strategy as follows: „Whereas strategy is only concerned with the problem of winning military victory, grand strategy must take the longer view – for its problem is the winning of the peace"(ibid., p. 362).

However, the domain of strategy development is not unique to the military. At least since 1980, when the "Strategic Management Journal" was founded, strategic management has been a fixture on business studies curricula (cf. Hofer & Schendel 1978) Strategy planning processes are also integral to the longterm success of business management: "Strategy differs considerably from vision, aims, measures or tactics. A vision is intended to inspire, the mission defines the raison d'être, an aim designates a target state and the tactics and measures indicate the action needed to reach that state. A strategy, however, defines the distinctive competitive approach of a company and the competitive advantages on which that approach is based" (Strategieplanung).

Politics without strategies is inconceivable, since politics is always a form of strategy. The relational structure of democracy and strategy is well documented from a scientific perspective (cf. Gohl; cf. Lechner). In the field of political science in Germany, Joachim Raschke and Ralf Tils have made an important contribution to the research on the issue of political strategy (2007, 2010). According to them, strategies are "success-oriented constructs based on calculations of the objectives, the means and the environment" (ibid, pp. 127-128). A slightly broader definition of political strategy states that it is "a plan-based, calculated, forward-looking, end-to-end thinking (feedback loops), success-oriented purpose-time-objective-means-environment continuum. The validity of strategies should not be subject to any orthodoxy. It is therefore necessary to continually evaluate the effectiveness of strategies" (Lapins 2018, p. 378). Moving now from the theoretical level to political practice, the "grandmaster" of US foreign policy and diplomacy, Henry Kissinger, defined strategy as a doctrine that translates power into policy. For him, this political art was also what set the statesman apart: „A statesman's test is whether he can discern from the swirl of tactical decisions the true long-term interests of his country and devise an appropriate strategy for achieving them"(Kissinger 1994, p. 109).

It is clear from the foregoing problematisation that the term strategy can be interpreted in a variety of ways. Therefore, it is not surprising that the same applies by analogy to the term "strategic culture".

2.   Genealogy of strategic culture

The intellectual concept of "strategic culture" was developed in 1977 by the political scientist Jack Lewis Snyder[2] at Columbia University in the context of a "RAND study" (Snyder 1977) for the Office of the Deputy Chief of Staff for Plans and Operations, Headquarters, United States Air Force, and it critically examined the US doctrine of nuclear deterrence prevailing at that time. The objectives of the research project were "(1) providing a context for a better understanding of the intellectual, institutional, and strategic-cultural determinants that would bind the Soviet decision-making process in a crisis and, (2) speculating on the dominant behavioral propensities that would motivate – and constrain – the Soviet leaders during their efforts to cope with a situation, where limited nuclear use by either side loomed as a possibility" (ibid., p. iii). Snyder observed that the US strategy of deterrence was strongly characterised by game-theoretical assumptions, which implied that the USSR would proceed on the basis of similar assumptions. He argued that US thinking on deterrence did not sufficiently take into account the possibility that the US doctrine could be ineffective due to the different notions of rationality in the Soviet Union. Deterrence would only function effectively if the political opponents were operating on the basis of the same premises. For this reason, nuclear strategy should not be limited to a mere analysis of the opponent's power potential, but should also take into consideration the given normative and non-material/ideological basis for the use of nuclear weapons. From this, Snyder drew the conclusion that the respective elites had developed a specific strategic culture as the product of differing organisational, historical, political and technological contexts, and that these cultures manifested themselves in a specific way of thinking regarding military matters.

He believed that the Soviet military leadership had a preference for the pre-emptive and offensive use of nuclear weapons, an attitude that had its origins in Russia's history of insecurity, confusion, attacks by foreign powers and the

---

2 In his 1991 book, Myths of Empire. Domestic Politics and International Ambition, Cornell University Press, Jack L. Snyder then conceptualised the distinction between offensive and defensive realism in international relations.

authoritarian system. His conclusion resulted in the position that new developments should only be viewed in terms of strategic culture; that they were, in a way, semi-permanent.

Until the 1970s, cultural theory played no role in the US strategic discussion. Instead, it was characterised by the prevailing doctrine of nuclear deterrence. The design of the systems in the "political West" and its implications for political practice was the subject of comparative government and what was known as Sovietology in relation to the USSR. Game-theoretical[3] and (neo)realistic[4] approaches were at the forefront of US strategic thinking on security policy. Rational choice models (Cf. Steinbrunner 1975, pp. 223-245)[5] were also completely abstracted from cultural factors and characteristics of the two Cold War superpowers. From this, it was concluded that the Soviet leadership would behave in a comparable way to the USA in similar situations.

Dialectics of strategy and strategic culture

But what is meant by strategic culture – what question does it set out to answer? Its object of inquiry clearly relates to values, norms, attitudes and opinions – in short, to the ethical essentials for the use of military tools and methods. However, do these relate merely to the political elites, as argued by Jack L. Snyder in the above-mentioned study of 1977, when he referred to strategic culture as "a set of semi-permanent elite beliefs, attitudes, and behavior patterns socialized into a distinctive mode of thought"(Snyder 1977, p.8)? In the light of the fact that it is ultimately still the elite actors that determine when and to what extent military means are used, these were still considered to be the gatekeepers or carriers of strategic culture nearly 20 years later (cf. Griegerich 2006, p. 201).

---

[3] On game theory: cf. Leininger & Amann; Hesse.
Thomas Schelling is one of the most influential protagonists in the field of deterrence theory, which has its basis in game theory; cf. Schelling 1960 & 1966; also cf. Blendin & Schneider.
[4] Cf. Herz 1959; Hans J. Morgenthau is indisputably the founder of the realist theoretical structure in international politics (cf. Morgenthau 1962, p. 76). In an obituary for Morgenthau, Henry Kissinger stressed his importance when he wrote: "Hans Morgenthau was my teacher. And he was my friend. (…) Hans Morgenthau made the study of contemporary international relations a major discipline. All of us who taught the subject after him, however much we differed from one another, had to start with his reflections. Not everybody agreed with Hans Morgenthau, but nobody could ignore him" (1980, p. 12). For a critical analysis of the logic and practice of nuclear deterrence: cf. Morgan 1977. While conventional realism tended to present a theory of foreign policy, neorealism, or structural realism, as a systemic theory, analyses the structure of international relations and attempts to draw conclusions about the actions of the state. One of the most prominent proponents of neorealism was Kenneth Waltz (cf. 1979). For a good comparison of realism and neorealism: cf. Zürn 1994.
[5] A very good overview of the overall matter of nuclear deterrence: cf. Sauer 2016.

As Peischel argues regarding the two concepts of strategy and strategic culture with reference to Carl von Clausewitz: "As with the attempt to grasp the concept of strategy per se, here, too, the question is not how strategic culture can best be circumscribed semantically, but, rather, what benefit or added value a concept, which is to be constructed around the term strategic culture, would have to yield. In order to do this, it must first be clarified whether the terms strategy and strategic culture do not simply comprise for the most part synonymous contents. If this were the case, then strategic culture would be a mere linguistic creation of no identifiable explanatory value. The question of whether strategy and strategic culture can actually be distinguished will ultimately determine whether a concept of strategic culture is actually required. Assuming that the two concepts are not congruent, a further question arises whether strategic culture represents a subset of the concept of strategy – not in the sense of a functional element, a cogwheel in the gearbox, but merely in the sense of a conspicuous designation of individual elements, which would facilitate a common approach. In this case it would again only be a formal system of ordering and processing elements which represent a subset of strategy but have no significant controlling influence on its functional mechanism. A further hypothesis could be based on the idea that strategic culture largely coincides with the spiritual dimension of warfare, with which Carl von Clausewitz went beyond the deterministic-technical view – and, just like the aforementioned spiritual dimension, has been neglected or forgotten. If this thesis were to substantiated, Clausewitz' wonderful trinity would serve as an excellent illustrative, diagnostic, and development model for strategic culture. Carl von Clausewitz, the theorist of war, introduced the terminological distinction between purpose, aim and means, which underpins any definition of strategic intentions. In this, purpose is the ultimate reason for any strategic effort, the logic which all measures derived should serve. Aims refers to the operational-level steps towards implementation (action) derived from the purpose, the means are the resources released by the leadership, which are required for goal achievement and, by enabling goal achievement, indirectly key to the realisation of the strategic purpose. Following this logic, determining the purpose would be the task of the strategic echelon. The feasibility analysis, part of every assessment cycle, the derivation of subgoals, which, in their totality, serve to enable the achievement of purpose, and the determination of resources required to achieve the sub-goals, would be tasks of the operational level implementation planning and /or echelon. The decision of the political echelon concerning the release of the resources deemed necessary will either lead to a feasible proposal for a strategic determination of purpose or to the task of formulating a new working hypothesis, which can make do with fewer resources. With Clausewitz any decision concerning the strategic purpose is clearly the responsibility of the political leadership. However, given its scientifically sound and competence-based expert evaluation ability, the highest military leadership would be tasked with giving substantive advice to the political leadership in the process of its decision, whereby it becomes an indirect constituent of the determination of the strategic purpose while the primacy of politics is maintained" (Peischel 2018, p.14).

3.   Strategic culture – schools of thought

Towards the end of the 1970s, it became apparent that a number of rational game-theoretical analyses and predictions made by Western analysts were incorrect. Meanwhile, it had become clear in the course of the empirical experience acquired in the context of international relations that states in similar situations did not always act in similar or predictable ways, but analysed and interpreted the security situation in different ways and ultimately reacted in different ways. An attempt was made to explain this phenomenon on the basis of culturalistic approaches, which once again placed the attention on issues of national culture. This ultimately resulted in three different approaches to "strategic culture", being generations/schools of thought that differed from one another in their respective approaches (cf. Biehl, Griegerich, & Alexandra 2013, p. 11).

The first approach understood the state's security posture as being implemented in the strategic culture (cf. Gray 1981, pp 21-47). According to this understanding, strategic culture therefore forms the context of the behaviour, but is simultaneously also a part of this behaviour; in other words, the mutual influence of strategic culture and security behaviour is assumed. One of the basic assumptions is that the strategic culture influences tendencies, but is not the only aspect to affect the behaviour and political decisions. However, this approach fundamentally lacked cohesion and a stringent methodical procedure. In addition, it was not possible to explicitly establish the connotation between actual behaviour and strategic culture.

In the 1980s and 1990s, the discussion regarding strategic culture moved away from the issue of nuclear deterrence that had previously been of central importance. It was extended to include fundamental questions regarding normative, non-material, cultural and ethical ideas about the use of military means in general. This idea continues to be one of the central tenets of the common approaches to strategic culture.

The main focus of the second generation was working out the differences between the formal strategic culture that was declared valid and the motives and objectives of the decision-making elites that were pursued in reality, in the tradition of critical theory (critical deconstruction) (cf. Klein 1988, pp.

144

133-148). One substantial criticism of the second generation was that it decoupled strategic culture from strategic behaviour by equating the features of strategic culture to merely spurious arguments used by dominant groups to justify security policy and conceal their actual motives.

In a third interpretation, strategic culture exists as an independent, sovereign entity that controls state security policy (cf. Johnston 1995, pp. 32-64). Proponents of the first generation are commonly perceived to focus on norms, attitudes and values regarding the use of military means, as they are considered to be of particular relevance to the behaviour of states in matters of foreign and security policy. Another shared feature is the firm rejection of historical and anti-culturalist paradigms such as those advocated by neorealism.

One of the central ideas behind the concept of strategy culture was and continues to be the attempt to explain the behaviour and behaviour patterns of states that fall outside of the predictions based on the rationality of the state. From this, it is possible to conclude that there is not a single, universal rationality, but various notions of rationality. What one actor may consider to be logical and worthwhile may seem irrational to another. Furthermore, each strategic actor is influenced by his own strategic culture. This includes values, norms, world views, culture, history, experiences, fears, etc (cf. Fischer; cf. Winter 2013).

The political scientists Sven Biscop and Thomas Renard of the Royal Institute for International Relations (Egmont) rightly ask in their study "A Need for Strategy in a Multipolar World: Recommendations to the EU after Lisbon. European Strategy in the 21st Century": "The first rule of strategy-making is to know thyself. (...) Which values and interests should our grand strategy safeguard?" (2013, pp. 1-2) An example of how such central issues are addressed is provided by the US National Security Strategy of November 2017, the first page of which states: "An America that is safe, prosperous, and free at home is an America with the strength, confidence, and will to lead abroad. It is an America that can preserve peace, uphold liberty, and create enduring advantages for the American people. Putting America first is the duty of our government and the foundation for U.S. leadership in the world. A strong America is in the vital interests of not only the American people, but also those around the world who want to partner with the United States in pursuit of shared interests, values, and aspirations. This National Security Strategy puts America first" (White House 2017, p. 1).

4. New approach due to constructivism

After a brief lull in interest in the research field of strategic culture following the end of the Cold War, the discussion was revitalised in the mid-1990s. This was influenced in particular by the emergence of constructivism as an additional political science metatheory in international relations (cf. Martinsen 2014). Its rapid increase in significance was based on the inability of the methods espoused by the previously dominant field of neorealism to predict the end of the East-West conflict, essentially due to its unwavering theory that a change in the international system was not possible. In constructivism, international relations are seen and evaluated through the prism of social theory. The German-US political scientist Alexander Wendt is considered to be one of the pioneers in the field (cf. Wendt 1999). One of the main tenets of constructivism is that human behaviour acquires its relevance through language and interpretation of the material environment. He believes that historical experiences and cultural conventions/traditions/rituals provide a repertoire of ways to assign meaning and patterns for interpreting social behaviour. A further central assumption of this approach is that the identities and interests of actors should not be understood as given variables but that they arise only from the interaction of material and non-material factors (cf. Biehl et al 2011, p.9). Interests are understood to be the result of ideas. It is thus the social construct of friend/foe that determines the corresponding behaviour of the state (cf. ibid., p.133). The constructivist approach places great emphasis on the identification of formation in connection with organisational processes relating to history, tradition and culture.

The approaches of this new school of thought differ from the three generations described above in two aspects in particular (cf. Biehl et al 2013, p. 10). First, strategic culture is seen as neither an independent nor a dependent variable, but as an interceding variable that influences the behaviour of actors in conjunction with other factors. Strategic culture provides a framework for understanding which options are considered to be legitimate within a society, for example with regard to using military means in the context of security policy. Second, the opinions, attitudes and preferences of the population are taken into account.

This brief description of how generations of thought in the field of strategic culture developed makes it clear that strategic culture describes actor-specific ideas, values and norms, opinions, attitudes, assumptions or expectations, which (among other things) determine the identity, patterns for interpreting the surrounding world, positions and behaviour of the respective actor in matters relating to foreign, security and defence policy. It is usually the state or its political and military elites that are seen as the central subjects in this regard. It is their task to provide a frame of reference and thus contribute to the success of a strategy. The absence of this leads to disorientation, unpredictability, implementation problems, a limited scope for action, heteronomy, legitimation issues and many other phenomena.

Accordingly, various material, social and non-material factors that can be considered as sources of strategic culture have been identified. These factors interact with the actor in question and thus contribute to their socialisation, as it were. Geofactors, such as topographic features, access to the sea or being a landlocked country, demographic factors, access to important resources and the climate are seen as key factors. Proximity to a major power is often mentioned in this context (cf. Lentis & Howlett 2013, pp. 77-95). Further central factors are undoubtedly historical experiences and narratives, the political system and national, international and transnational norms. However, there has not yet been a uniform definition or a coherent theoretical structure.

Nayef Al-Rodhan, a British neuroscientist and pioneer in researching the interaction between neuroscience and strategic issues in international relations, additionally emphasises the importance of narratives in the context of strategic culture:

"The strategic culture of any given country has numerous sources and it is bound to remain an "elastic" term given that there are various factors that influence the formation of national culture and a subsequent rationality for security policy and strategic thinking. Factors such as geopolitics, norms and customs, perceptions of regional and international roles, political systems and power sharing (including the balance between military and civilian actors or how military power and institutions are structured) are solidified in collective memory and identity through political narratives, education, artistic and popular renderings of (often carefully) selected historical episodes, interpretations of common memories" (Al-Rodhan 2015).

Wolfgang Peischel, the "strategy connoisseur" mentioned above, summarises his thoughts on the trinity of strategic interest, strategy and strategic culture as follows: "Strategic interest requires a definition that goes beyond security issues and the classical instruments of strategy – the term strategic culture would have to follow this expansion. Strategic culture is a functional, by necessity complementary, element of strategy. A concept of strategic culture is required, because it facilitates a value-based, escalation-averting containment of a predominantly power- and interest-driven concept of strategy. Another possible approach would result from the numerous overlaps between the concept of strategic culture and the intellectual dimension of warfare according to Clausewitz. The awareness of the cultural area-related specificity of strategic culture should be raised, so that one's own strategy can be developed meaningfully and the opponent's strategy be assessed accurately. Furthermore strategic ability requires tamed enlightenment and enhanced classical education, and an awareness of one's own set of values or one's own cultural identity. With opposing hegemons being present, a unilateral renunciation of a claim to power would inevitably lead to the opponent's victory, whereas offset strategy thinking would inevitably lead to an escalation and acceleration in the arms race. The symmetrical withdrawal of the enforceable strategic interest in favour of a more value-driven strategic culture would indeed be an extremely idealistic concept, but it would at least serve as a theoretical model for the containment of a predominantly power-politically motivated strategy. And last but not least, in the future, a responsible strategy will increasingly be defined by a dialectical synthesis between value-free power interests and a value-based strategic culture, is any advantage to be utilised in war, as Friedrich Schiller stated, is everything fair in love and war as Napoleon said – or isn't it? (Peischel 2018, p. 16)

5. The actors of strategic culture at the level of nation states

Under the original state-centric approach, the carrier of strategic culture is identified as the political elite (the "strategic community") on account of its prominent position in the decision-making processes. An important question here is what role is assigned to the population in the strategic culture process. Newer approaches highlight the importance of taking into account the preferences and attitudes of the population (cf. Meyer 2004). It is evident that, in representative democracies, citizens influence those who are politically responsible for foreign and security policy through the conventional method of electing parties and representatives, but also through newer participation models (cf. Bertelsmann Stiftung; cf. Helmut-Schmidt-Universität 2018). But to what extent can/should the political system take voter preferences into account? (cf. Oberreuter) After all, citizens' attitudes about foreign and security policy are simultaneously a valuable resource(cf. Steinbrecher, Biehl, & Rothbart 2017) and a restriction (cf. Stein 2017, pp. 59-77). The population is an essential factor influencing strategic culture. However, historical experiences, myths, demographic developments, patterns of behaviour, international norms, fears, expectations, organisations, external influences, geofactors and the attitudes of the elites are important as well.

Each and every state enters the international arena with its historical baggage of accumulated experiences, beliefs, cultural influences, and geographic and material limitations – all of which define its conduct. Moreover, due to a variety of reasons a country may have either a strong or a weak strategic culture.

Therefore, the deeper analysis and discussion on this topic may yield recommendations on how to build and/or strengthen the strategic thinking in security institutions, at both practitioner and policymaking levels (Dymshi 2018, p. 7).

There is broad consensus in the research sector that, in addition to political institutions, such as parties, bureaucracies also have a significant influence on the behaviour of states in terms of foreign and security policy (cf. Jäger & Oppermann 2006, pp. 105-134).

6. The construction of a strategic culture in the EU?

The concept of strategic culture has also been transferred to supranational entities such as the EU. In 2005, Paul Cornish and Geoffrey Edwards defined the strategic culture of the Union as "political and institutional confidence and processes to deploy military force, coupled with the external recognition of the EU as a legitimate actor in the international sphere" (Cornish & Edwards 2005, p.802). This was unsurprising, since, two years prior to this, the European Council had already made the following categorical demand in its European Security Strategy "A Secure Europe in a Better World": "We need to develop a strategic culture that fosters early, rapid, and when necessary, robust intervention" (European Security Strategy 2003, p. 11). In June 2016, the then High Representative of the Union for Foreign Affairs and Security Policy and Vice-President of the European Commission, Federica Mogherini, published the EU's Global Strategy (EU-Commission 2016). However, without steadily building up the corresponding financial resources and diplomatic and military capacities, this amounts to no more than another example of "Brussels" rhetoric, in other words another declaration for the political archive.

It remains to be seen whether this will also apply to the direction strategic culture is given under under the President of the new EU Commission, Ursula von der Leyen. At the Paris Peace Forum in November 2019, she accurately characterised the upheaval in the global political order: "Existing powers are going down new paths alone. New powers are emerging, re-emerging and consolidating. We also see the need for stable and responsible leadership." However, she then promised more for the EU than is certainly achievable in real-political terms due to the disparate interests of the EU member states: „This is why, as President of the next European Commission, I want to build a truly "geopolitical" Commission. I want a more outward-looking Europe. A Europe which collectively defends our common values and interests in the world. My vision is of a Europe that helps to reconcile those who are divided, a Europe that brings together those who are apart, but at the same time demands responsibility. From ourselves, from our friends and from our partners. A responsible approach to our planet. Good governance, fight against corruption and respect for the rule of law and dignity of people. The point is that Europe needs to develop a common strategic culture and comprehensive answers" (von der Leyen 2019)[6]

Hinted at, but not articulated by, the President of the Commission was the formation of a European Security and Defence Union. The discourse on this is comprehensive[7], but it is not yet effective from a political or practical perspective. In the future, this will be driven by the EU defence initiative for Permanent Structured Cooperation (PESCO), which was initiated in 2017 and now has 46 projects. Although still in the embryonic stage, the formation of a European defence union is already coming under strong political pressure. The Trump administration is threatening with consequences due to fears of US companies being put at a disadvantage in terms of defence projects (cf. DPA 2019) and, since President Emmanuel Macron's Sorbonne speech in September 2017, France is intensively promoting the creation of a European Intervention Initiative (EI2), which has, however, been received with scepticism/hesitancy in Germany (cf. Kunz 2018). "He identified the lack of a shared strategic culture as the biggest obstacle to an ambitious European defence union, which prevents Europeans from acting in harmony and being able to respond to crises quickly" (Kahlert & Major 2019, p. 4) It should also be no surprise that the democratic left in the European Parliament vehemently rejects PESCO for ideological reasons. In their opinion, PESCO means: "Securing economic and commercial interests also through military structures and building up the EU's (military) superpower status on the world stage."

7. A change in strategic culture?

Of enormous significance is the question of whether strategic culture should be understood as a constant factor or whether it can and should change, and if so under what circumstances? In principle, it seems obvious that it should be understood as relatively constant, since, as argued for example by Eckstein, the socialisation of values, ideas, opinions and attitudes is a relatively long

---

[6] Speech by President-elect Ursula von der Leyen at the 2019 Paris Peace Forum. Criticisms of this can be found in: Müller-Hennig 2019.
[7] Examples from the large number of publications: Bartels, Kellner, & Optenhögel 2017; Bartels 2019.

process (Pankratz 2019, p. 29).[8] Lessons from the past function as lenses through which the present and the future are interpreted, which results in a certain permanence, stability and thus a tendency to be unresponsive to changes in the surrounding system.

Russia exemplifies the position of a solid and unwavering strategic culture: "The strategic culture of the country remained largely stable throughout the ages up until the present day. Fluctuations were apparent in particular in the preference for isolating Russia from the outside world. Rifts in the strategic culture were expected both during the dissolution of the Tsarist empire and during the collapse of the Soviet Union. In both cases, the existing system had no answers to fundamental questions of society. (...) However, the traumatic shock associated with the historical origin of the Soviet Union did not lead to a permanent change in the strategic culture, but to a further deepening of the already strong desire for security. Only the collapse of the Soviet empire and the delegitimisation of the ideology underpinning the state constituted a similarly drastic shock that changed the strategic culture. (...) Russia's preference for a strong state and authoritarian leadership remained largely unchanged by the events of the early 1990s. In order to get to grips with the upheaval at that time, the strategic culture provided an inwardly strong state as a suitable solution. (...) [Putin] therefore does well to orient his governance to the strategic culture of his country. In order to safeguard the cohesion of society, he increasingly draws on identity-building images – and thus norms and values – from history. The importance of strategic culture to the development of society and the formulation of foreign and security policy will, therefore, only continue to rise" (Eitelhuber 2015,pp. 2-3).

In Germany, by contrast, the positive shock of reunification led to a disengagement from the fixed strategic culture that had prevailed for many years during the division. This was due to the 40 years during which the raison d'être across all party lines was one of unconditionally condemning war, as well as the inevitable cooperation in terms of foreign and security policy. "The reunification of Germany dissolved the harmony between alliance orientation and military restraint. German federal policy had to repeatedly decide between the following two maxims: should the Federal Republic of Germany stand by its partners and send soldiers into wars and conflicts? Or should it exercise military restraint, thus going against its closest allies?" (Biehl 2019, p. 37)

---

[8] – including a reference in footnote 6 to Harry A. Eckstein, A Culturalist Theory of Political Change, in: American Political Science Review No. 82/1998; p. 796.

8.   Ideas and problems regarding the extension of the scope of strategic culture

Differences in the discussion surrounding strategic culture mainly relate to the assessment of its influence on the behaviour of states and their elites in terms of foreign and security policy. The role of the potential carriers of strategic culture is also widely discussed. However, in addition to these two issues, there are other problem areas that have received little or no attention.

Strategic culture can take a wide variety of forms. The interpretation of one's own position, perception of the outside world and the interpretation of the perception by others results in an understanding of self-perception and the perception by others. Sociopolitical orientation is characterised by the configuration of a sociopolitical system/value system, foreign policy orientation and the dichotomy of isolationism and multilateralism. Strategic processes are initiated and steered by strategic discussions, strategic awareness and also by the creation and implementation of strategic concepts.

One basic point, similar to the discourse on strategy, is that a differentiation has not been explicitly made as to whether strategic culture is a phenomenon per se, in other words the ideas, attitudes, opinions, etc. of an actor, which manifest in the behaviour of that actor, or whether it is a methodical and analytical concept that attempts to explain this phenomenon.

A fundamental problem of scientific theory should be mentioned in this connection. Central to the scientific approach is the idea of using the concept of strategic culture to interpret the other party's strategic culture on the basis of a specific analytical grid, to explain the behaviour of this other party and thus understand it. The question then arises as to whether or what extent it is possible to understand the other party at all if one does not have the same strategic culture. This becomes apparent in particular when one considers that strategic culture is a Western concept, in other words it is based on certain Western parameters. It is conceivable that one's own ideas or attitudes are unconsciously, or even consciously, projected onto the ideas or attitudes of the other party, which in turn leads to prejudices. The attempt to understand the other party raises it to the same level, to a certain extent that also assumes that the other party will act in a goal-oriented way. In this respect, it is therefore also logical to refer to action rather than behaviour. The concept of strategic culture thus exerts a certain pressure to make sense of this. However, the precondition for this is, firstly, clarifying one's own position in the sense of self-introspection, and then recognising that this attempt is subject to limits due to the differences in culture.

A further central issue in this discussion relates to the carriers of strategic culture. Although there are advanced approaches to determining the carriers of strategic culture, the state's and elite's approach continues to dominate. This is closely connected to the view, firstly, that only states are capable of strategy and, secondly, that states continue to be the central actors in the field of international relations. It is advantageous to concentrate on the elites in this case, since they are responsible for state strategies. This raises, however, two questions: First: who are the elites eventually? Do they include only the formal elites (government, bureaucracy) or others too (civil society, economic system)? Second, it should be pointed out that even elites are not homogeneous entities, but that they in turn consist of individuals who often put their own interests above those of the state.

Even though states and their elites continue to be the central objects of reference under a generalised understanding of strategy, an expanded understanding of strategic culture would require us to introduce the concept of the "strategic actor". This would remove the focus from states and also considerably expand the circle of potential carriers of strategic culture. Basically, therefore, any actor may be a strategic actor if he thinks and acts strategically. Raschke and Tilfs describe the "strategic actor" as follows: "The category of the strategic actor is a pointed emphasis. It refers to agents who think and act strategically. Strategic actors are not automatically identical to individual, collective or corporate actors. All actors must first acquire and continuously reproduce strategic capability in order to be able to pursue strategic policies. The strategic actor is thus important not only to identify the agent but also as a field of activity (developing strategic capability). In principle, strategic agents can be individuals or collectives" (Raschke & Tils 2013, p. 140).

A further issue that has hardly received any attention to date is whether or not, based on the comprehensive concept of security, the concept of strategic culture should also be expanded to include economic, financial or climate policy.

To complete the arc of scientific-theoretical considerations, in a modern understanding, both culture and strategy require a transdisciplinary approach. This has so far been missing in the context of strategic culture. If strategic culture is made up of attitudes, ideas, historical experiences and geopolitical factors, this also requires the use of different scientific disciplines.

The advanced approach to strategic culture outlined here can be summarised as follows: from a phenomenological perspective, strategic culture describes the attitudes, ideas, norms, values, etc. of a strategic actor, which are internalised in an extremely wide variety of ways, and influence the strategic beliefs and actions of this actor. In this case, strategy relates to a success-oriented calculation based on the categories "objectives-means-strategically relevant environment of a strategic actor". From a methodological perspective, it should be understood as an approach that incorporates as many disciplines as possible for interpreting this strategic culture using various analytical grids. The aim is to explain and understand present and possible future actions, or the options for action on which they are based, of actors at a strategic level. However, these attempts to explain and understand are subject to certain limits, not the least due to strategic culture.

9.   References

Al-Rodhan, N. (2015). *Strategic culture and pragmatic national interest.* Retrieved from: https://www.globalpolicyjournal.com/blog/22/07/2015/strategic-culture-and-pragmatic-national-interest (29.08.2020)

Bartels, H. P., Kellner, A. M., & Optenhögel, U. (Eds.). (2017). *Strategische Autonomie und die Verteidigung Europas.* Bonn.

Bartels, H. P. (2019). *Deutschland und das Europa der Verteidigung.* Bonn.

Bertelsmann Stiftung. *Politik beleben, Bürger beteiligen.* Retrieved from: https://www.bertelsmann-stiftung.de/fileadmin/files/user_upload/Politik_beleben__Buerger_beteiligen.pdf (29.08.2020)

Biehl, H., Fiebig, R., Giegerich, B., Jacobs, J., Jonas, A. (2011). *Strategische Kulturen in Europa. Die Bürger Europas und ihre Streitkräfte September.* Retrieved from: http://www.zmsbw.de/html/einsatzunterstuetzung/downloads/forschungsbericht96.pdf?PHPSESSID=3bbda6452471265d4df91fbddad9b18c (29 August 2020)

Biehl, H., Giegerich, B., & Alexandra, A. (2013). *Strategic Cultures in Europe.* Wiesbaden.

Biehl, H. (2019). Zwischen Bündnistreue und militärischer Zurückhaltung. Die strategische Kultur der Bundesrepublik Deutschland. In I.-J. Werkner M. Haspel (Eds.). *Bündnissolidarität und ihre friedensethischen Kontroversen.* Wiesbaden

Biscop, S. Renard, T. (2013). A Need for Strategy in a Multipolar World: Recommendations to the EU after Lisbon. Retrieved from: http://www.egmontinstitute.be/content/uploads/2013/09/SPB-5_EU-Strategy-for-a-Multipolar-World.pdf?type=pdf (29.08.2020)

Blendin, H. & Schneider, G. *Grenzen der rationalen Abschreckung: Psychologische Korrelate von aggressivem Verhalten in experimentellen Krisenverhandlungsspielen.* Retrieved from: https://www.polver.uni-konstanz.de/typo3temp/secure_downloads/79876/0/f53bbea7a6ba6a063563de1da86443a334d   6f437/Blendin_Schneider_2015_03_11_mit_Anhang.pdf (29.08.2020).

von Clausewitz, C. *On War*. Retrieved from: https://www.clausewitz-gesell-schaft.de/wp-content/uploads/2014/12/VomKriege-a4.pdf (29.08.2020).

Cornish, P. Edwards, G. (2005). Beyond the EU/NATO Dichotomy: The Beginnings of a European Strategic Culture. *International Affairs No. 3/2005*.

DPA. (2019). *USA senden Drohbrief an die EU*. Retrieved from: https://www.t-online.de/nachrichten/ausland/internationale-poli-tik/id_85753206/plaene-fuer-verteidigungsunion-usa-senden-drohbrief-an-die-eu-.html (29.08.2020)

Dymshi, A. (2018). *National Security Policymaking and Strategic Culture: European and Albanian Perspectives*. Friedrich Ebert Stiftung.

Eitelhuber, N. (2015). *Die strategische Kultur Russlands – Russland begreifen*. https://www.laender-analysen.de/russland-analysen/306/RusslandAna-lysen306.pdf (29.08.2020)

European Security Strategy. (2003). Brussels.

EU-Commission. (2016). *Shared Vision, Common Action: A Stronger Europe*. https://eeas.europa.eu/sites/eeas/files/eugs_review_web_0.pdf (29.08.2020)

Fischer, L. *Strategische Kulturen im Vergleich Russland und die Türkei oder die Wie-derbelebung einer geokulturellen Konfrontation*. Retrieved from https://www.an-drassyuni.eu/pubfile/de-221-3-zedem-lorenz-fischer-strategische-kul-turen-1.pdf (29.08.2020)

Gray, C. S. (1981) National Style in Strategy. The American Example. *International Security, Vol. 6* (No. 2), 21-47.

Gohl C. *Organisierte Dialoge als Strategie*. Retrieved from: https://www.bertels-mann-stiftung.de/fileadmin/files/BSt/Publikationen/GrauePublika-tionen/GP_Organisierte_Dialoge_als_Strategie.pdf (29.08.2020).

Giegerich, B. (2006). *European Security and Strategic Culture. National Responses to the EU's Security and Defence Policy*. Baden-Baden.

Helmut-Schmidt-Universität. (2018). *Bürgerbeteiligung in der Außen- und Sicher-heitspolitik: Motivation, Prozesse, Ergebnisse*. Retrieved from: https://www.hsu-hh.de/isk/wp-content/up-loads/sites/682/2018/01/Synopse-Geis-Pfeifer-Beteiligung.pdf (29.08.2020)

Herz, J. H. (1959). *International Politics in the Atomic Age*. Columbia University Press.

Hesse, R. *Game-theoretic Approaches to Deterrence*. Retrieved from: http://the-oryofcomputation.asia/THESES/13Hesse.pdf (29.08.2020)

Hofer, C. W. & Schendel, D. (1978). *Strategy Formulation: Analytical Concepts*. St. Paul.

Jäger, T., Oppermann, K. (2006). Bürokratie- und organisationstheoretische Analysen der Sicherheitspolitik: Vom 11. September zum Irakkrieg. In A. Siedschlag (Ed.). *Methoden der sicherheitspolitischen Analyse. Eine Einführung* (pp. 105-134). Wiesbaden.

Johnston, A. I. (1995). Thinking about Strategic Culture. *International Security Vol. 19(*No. 4), 32-64.

Kahlert, M., & Major, C. (2019). *Frankreichs Europäische Interventionsinitiative (EI2): Fakten, Kritik und Perspektiven*. Retrieved from: https://www.swp-berlin.org/fileadmin/contents/products/arbeitspapiere/Major__Kahlert_Arbeitspapier_01072019.pdf (29.08.2020)

Kissinger, H. (1980). A Gentle Analyst of Power – Hans Morgenthau. In *New Republic*.

Kissinger, H. (1994). *Diplomacy*. New York.

Klein, B. S. (1988). Hegemony and Strategic Culture. American Power Projection and Alliance Defence Politics. *Review of International Studies, Vol. 14* (No. 2), 133-148.

Kommunist. (1953). Strategie und Taktik des Kommunsismus. *Moscow issue 4*. Retrieved from: https://www.jstor.org/stable/44923869?seq=1 (29.08.2020).

Kunz, B. *Wann wird Deutschland endlich „normal"?* Retrieved from: https://internationalepolitik.de/de/wann-wird-denn-deutschland-endlich-normal (29.08.2020)

Lapins, W. W. (2018). Geopolitisierst Du noch – oder digitalisierst und cyberst Du schon? In: W. Peischel (Ed.). *Wiener Strategie-Konferenz 2017. Strategie neu denken* (378-395). Norderstedt: Miles-Verlag.

Lechner A. *Zum Verhältnis von Strategie und Demokratie – am Beispiel der FTI-Strategie*. Retrieved from: https://core.ac.uk/download/pdf/11595432.pdf (29.08.2020)

Leininger, W. & Amann, E. *Einführung in die Spieltheorie*. Retrieved from: https://ethz.ch/content/dam/ethz/special-interest/gess/chair-of-sociology-dam/documents/education/spieltheorie/literatur/Leininger%20Amann%20Einf%C3%BCchrung%200708-ST1-Vorlesung-Skript.pdf (29.08.2020);

Lentis, J. Howlett, D. (2013). Strategic Culture. In J. Baylis, J. Wirtz & C. S. Gray (Eds.). *Strategy in the Contemporary World*, pp. 77-95. Oxford.

von der Leyen, U. (2019). *Speech at the 2019 Paris Peace Forum*. Retrieved from: https://ec.europa.eu/commission/presscorner/de-tail/en/speech_19_6270 (29.08..2020).

Liddell Hart, B. H. (1956). *Strategy*. New York.

Martinsen, R. (2014). *Spurensuche: Konstruktivistische Theorien der Politik*. Wiesbaden.

Meyer, C. (2004). *Theorising European Strategic Culture: Between Convergence and the Persistence of National Diversity*. Brussels.

Morgan, P. M. (1977). *Deterrence: A conceptual analysis*. Beverly Hills, Calif.: Sage Publications.

Morgenthau, H, J. (1962). *The decline of democratic politics. Politics in the twentieth century*, volume 1. Chicago: University of Chicago Press.

Müller-Hennig, M. 2019. *Brüsseler Großmachtphantasien*. Retrieved from: https://www.ipg-journal.de/rubriken/aussen-und-sicherheitspoli-tik/artikel/bruesseler-grossmachtphantasien-3891/ (29.08.2020)

Oberreuter, H. *Entfremdung. Über Defizite in der „kommunikativen Demokratie"*. Retrieved from: https://www.kas.de/documents/252038/253252/7_doku-ment_dok_pdf_51472_1.pdf/034e1c0c-c2e5-1d9a-c711-b3ed58db7a4e (29 August 2020)

Pankratz, T. (2019). *Zur Weiterentwicklung des Konzepts der Strategischen Kultur – Ideen zu einem ganzheitlichen Ansatz*. Retrieved from: https://www.ka-rierre.bundesheer.at/pdf_pool/publikationen/17_2019_s_fom-ngt_lvak_symposion_2018_webversion.pdf (29.08.2020)

Peischel, W. (2018). *National Security Policymaking and Strategic Culture: European and Albanian Perspectives*. Tirana: Friedrich Ebert Stiftung.

Peters, W. (1972). *Untersuchungen zu Onasander*, Bonn.

Raschke, J. & Tils, R. (2007). *Politische Strategie. Eine Grundlegung*. Wiesbaden.

Raschke, J. & Tils, R. (Eds). (2010).*Strategie in der Politikwissenschaft. Konturen eines neuen Forschungsfelds*. Wiesbaden.

Raschke, J. & Tils, R. (2013). *Politische Strategie*. Wiesbaden.

Sauer, F. (2016). *Nuklearwaffen und internationale Politik*. Wiesbaden: VS Verlag für Sozialwissenschaften. Retrieved from: https://link.springer.com/content/pdf/10.1007%2F978-3-531-19954-2_38-1.pdf (29.08.2020).

Schelling, T. C. (1960). *The Strategy of Conflict* 1960. Harvard University Press. Retrieved from: https://www.elcenia.com/iamapirate/schelling.pdf (29.08.2020).

Schelling, T. C. (1966). *Arms and influence.* New Haven: Yale University Press.

Snyder, J. L. (1977). *The Soviet Strategic Culture. Implications for Limited Nuclear Operation.* Santa Monica: Rand Corporation.

Snyder, J. L. (1991). *Myths of Empire. Domestic Politics and International Ambition.* Cornell University Press.

Stahel, A.A. (1996). *Klassiker der Strategie – eine Bewertung.* 2nd revised edition. Zürich: Vdf Hochschulverlag.

Strategieplanung, Retrieved from: https://www.die-unternehmensplanung.de/strategieplanung (29.08.2020)

Stein, T. (2017). Das Geheimnis in der Außen- und Sicherheitspolitik, Zwischen Staatsräson und öffentlicher Kontrolle. In A. Gawrich, W. Knelangen (Eds.). *Globale Sicherheit und die Zukunft politischer Ordnungen* (pp. 59-77). Opladen/Nerlin/Toronto.

Steinbrecher M., Biehl, H., Rothbart, C. (2017). *Sicherheits- und verteidigungspolitisches Meinungsbild in der Bundesrepublik Deutschland 2017.* Retrieved from: http://www.zmsbw.de/html/einsatzunterstuetzung/downloads/1_171220kurzberichtbevoelkerungsumfragezmsbw2017aktualisiertneu.pdf (29.08.2020)

Steinbrunner, J. (1975). Beyond rational deterrence: The struggle for new conceptions. *World Politics*

28(1), 223–245.

Sun Tzu. *The Art of War.* Retrieved from: https://zielniok.de/sunzi-die-kunst-des-krieges.pdf_(29.08.2020).

Wagner, J. (2019). *PESCO. Das militärische Herz der Europäischen Verteidigungs Union.* Retrieved from: https://oezlem-alev-demirel.de/wp-content/uploads/2019/10/PESCO-interaktiv.pdf (29.08.2020)

Waltz, K. (1979). *Theory of international politics.* Boston.

Wendt, A. (1999). *Social Theory of International Politics.* Cambridge University Press.

White House. (2017). *National Security Strategy of the United States of America.* Retrieved from: https://www.whitehouse.gov/wp-content/uploads/2017/12/NSS-Final-12-18-2017-0905.pdf (29.08.2020)

Winter, T. (2013). *Sicherheit und außenpolitische Rolle. Zu den sicherheitspolitischen Kulturen und der Ukrainepolitik Polens und Tschechiens.* Dissertation at the University of Trier.

Zürn, M. (1994). Neorealistische und Realistische Schule. In: A. Boeckh (Ed.): *Lexikon der Politik.* Band 6: Internationale Beziehungen (pp. 309-322). München: C.H. Beck. Retrieved from: https://www.econstor.eu/bitstream/10419/112623/1/208610.pdf (29.08.2020)

10. Further Reading

Almond, G., & Verba, S. (1965). *The Civic Culture. Political Attitudes and Democracy in Five Nations.* Boston.

Baylis, J., Wirtz, J J., Gray, C. S., Cohen, E. (Eds.). (2007). *Strategy in the Contemporary World. An Introduction to Strategic Studies.* Oxford, New York: Oxford University Press.

Booth, K. (1979). *Strategy and Ethnocentrism.* New York.

Farrell, T. (2005): The norms of war. Cultural beliefs and modern conflict. Boulder: Colo.

Gray, C. S. (1984). *Nuclear strategy and strategic planning.* Philadelphia: Foreign Policy Research Institute.

Gray, Colin S. (1999): Strategic Culture as Context. The First Generation of Theory Strikes Back. *Review of International Studies 25* (1), 49–69.

Johnston, A. I. (1995). Thinking about Strategic Culture. *International Security, 19(* 4), 32–64.

Lantis, J. S. (2003). Strategic Culture and National Security Policy. *International Studies Review, 4(* 3), 87–113.

Longhurst, K. (2000). The Concept of strategic Culture. In G. Kümmel, A. Prüfert (Eds.), *Military sociology. The richness of a discipline.* Baden: Nomos Verlagsgesellschaft.

Meyer, C. O. (2004). *Theorising European Strategic Culture. Between Convergence and the Persistence of National Diversity.* Centre for European Policy Studies. Retrieved from: http://aei.pitt.edu/6634/1/1126_204.pdf (29.09.2020).

Waltz, K. N. (1993). The Emerging Structure of International Politics. *International Security 18* (2), 44–79.

Wendt, Alexander (1992): Anarchy is what States Make of it. The Social Construction of Power Politics. *International Organization 46* (2), 391–425.

Chapter 7: Strategy and Economics

Univ.-Prof. Dr. Werner H. Hoffmann, Dr. Michael König, MBA, MG (retd.) Hon.Univ.-Prof. Mag. Dr. Dr.habil. Harald Pöcher

Keywords: Geo-Economy; Economic Warfare; Institutional View; Market-Based View; Relational View; Resource-Based View; Scenarios; Strategy Schools; SWOT; TUNA; Uncertainty; VRIO;

0. Abstract

There are many ways to define strategy. Multitudinous perspectives fall into place when addressing a term used in nearly all realms of our life. We endeavor to focus exclusively on one of them, namely strategy from an economics and business administration perspective. We therefore provide an overview of the origins and main theoretical frameworks of strategy in economics and business administration, juxtapose them to the notions of strategy in a military context, unpack and address common ground, striking similarities and joint future avenues. A particular emphasis is put on uncertainty and how strategic thinking prevails in turbulent, uncertain, novel and ambiguous environments. Further, we showcase some non-military means of geo-economy and economic warfare, phenomena that gain increasing global importance. Finally, we come full circle by presenting trajectories for joint theoretical research and practical collaboration between economics and the military. Readers are equipped with references and suggestions for further in-depth readings.

1. Introduction

The history of the term strategy seems to be one of forking paths.[1] Rooted in war theory, military strategy, and historical strategy theories, modern economics and business administration seem to have developed their own notion of strategy, independent from military connotations (Hoskin, 1992). In a turbulent, uncertain, novel and ambiguous (in short: TUNA[2]) global setting, however, it is time to rethink and reconsider the different paths taken and to explore common grounds in the perception of the term strategy from a military

---

[1] To the notion of forking paths, see Borges (2018).

[2] TUNA is an acronym, coined by Ramírez and Wilkinson at the Oxford Scenarios Programme, Said Business School, University of Oxford. It is since customary internationally. It is different from the earlier acronym VUCA (volatile, uncertain, complex, ambiguous) as it also addresses turbulence, novelty and novel phenomena.

and an economics perspective. Scholars frequently address the etymological foundation of the word strategy referring to the ancient Greek expression στρατός ἄγειν, which means leading an army. Clearly, this is not what modern economics and business administration scientists usually have in mind when they talk about strategy. At a closer look, there is more commonality than first expected.

In the military, strategic thinking is influenced over the centuries by strategists like Sun Tsu (approx. 500 b.c.), Machiavelli (1469-1527), Montecuccoli (1609-1680), von Clausewitz (1780-1831), or Liddell Hart (1895-1970), just to name the most notorious ones.[3] In economics, however, dominant strategists like Ansoff (1918-2002), Chandler (1918-2007), Mintzberg (born 1939) or Porter (born 1947) only emerged in the 20th century. Can we really talk about two different paths, though? One established over hundreds of years, and the other comparably still in an embryonic stage? Trade is as old as warfare, so one should assume that economics and war theory would co-exist for quite some longer time; or does it have to do with the object of desire, that might be different, i.e. competing for resources and market shares in economics, and competing for survival and territory in war conflicts in the military? As follows, we will first elaborate where and when indeed those paths did fork, and second where, in the 21st century, they come together again.

2. Where the paths fork: Foundations of strategy in economics and business administration

The notion of strategy has indeed entered economics not before the 20th century, mainly as a logical aftermath of the second industrial revolution.[4] When technological progress bore businesses that transformed classic agricultural and traditional trade systems, a longer-term view for policy-making related to newly emerging business styles and cycles became inevitable. Exploiting resources more efficiently and allocating investments to interest-bearing projects was of the essence. Initially called business policy, one of the first academics to coin it strategy and the practice of strategizing as strategic management, was Ansoff (1965). He is hence one of the "fathers" of strategic management, as we know it, together with his contemporaries Chandler (1962), who emphasized that strategic management needs to be a separate function

---

[3] For further reading on grand strategy, battle strategy, and modern analogies: Lampel, Mintzberg, Quinn, Goshal (2014, pp. 10).

[4] The second industrial revolution is usually associated with the time of important technological leaps between the end of the 19th century and the beginning of the 20th before WW1, amongst them the emergence of new transportation systems (railways), requiring new managerial thinking.

within an enterprise, and Andrews (1971), who presented the importance of focusing on both, internal strengths and weaknesses and external opportunities and threats, in his SWOT analysis.[5] A little earlier, von Neumann and Morgenstern (1944) published on a subject that ever since not only influences economic thinking but also created a distinctive stream in economics, termed game theory.[6]

After WW2, there was an urgency to change business policy into a more systematic and future-oriented approach. *This is where – to our reading – the strategy paths between economics and the military started to fork in different directions.* High ranking and well-educated military officers took over managerial responsibilities after the war, and their experience in planning and quantitative diagnostics was highly welcomed in recovering economies (McKiernan, 2002; Burnes, 2009, pp. 247). Eventually, during the economic upturn of the 50ties, new views of strategy, detached from their historical and military roots, emerged.

To provide a succinct landscape of these different new "schools" of strategy, we would like to refer to Mintzberg, Ahlstrand and Lampel (1998) who classify ways of seeing strategy in economics and business administration threefold: First, there is a prescriptive approach, explaining and guiding how to build and formulate strategies. Second, there is a descriptive approach, displaying the reality of strategic management in an enterprise context, and third, there is a combined approach addressing both. Mintzberg, Ahlstrand, and Lampel (1998) list *ten schools of strategy*, accordingly:

2.1 Prescriptive schools:

(1) Design school: "Senior Management formulates clear, simple, and unique strategies in a deliberate process of conscious thought" (Lampel, J., Mintzberg, H., Quinn, J.B., Goshal, S., 2014, p. 21). Conducting a SWOT analysis provides managers with internal strengths and weaknesses and external threats and opportunities (Selznick, 1957, Chandler, 1962, and more explicitly on SWOT Andrews, 1971). The target is to design a strategy that enables a well-balanced fit between them.

(2) Planning school: Ansoff (1965) supports the reasoning of the design school and adds an additional layer of professionalism to it. Formulating strat-

---

[5] Andrew's basic SWOT analysis was developed further in several directions: enriched as dynamic TOWS analysis (Johnson et al., 2016) or as strategic SWOT analysis analyzing past, present and the future of an enterprise (König, 2012).

[6] We will come full circle with their approach to dealing with uncertainty in the next section of this chapter.

egies needs qualified methods, formal steps and checklists, and planning capabilities (like budgeting and long-term planning). Hence, enterprises need corporate planners to fulfill those tasks, in addition to senior management.

(3) Positioning school: This is probably the school with the most direct links to classic military strategy, addressing insights from military strategists. It represents the switch from mere planning to analyzing.[7] Main contributor to this analytical approach is Porter (1980 and 1985), who introduced basic instruments like the five forces analysis and established generic strategies: overall cost leadership, differentiation, and a focus/niche positioning, applicable to any competitive situation in a given industry.

2.2   Descriptive schools:

(4) Entrepreneurial school: Contrariwise to Ansoff's planning logic, the entrepreneurial school emphasizes the role of non-prescriptive, non-formal aspects of formulating strategies, like the intuition or vision of a CEO. This refers to pivotal publications in economics by Schumpeter (1934), and Cole (1959).

(5) Cognitive school: The cognitive school sees strategizing and strategy formulation as a mental process. It is about framing, modelling and conceptionalizing entrepreneurial futures, as outlined in Simon (1947), and March and Simon (1958).

(6) Learning school: This view assumes that organizational learning and (ex post) sense making are key to enabling emerging strategies. Main representatives of this approach to bundle strategy formulation with strategy implementation are Braybrooke and Lindblom (1963), Weick (1969), Quinn (1980), and Hamel and Prahalad (1994).

(7) Power school: Enterprises derive strategies as a consequence of internal "micro" power play (by bargaining, negotiating and juxtaposing) or external "macro" power play by utilizing competitive advantages, unique or complementary resources, market position, etc. The latter stream is relevant for network strategies, like co-operation, co-opetition, (strategic) alliances, joint ventures and other forms of joint strategies. For the micro view compare Allison (1971), for macro Pfeffer and Salancik (1978).

(8) Cultural school: Culture as a source for formulating strategies became particularly influential when Japanese management techniques (as described in e.g. Ohmae, 1982) found their way into Western enterprises.

---

[7] This also created an enormous boost for the consulting business that approaches strategy with an analytical lens.

(9) Environmental school: This school is based on contingency theory (Pugh, Hickson, Hinings, Turner, 1968) and focuses on how enterprises use their degrees of freedom when making choices framed by their environments.

2.3 Combination:

(10) Configuration School: This last school, introduced by Mintzberg, Ahlstrand, Lampel (1998), tries to marry and integrate prescriptive and descriptive views (rather than viewing them to be mutually exclusive). Strategies is seen as a process, and can be planned as well as emerge, a phenomenon dubbed "planned emergence" by Grant (2010, p-22). Mintzberg, Lampel, Quinn, Goshal (2014, p. 24) see this as a process of transformation, recommending to utilize more prescriptive attempts when acting in tranquil environments and more descriptive, intuitive elements when in more dynamic settings.

The first tipping point (and major difference to military strategy) for a theoretical foundation of strategic management is the *market-based view*, developed from classic economics and industrial economics. The long-term success of an enterprise is thus determined by five particular (external) competitive forces: rivalry amongst existing firms of an industry, threats of new entrants, bargaining power of buyers, threat of substitute products of services, and bargaining power of suppliers (Porter 1980 and 1981). Companies should therefore always strive to remain in attractive industries where those forces are managed favorably. This market-based view, however, has a limitation: By addressing external forces only, internal strengths and weaknesses are somewhat neglected.

The second tipping point is the *resource-based view* of strategic management, embracing exactly that conundrum (Wernerfelt, 1984, Barney, 1991). Instead of solely looking at external and market forces, the resource-based view complements the process of strategic management by (also) taking an internal perspective, as already recommended by Andrews (1971) in his SWOT analysis. To detect and assess internal strengths and weaknesses, Barney (1991) introduced his VRIO model. VRIO is an acronym for Value (does a certain resource enable an enterprise to benefit from opportunities?), Rarity (is a certain resource ubiquitous or rare?), Imitability (does a certain resource provide an enterprise with cost advantages as it is not easy to imitate?) and Organization (is the organizational structure of an enterprise able to support the exploitation of this certain valuable, rare and inimitable resource?).

More recent directions in strategic management are the *institutional view*, expanding the focus of strategic management to include other institutional frames like laws, culture, norms and ethical rules to complement the internal and external analysis (Peng, 2002), and the *relational view* which instead looks at networks and dyads of firms to explain relational rents of an enterprise (Dyer and Sing, 1998; Lavie, 2006). A relational rent is defined as "a supernormal profit jointly generated in an exchange relationship that cannot be generated by either firm in isolation and can only be created through the joint idiosyncratic contributions of the specific alliance partners" (Dyer and Singh, 1998, p. 662). For a contemporary view on managing portfolios of strategic alliances, see Hoffmann (2007).

Economics and business administration as briefly outlined in this section[8] have indeed produced new and distinctive approaches to strategy and strategic management that are not necessarily related to the classic strategy approaches of the military sciences. There is one aspect, however, where the forking paths of economics and the military merge again, as outlined in the following section.

3. Where the forking paths merge again: The cunning of uncertainty

In 2008, Bostrom and Circovic edited their seminal work Global Catastrophic Risks and presented several sections of risks that might affect the global economy substantially: risks from nature, risks from unintended consequences, and risks from hostile acts. In the class risks from unintended consequences, Kilbourne (2008) widely discusses plagues and pandemics. Hithereto, such risks were deemed to be merely of a statistical nature, and their occurrence judged as rather unlikely. Therefore economies, health systems, civil and military entities, and in the end whole nations worldwide were rather unprepared and hit heavily in spring 2020, when COVID-19 brought about what no one would either have expected or wished for: a real pandemic. With all its lethal and detrimental consequences, the COVID-19 pandemic turns out to be a real inflection point and a striking example for what Novotny (2015) called the cunning of uncertainty: "It appears at unexpected moments. Its logic shuns the direct line. It indulges in taking the oblique route and occasionally unexpected shortcuts (...) In the context of contemporary societies, the cunning of uncertainty may act as a wholesome counterforce to the false certainties induced by hubris and over-reliance on the assumptions that undergird what people think they know." (Novotny, 2015, preface, p. X). While this

---

[8] For an exhaustive and in-depth reading and description of the theoretical foundations of (economic and business administration) strategy, we recommend Grant (2010), Lampel, Mintzberg, Quinn, Goshal (2014), and Johnson et al. (2016).

chapter is written, COVID-19 still prevails and has spellbinding consequences for all parts of life. Many lessons will have to be learned from this pandemic, amongst them certainly about how to better anticipate, cope and manage such global catastrophic risks that know no national borders. It is a natural experiment in many ways and shows research avenues that are highly relevant for economics and military, likewise. Safeguarding of lives and assets under unprecedented, unexpected and even unthinkable circumstances affects them both.

To better grasp the nature and character of uncertainty, however, it is first necessary to classify what the term stands for, and how to differentiate the underlying phenomena that create it. This is a field, where economics and military have many communialities, indeed. It is not a new topic, either. Whitehead addressed uncertainty and its importance for enterprises as follows: "The whole of this tradition is warped by the vicious assumption that each generation will substantially live of its fathers and will transmit those conditions to mould with equal force the live of its children. We are living in the first period of human history for which this assumption is false." (Whitehead, 1933, 93). This was nearly a century before COVID-19. Unexpected changes, volatile markets, chaos and complexity have since become regular phenomena.

Uncertainty is usually divided into two distinctive categories, one where rationally acting players maximize their utilities (game theory), and another where the game is not orchestrated against other players but against chance (uncertainty theory). This distinction is crucial. The first is the arena of strategic reasoning in games, pioneered by Morgenstern and von Neumann (1944) and notably Nash (1950), while in the second agents strive to minimize uncertainty in their decision-making by assigning probabilities to each future outcome. Here we are in the arena of risk management. *Risk can be described as impact * probability*. So, if the potential impact is well-estimated and probabilities can be assigned, proper risk management techniques can be put in place to assure optimal future outcomes. This certainly holds true for so-called "known unknowns". However, why did classic risk management approaches fail to embrace existential risks like the COVID-19 pandemic? Dealing with uncertainty in the sense of uncertainty theory starts to become problematic when risks are not easy to measure and hence impossible to calculate. If the probability of an event is not known, or its impact is not known, or sometimes even both are unknown, traditional risk management will fail. This is the arena of so-called Knightean uncertainties (Knight, 1921). Rumsfeld (2002) famously used the expression "unknown unknowns" for exactly such a situation in a military and war context. Another issue companies face are so-called near-certainties, as pointed out by Ringland, Sparrow, Lustig (2010, p. 1):

"The uncertainty of the future offers us some near-certainties. Life in large organisations will become even more complex, time and resource constrained. Competition will become more intense, and scrutiny will be unrelenting. At the same time, the world has seen a financial crisis and faces ongoing changes in the world balance and global systematic challenges. We seem to have reached a number of global tipping points." This certainly concerns the military, too. Under such circumstances of "real" uncertainty and/or near-certainties, coloured by irrational behavior of market and policy agents and the change from a homo oeconomicus assumption to a homo emotionalis assumption, probabilistic approaches might fall short (König, 2017). Wrong decisions have an enormous impact on the going concern of enterprises and – as we can see in the current pandemic – even whole industries, military services and nations. It is therefore of the essence to complement probabilistic methods with methods that create plausible alternative futures. One way of doing this is to employ scenarios: "Scenario planning is a process within strategic management that combines the creation of several stories of plausible futures with the practical strategic responses that are required to deal with them. The creation of stories maps the future terrain through a systematic analysis of the key drivers of contextual change." (McKiernan, 2008, p. 1391).

Scenario creation is a tool that is deeply embedded in classic military strategy. *This is where – to our reading – the forking paths of strategy between economics and the military merge again.* When dealing with uncertainty, economics and business administrations' perception of strategic decision making is very similar to that of the military. There is a common field of problems (although with different agents), a wide toolbox that suits both[9], and both sides could benefit from joint research efforts. A very instructive example for a successful cooperation of economics, politics, and the military to tackle uncertainties and future challenges is the nuclear scenarios work of Kahn (1960, 1974, and 1984) which turned out to be highly influential for nuclear strategies worldwide and for establishing scenario planning as a useful tool to create plausible futures. Kahn is one of the forefathers of scenarios, together with Wack (1985).[10]

---

[9] The toolbox comprises of several generations of foresight tools and techniques, like (just to list a few): ratio analysis, indicator-based analysis, weak signals analysis, cross-impact-vulnerability analysis, wild cards, multiple scenarios, skunk works (from the military), etc. For further reading on foresight practices we recommend the following academic journals: Futures; Futures & Foresight Science; European Journal of Futures Research; Foresight – The journal of future studies, strategic thinking and policy; Long Range Planning; Technological Forecasting and Social Change; World Futures Review.

[10] In-depth reading on the enormous interdisciplinary contributions of Kahn and Wack to scenario planning can be found in Ghamari-Gabrizi (2005) and Chermack (2018).

168

The whole arena of corporate and strategic foresight is one where both realms, economics and the military have high stakes.[11] There is overwhelming empirical evidence for the effectiveness and bottom-line consequences of foresight (Rohrbeck, 2011, Rohrbeck and Kum, 2018)[12]. Makridakis (2004) provided a general definition for the purpose of foresight: "(. . .) to provide business executives and government policy makers with ways of seeing the (long term) future with different eyes and fully understanding the possible implications of alternative technological/societal paths. (. . .) Thus the purpose of foresight is neither to provide recipes nor specific forecasts. Its aim is to enhance an organizations' ability to consider various future scenarios without any preconceptions, debate their implications, examine the risk involved, estimate potential benefits, predict the cost/investments involved to arrive with practical alternatives that can be translated into executable actions."

When considering how to deal with uncertainty, one must however be careful which approach to choose. Ramírez and Ravetz (2011) demonstrated that there is a danger to choose tools for an environment that they are not wished for and consequently this might cause a problem to deteriorate rather than to improve. They distinguish between three types of futures, "tranquil" futures (such with rather static and placid environments), "wild futures" (such with a high degree of volatility, constant change and novelty), and "feral futures". Feral futures can happen, when tranquil futures are tackled with tools for wild futures, and vice-versa (Ramírez and Ravetz, 2011) and worsen a situation. This is of relevance not only for enterprises but also for geo-strategy and geo-policy of nations.

4. Non-military means of warfare in geo-economics

Geo-economics is a branch of geo-politics and geo-strategy. "In its strategic, foreign policy essence, geoeconomics is about the geostrategic use of economic power" (Vihma, 2017, p. 48). Luttwak argues that the same logic that underlies military conflict also pertains to international commerce: "Just as in war the artillery conquers by firepower territory that the infantry can then occupy, R&D can conquer the industrial territory of the future by achieving

---

[11] For a discussion on innovations in business administration and a juxtaposition of foresight thinking: König (2017).

[12] In a longitudinal study, Rohrbeck and Kum (2018) looked at 70 European stock exchange listed companies over a period of 7 years and investigated their future-preparedness. Based on their maturity model (Rohrbeck, 2011) companies were classified as being „vigilant", „neurotic", „vulnerable" or „in danger".12 For vigilant companies they could observe an increase of EBITDA of 16% and an average growth of market capitalization of 75%, whereas such effects could not be observed with companies not showing a high maturity in their foresight practices.

a decisive technological superiority" (Luttwak, 1993, p. 307). Conflicts and wars were never solely fought by well-armed and equipped soldiers but also with weapons of economic nature. Both kinds of warfare, however, led to heavy damage. Because of the use of different weapons or weapon-systems, the war with military weapons mostly goes hand in hand with bloodshed while the economic warfare leads to heavy economic damage without bloodshed.

The war, as Clausewitz asserts, is an act of power to force an enemy (opponent) fulfilling the own intention (Clausewitz, 1832). While those acts of power fought with military methods are well investigated, economic warfare is still an under-researched topic. Since there is no established definition, the following working hypothesis is proposed: "Economic warfare is a warfare based on non- military methods and means with the purpose to hit the opponent economy. At the end of the warfare the opponent's economy should have lost market shares and the own economy should be better off." Warfare in this sense does not include the warfare against the enemies' armament industry and pivotal infrastructure for daily life during a war with military forces. Human history offers a plethora of examples for economic warfare. As early as in the 14th century biological economic warfare was employed to destabilize an enemies' economy, by spreading contagious plagues (Wheelie, 2002). In 1806, after Napoleon could not invade the British Isles with military methods, he imposed an economic embargo by a naval blockade, also known as Continental System, albeit ultimately not successful (Aaslestad and Joor, 2014). Similarly unsuccessful, in WW2, Germany tried to utilize means of economic warfare against the United Kingdom, by producing forged bank-notes and planning to float the British economy with fake money, renowned as Operation Bernhard (Bower, 2001). In more recent times, economic warfare became visible more frequently as e.g. through the currency speculations against whole nations on Black Wednesday 1992 (Aykens, 2002).

4.1 Methods of economic warfare

Methods comprise of fiscal methods, monetary methods, trade methods, strategic intelligence methods, head hunting, biological economic warfare, and economic cyber warfare. Fiscal methods aim to improve economic competiveness with the purposeful use of taxes, contributions, and customs duties. Monetary methods are e.g. stock exchange speculation, devaluation of own currencies to support export prices, or money laundry. Closely related to it are trade methods. Trade can be steered by exchange rate regimes, depreciation or appreciation of currencies, and by trade embargoes. An increasingly prevalent sector or economic warfare is strategic business intelligence and organized corporate espionage.[13] In the 21st century, economic warfare is characterized by the use of electronics and communication technology, allowing for a more efficient reconnaissance and deception. Receiving and veiling information is an important branch of strategic business intelligence. Not entirely new, but effective nevertheless, is head hunting. Key personnel is approached and poached away to e.g. harm crucial R&D activities or scientific research. Biological economic warfare is part of general biological warfare, attacking economic with e.g. viruses, plagues or other biological perils. Cyber warfare can present a multitude of threats towards a nation. At the most basic level, cyber-attacks can be used to support traditional warfare. Essential systems providing water, electricity, healthcare, finance, food, and transportation are now increasingly software dependent, distributed, and interconnected. The Internet has made information exchange easier and more efficient, and malware can operate almost undetected. No longer is modern human conflict confined to the physical world; it has spread to cyberspace. Cyber attacks attempt to expose, alter, disable, destroy, steal or gain unauthorized access to or make unauthorized use of an asset, resulting in high direct losses and protection expenses.

4.2   Types and organization of economic warfare

There is conventional and asymmetric economic warfare. Conventional economic warfare is an economic war between two or more countries. Such an economic war is planned and implemented by official authorities of the countries involved. An asymmetric economic warfare is fought between opponents of different levels of capabilities, i.e. between an official authority of a country and a private enterprise or between two or more private enterprises. Only a few of the 194 independent states worldwide recently fought wars, but all of them established a Ministry of Defence. None of them, however, maintains a Ministry of Economic Warfare. Merely the great powers have installed special governmental institutions to collect information, which are useful for managing the economic warfare to impose the nation's economic interests on other nations. A planning process of economic warfare is not necessarily the responsibility of a government alone; it could also be made by enterprises. Successful leaders in the economic warfare normally act in the same way as military leaders do. What are the main responsibilities of planners or who are the leaders of the economic warfare? Today, it is state of the art in training of military leaders to teach the estimate process. The estimate process had its

---

[13] For further reading on strategic intelligence we recommend Andrew (2018), Andrew (2009), Jeffery (2010) and Omand and Phythian, M. (2018).

origins in the Prussian Army's attempt in the early 1800ies to develop a systematic and logical approach to the solution of military problems. In economic warfare the estimate of the situation also plays an important role, and it therefore has to be trained similar to the programs of military education institutions. In the warfare with military means the success of military leaders depends on the use of a balanced combination of talent and wise use of military knowledge obtained at military universities. In economic warfare success also is the result of well-based use of knowledge about the influence of the taken measures on the economic process and the talent for analyzing economic relationships trained at universities. The complex requirements for leaders of economic warfare more or less require an all-in-one solution of education and training suitable for all purposes. The best possible preparation to achieve well educated and trained leaders for economic warfare could be taken place in military universities which are not only teaching the military core subjects like assessment of situation, issue of orders, leadership and control but also economics and business administration as a distinctive disciplines.[14] In 1997, general Jean Pichot Duclos founded the *Ècole de Guerre Èconomique* (www.ege.fr) in Paris. Since its founding, the école de guerre économique has been educating students to learn all the necessary knowledge to fight an operation in an economic war successfully.

For a long time power and influence of states have been based not only on military power but also on economic strength. With their economic policy, states attempt to guarantee the best possible standard of living for their population. This could be achieved by conquering desirable roles in the world economy and by further protection against attacks from opponents. For this reason states have vital interests to strengthen their economies. A strengthening of the economy could be achieved by organizing the national economy in the best possible way and by being prepared to counteract an economic warfare. Hence, every country is well advised to establish academic educational training centers that are able to teach leadership and economics for an economic warfare.

5.   Summary

After discussing the origins and theoretical foundations of strategy and strategic management from an economics and business perspective, we arrive at the following hypothesis: the term strategy took different directions for economics and the military. In economics, it forked into a new and distinctive

---

[14] For further reading on defense economics, we recommend Pöcher and Strunz (2015).

perception of strategy, mainly disassociated with its historic roots. Notwithstanding, ends (goals and objectives), ways (action) and means (resources) do not differ substantially between economics and the military, quite the opposite. It is just the stakeholders, the arena of competition, and the agents that might differ. The schools of strategy and new trends in strategic management illustrate that there is quite a lot of common ground. This certainly holds true for dealing with uncertainty, one of the grand challenges of the 21st century. This is where the forking paths merge again and joint (research) efforts to improve the anticipation of alternative futures to be better forearmed against unexpected surprises and quasi-unthinkable events, to be more agile and resilient, and to act future-oriented and sustainably, will pay off. The treasure of knowledge needs to be bundled and expanded together.

6.   References

Allison, G.T. (1971), Essence of Decision: Explaining the Cuban Missile Crisis, Boston.

Andrew C. (2009), Defense of the Realm. The authorized history of MI5, London.

Andrew, C. (2018), The Secret World, A History of Intelligence, London.

Andrews, K.R. (1971), The Concept of Corporate Strategy, Homewood, Illinois.

Ansoff, H.I. (1965), Corporate Strategy, New York.

Aykens, P. (2002), Conflicting Authorities: States, Currency Markets and the ERM Crisis of 1992-93, Review of International Studies, 28, 2, pp. 359-380.

Aaslestad, K.B., Joor, J. (eds) (2014), Revisiting Napoleon's Continental System: Local, Regional and European Experience, Palgrave Mcmillan, London.

Barney, J.B. (1991), Firm resources and competitive advantage, Journal of Management,17, 1, p. 99-120.

Borges, L. (2018), The Garden of Forking Paths, Penguin Classics.

Bower, P. (2001), Operation Bernhard: The German Forgery of British Paper Currency in World War II. In Bower, P. (ed), The Exeter Papers. London, The British Association of Paper Historians, pp. 43-65.

Braybrooke, F.D., Lindblom. C.E. (1963), A Strategy of Decision, New York.

Burnes, B. (2009), Managing Change, Harlow, Essex.

Chandler, A.D. (1962), Strategy and Structure: Chapters in the History of Industrial Enterprise, Cambridge, Massachusetts.

Chermack, T. (2018), Foundations of Scenario Planning, New York.

Clausewitz, C.P.G von (1832), Vom Kriege, Buch 1, Kapitel 1, Abschnitt 2, Berlin.

Cole, A.H. (1959), Business Enterprise in Its Social Setting, Cambridge, Massachusetts.

Dyer, J.H., Singh, H. (1998): The relational view: Cooperative strategy and sources of interorganizational competitive advantage. Academy of Management Review, 23, pp. 660–679.

Ghamari-Gabrizi, S. (2005), The worlds of Herman Kahn: The Intuitive Science of Thermonuclear War, Cambridge, Massachusetts.

Grant, R.M. (2010), Contemporary Strategy Analysis, Chichester.

Hamel, G., Prahalad, C.K. (1994), Competing for the Future, 1994.

Hoffmann, W.H. (2007), Strategies for managing a portfolio of strategic alliances, Strategic Management Journal, 28, p. 827-856.

Hoskin, K.W. (1990), Using history to understand theory: A re-consideration of the historical genesis of 'strategy', EASIM workshop on Strategy, Accounting and Control, Venice, Italy.

Jeffrey, K. (2011), MI6, The History of the Secret Intelligence Service, London.

Kahn, H. (1960), On thermonuclear war, Princeton.

Kahn, H. (1962), Thinking about the unthinkable, Michigan.

Kahn, H. (1984), Thinking about the unthinkable in the 1980s, New York.

Kilbourne, E.D. (2008), Plagues and pandemics: past, present, and future, in: Global Catastrophic Risks, Bostrom, N., Circovic, M.M., (eds.) (2008), Oxford, pp. 288-307.

König, M. (2012), Strategische SWOT, in Heimerl, P., Sichler, R. (eds.), Strategie, Organisation, Personal, Führung, Wien, pp. 127-132.

König, M. (2017), Innovations in Business Administration, in: Carayannis, E.G. (ed.), Encyclopedia of Creativity, Invention, Innovation and Entrepreneurship, pp. 1-7.

Knight, F.H. (1921), Risk, uncertainty and profit, Boston.

Lavie, D. (2006): The competitive advantage of interconnected firms: An extension of the resource- based view. Academy of Management Review, Vol. 31, pp. 638–658.

Luttwark, E.N. (1993), The Endangered American Dream: How to stop the United States from becoming a third world country and how to win the geo-economic struggle for industrial supremacy, Touchstone, Simon & Schuster, New York.

Makridakis, C. (2004), Foreword: foresight matters. In: Tsoukas, H. , Shepperd, J., (eds.), Managing the future – foresight in the knowledge economy. Oxford, p. XIII.

March, J.G., Simon, H.A. (1958), Organizations, New York.

McKiernan, P. (1992), Strategies of Growth: Maturity, Recovery and Internationalization, London.

McKiernan, P. (2008), Scenario Planning, in: Clegg, S.R., Bailey, J.R. (eds.), International Encyclopedia of Organization Studies, London.

Morgenstern, O, von Neumann, J. (1944), Theory of games and economic behavior, Princeton.

Nash, J. (1950), Non-cooperative games, Doctoral dissertation, Princeton.

Novotny, H. (2015), The Cunning of Uncertainty, Cambridge/Malden.

Ohmae, K. (1982), The Mind of the Strategist, New York.

Omand, D., Phythian, M. (2018), Principled Spying. The ethics of secret intelligence, Oxford.

Peng, M. W. (2002), Towards an institution based view of business strategy, Asia Pacific Journal of Management, 19, 2/3, p. 251-267.

Pfeffer, J., Salancik, G.R. (1978), The External Control of Organizations: A Resource Dependence Perspective, New York.

Porter, M. E. (1980), Competitive Strategy: Techniques for Analysing Industries and Competitors, New York.

Porter, M.E. (1981), The contribution of industrial organization to strategic management, Academy of Management Review, 6, p. 609-620.

Porter, M.E. (1985), Competitive Advantage: Creating and Sustaining Superior Performance, New York.

Pöcher, H., Strunz, H. (2015), Security and Defense Economics. Selected Essays, Brussels.

Pugh, D.S., Hickson, D.J., Hinings, C.R., Turner, C. (1968), Dimensions of Organizational Structure, Administrative Science Quarterly, 13, 65-105.

Quinn, J.B. (1980), Strategies for Change: Logical Incrementalism, Homewood, Illinois.

Ramirez, R., Ravetz, J. (2011), Feral Futures: Zen and Aesthetics, Futures, S. 478-487.

Ringland, G., Sparrow, O., Lustig, P. (2010), Beyond Crisis: Achieving Renewal in a Turbulent World, Chichester.

Rohrbeck, R. (2011), Corporate Foresight. Towards a maturity model for the future orientation of a firm, Berlin, Springer.

Rohrbeck, R., Kum, E.M. (2018), Corporate Foresight and its impact on firm performance: A longitudinal analysis, Technological Forecasting and Social Change, S. 105-116.

Rumsfeld, D. (2002). DoD news briefing – Secretary Rumsfeld and Gen. Myers, http://www.defense.gov/Transcripts/Transcript.aspx?TranscriptID=2636.

Schumpeter, J.A. (1934), The Theory of Economic Development, Cambridge, Massachusetts.

Selznick, P. (1957), Leadership in Administration: A Sociological Interpretation, Evanston, Illinois.

Simon. H.A. (1947), Administrative Behavior, New York.

Vihma, A. (2018), Geoeconomics Defined and Redefined, Geopolitics, 23, 1, pp. 47-49.

Wack, P. (1985a), Unchartered Waters Ahead, Harvard Business Review, 9.

Wack, P. (1985b), Shooting the Rapids, Harvard Business Review, 11.

Weick, K.E. (1969), The Social Psychology of Organizing, Reading, Massachussets.

Wernerfelt, B. (1984): A resource based view of the firm. Strategic Management Journal, Vol. 5, pp. 171-180.

Whitehead, A.N. (1993), Adventures of ideas, New York.

7.   Further Reading

Books:

Bostrom, N., Circovic, M.M., (eds.) (2008), Global Catastrophic risks, Oxford.

Freedman, L. (2013), Strategy: A History, Oxford.

Johnson, G., Whittington, R., Scholes, K., Angwin, D., Regner, P. (2016), Exploring Strategy: Text and Cases, Harlow.

Lampel, J., Mintzberg, H., Quinn, J.B., Goshal, S. (2014), The Strategy Process; Concepts, Contexts, Cases, Harlow.

Mintzberg, H., Ahlstrand, B., Lampel, J. (1998). Strategy Safari, New York.

Ramírez, R., Wilkinson, A. (2016), Strategic Reframing: The Oxford Scenario Planning Approach.

Schelling, T. (1990), The Strategy of Conflict, Cambridge, Massachusetts.

Journals:

Strategic Management Journal

Journal of Economics and Management Strategy

Strategic Entrepreneurship Journal
Strategic Organization
Long Range Planning
Global Strategy Journal
Business Strategy and the Environment

Chapter 8: Military Strategy and Technology

Col (GS) Mag. (FH) Dr. Markus Reisner, PhD, BG (retd.)
Prof. Dr. Gerhard L. Fasching, Prof. Dr. Alfred Vogel

Keywords: Strategy; Military Strategy; Offset Strategy; Strategic Factors; Military Sciences; Natural Sciences; Environmental Sciences; Technical Sciences; Revolution of Military Affairs; Disruptive Technologies; Network Centric Warfare; Artificial Intelligence;

0.   Abstract

Human history has essentially been shaped by a process of ongoing technological advancement and the growth that has resulted from it. Whereas humans themselves have undergone hardly any visible evolutionary development from one generation to the next, they influence the world they live in at such tremendous pace that the transitions between the different technological cycles are becoming ever more rapid. The invention and creation of more and more new tools is allowing people to push the boundaries of what they can achieve. These new technological developments are having a major impact in ensuring that the way in which wars and conflicts are fought is constantly changing, threatening the very survival of humankind in the process. Conflict and war as well as the inherent primary objective of establishing supremacy over one's opponent are in fact often manifested in the constant quest for asymmetry, which is what really drives research and development. Such innovative technological developments and the developments consistently implemented in the military (referred to as the *Revolution in Military Affairs*) have in turn resulted in military actions and approaches, for example manoeuvre warfare and nuclear deterrence. These have ultimately manifested themselves in models of strategic thinking and action that are still used today. Strategic military thinking and the factors that influence military action (strength, space, time, information) have not been rendered invalid by ongoing technological developments. However, they have been and still are being constantly supplemented and enhanced by them. Military action with a strategic impact will therefore also increasingly be possible to an extent that was inconceivable just a generation ago. Successful military leaders are also actually able to grasp what effect a new technological development will have on the existing (military) strategic factors. They need to recognise in which domains (*land, sea, air, space, cyber/info*) these developments may deliver an advantage and thus decisively help them to achieve their own objective, or when their emergence (e.g.

in the case of disruptive developments, such as artificial intelligence) definitely needs to be taken into account.

1. Military Developments and Research in Natural and Environmental Sciences – a Trigger for Revolutions in Military Affairs

The (overall) strategy and the military strategy, which both form part of the foreign and security policies of states and supranational organisations, are very heavily influenced by military developments and by developments in natural, environmental and social sciences. The constant influence of technology on warfare and the change which it engenders was first described in the 1970s by the Soviet Marshal Nikolai Ogarkov as the theory of *Military Technological Revolution*. His ideas were adopted in English-speaking countries and have become well-known under the term *Revolution in Military Affairs (RMA) (cf. Ogarkov 1983)*. These developments have in fact been with us for thousands of years. One example is the development of the spoke wheel, because it enabled the construction of light chariots that could cope with all kinds of terrain. For instance, an Egyptian chariot made of wood and leather weighed just 24 kg. The crew of a chariot usually consisted of the charioteer and the archer. For the purpose of logistics, marching provisions as well as spare bows and arrows were also carried in suitably adapted chariots. A large group of chariots like this was highly mobile and had real firepower (armed with spears and bows). This meant that the opposing infantry or troops in chariots could either be intercepted in advance or attacked in a pitched battle in enemy territory (cf. Drews 2020).

Maxim: The use of horse-drawn chariots significantly increased the mobility of armed forces for the first time. Together with spears for the charioteer and the great firepower provided by the archers in the chariot crew, this led to a change in military strategy.

The clout and supremacy of the highly mobile and consistently numerically superior Asian cavalries – over the heavily armoured Occidental knights who fought as individuals – was based on the one hand on human factors (clever operational planning; mission-type tactics; strict hierarchy and discipline; lean organisation based on the decimal system; sophisticated battle tactics) and logistics (great mobility and supreme agility on the tough and tenacious horses; two to three horses per cavalryman, each with spare bows and arrows; provisions of very nutritious dried meat powder). On the other hand, a crucial advantage in combat was the use of the new technology of light horse saddles with metal stirrups – which meant that arrows could also be fired backwards – as well as composite bows with a long range and great penetrative force. Battles were decided by the newly developed battle tactic of feigned flight, which induced the enemy into a pursuit. It was then very easy to encircle and destroy the small groups of knights (cf. Morris 2013, 112ff).

Maxim: A new military strategy in the form of mass armies, mission-type tactics, logistics and new battle tactics first proved successful in the expansionist campaigns pursued by Asian light mounted soldiers to suppress whole peoples in East Asia, Central Asia and Eastern Europe.

Soon after people had begun to settle in the Middle East, abatises, palisades and earth walls were constructed around the villages to protect lives and property. The first city walls were built as the technology of building construction and civil engineering advanced with the development of mud brick and stone structures. Since ancient times, city walls have offered protection and also marked a settlement with a municipal charter. The world's oldest city is Jericho in Palestine, which has been settled for 11,000 years and been a city in its own right for 9,000. City walls only became less important with the invention of gunpowder and artillery. Most of them were then taken down to allow for new development within the city. However, to ensure they still presented an obstacle, from the Renaissance period through to the end of the 19th century some cities on operationally important transport routes were expanded to create fortresses surrounded by casemate walls. This defence system was heavily graduated and twisty – firstly, to withstand enemy artillery fire and, secondly, to ensure the optimum impact of fire from the fortress garrison. Fortresses from the 16th through to the 20th century were henceforth financed by the territorial lord or the state. The administrative council was also no longer led by a civilian mayor, but rather was run by a paid military fortress commander. The change in military strategy in the 20th century brought about by the evolution of mobile warfare with horizontal and vertical enclosures heralded the end of the traditional fortresses and rings of fortifications, such as the French Maginot Line against Belgium, Luxembourg, Germany and Italy, which was built between 1930 and 1940 (cf. Tuck 2008, pp. 83ff).

Maxim: For reasons of military strategy, to protect lives and property, walled cities and castles were constructed from ancient times. These

made it more difficult for the enemy to attack and thus made defence easier.

The invention of gunpowder in China in the 11th century and in Europe in the 14th century sparked a revolution in warfare. The first viable English cannons have been passed down from the Battle of Crécy in 1346. This led to the first arms race throughout Europe. The first cannons were developed during the Hussite Wars from 1419–1439. Together with the (horse-drawn) carriage, these artillery pieces could be used in a mobile manner for the first time. The invention of steel tubes by the German company Krupp and the development of breech loaders (guns for direct bombardment and firing in the lower register, mortars for firing in the upper register, and howitzers which can fire both in the upper and in the lower register) was a technological quantum leap. The use of tube artillery saw its heyday in the First World War. With a huge amount spent on gun materials and munitions (a total of 850 million shells were fired by all the warring parties), the way war was waged changed, because moving troops on open terrain would entail very heavy losses from a barrage of artillery fire. A new feature in the First World War was 'unobserved fire', a firing method based on using large-scale grid maps, which obviated the need for adjustment fire that would reveal your location. The lessons learned from this led to a change in military strategy in the inter-war period. Mobile warfare became possible again thanks to the increased mobility of the infantry and in particular thanks to mechanisation (new mechanised infantry). Self-propelled howitzers were developed to provide fire support (cf. Partington 1960).

Maxim: A key change to military strategy came with the invention of gunpowder in the 14th century. It meant that artillery dictated the pattern of war for centuries and many fortresses were rendered worthless. From then on, victory or defeat was decided by organisation and military resources.

Another milestone for the conduct of war on land and at sea – coupled with changes in military strategy – was the significant improvement in the power of the steam engine by James Watt in 1769 and the invention of the internal combustion engine by Nicolaus A. Otto in 1864. These engines, which were fitted in ships and locomotives or in vehicles, revolutionised transportation and also military affairs at every level of command. The invention of the diesel engine in 1893 by Rudolf Diesel facilitated motorisation and later mechanisation due to its high level of efficiency. Motorisation enabled large units to fight wars flexibly and independently. The heavy losses sustained in trench warfare without gaining any territory were the primary motivation to consider new technical and tactical solutions for breaking the mutual blockade. This led both of the warring sides to develop armoured tracked vehicles, because wheeled vehicles could not be used in muddy terrain or terrain covered by deeply echeloned trench systems. The British ultimately made a breakthrough with the development of their *tanks*, which revolutionised land warfare by combining firepower and mobility. Trench warfare, with the associated heavy losses, was thus avoided in the Second World War thanks to the blitzkrieg military strategy. Simultaneous and surprise advances by mechanised troops, in conjunction with ground attack aircraft from the air force to provide close support on the battlefield, firstly gave the enemy no opportunity to mount an effective defence, and secondly allowed for enemy forces to be encircled and destroyed. Israel has demonstrated how important and crucial the battle tanks are in the many wars it has fought with its neighbouring states. The invention of cheap, missile-based anti-tank weapons has made it difficult to deploy armoured tank units on their own. Battle tanks are therefore only used nowadays in combined arms warfare (cf. Tuck 2008, pp 86ff).

Maxim: Motorised and armoured military vehicles brought about a fundamental change in military strategy after the First World War, because mobile warfare involving large units then became possible.

The world's oceans and inland waterways had always been very important as transport routes for trade, but also for military operations. The oldest simple warships from the ancient world belonging to the Greeks, Persians and Phoenicians were equipped with a naval ram and had up to five rowers with three levels of oars one above the other. In terms of military strategy, the key development for naval warfare was the switch in propulsion from large rowing boats initially in the 15th century to sailing boats with naval guns and later to steamships with a paddle and propeller, to ships with a diesel engine and finally from 1955 onwards to nuclear-powered submarines and surface warships. The era of the large battleships came to an end in the Second World War with the invention of radar and air reconnaissance, while the importance of submarines and ships with torpedoes has increased since the First World War. Aircraft carriers are an essential part of modern naval warfare. Their development began back during the First World War, but they only became a key asset during the Second World War, primarily thanks to numerous innovations by the US Navy in the Pacific. This was because they allowed air support to be provided for the land invasions and the conquering of the many islands that had been occupied by Japanese armed forces. From 1961, the nuclear power of the USS Enterprise provided a technically satisfactory solution to the problem of the vast amount of power that aircraft carriers require. When reflecting on military strategy, it should always be borne in mind that nowadays the world's great geopolitical conflict zones are consistently shaped by what happens in the maritime arena. The major global trade flows in conjunction with regional conflicts can therefore only be managed at sea. Military deployments in such conflict zones are therefore always conducted across all services and generally on a multinational basis (cf. ibid., pp. 88ff).

Maxim: You can only project power globally if you have naval power. These forces are characterised by mixed fleet and aircraft carrier groups which operate on all the world's seas.

Air forces were first deployed under the Imperial Austrian Field Marshal Joseph Radetzky von Radetz[1] against insurgent Republicans during the Siege of Venice. For example, balloons were used for air reconnaissance and to drop bombs. Use of aircraft by the military only became established with the invention and constant evolution of motorised fixed-wing aircraft. In the First World War, the development of new types of aircraft and new aerial combat tactics meant that air forces became increasingly important for air reconnaissance over land and sea, for supporting land and naval forces in battle with close-support aircraft, for attacking military targets, such as transport hubs, port facilities and military infrastructure underground, for aerial combat with enemy aircraft and for airlifts. The Second World War was an initial high point for the development of air forces that had direct repercussions on military strategy. The significance of powerful air forces was recognised early on in particular in the German Reich, and reflected in the conception of the air force as an independent service within the armed forces. When the USA entered the conflict, the air campaign against the German Reich was stepped up, with long-range US bomber squadrons causing huge damage to armament facilities and transport infrastructure. Potent air forces are also important for small countries, such as Israel and Taiwan, because they enable them to protect their security interests against numerically far superior. The Second World War also saw the first use of long-range missiles, which in turn influenced military strategy. In the Cold War between the United States of America

---

[1] *Field Marshal Count Radetzky (1766-1858), with 72 years of service under five Emperors and retirement at the age of 90, was the longest-serving soldier in military history; he fought in 17 battles and was awarded 146 medals and decorations.*

and its allies in the North Atlantic Treaty Organization (NATO) and the Union of Soviet Socialist Republics and its allies in the member countries of the Warsaw Pact, there was an arms race in all aspects of military technologies. This included the field of air force and missile technology. The intercontinental missiles, which were fitted with nuclear warheads and could be launched from hardened silos or from nuclear submarines, presented a particular threat to world peace. Maintaining the balance of terror was the defining factor for the military strategy in the Cold War (cf. Walton 2008, pp. 379ff).

Maxim: The use of airspace to wage war in the air led to a major change in military strategy after the interwar period. The experiences of the Second World War and the Cold War mean that ensuring air supremacy with powerful air forces is regarded as an indispensable part of military strategy.

2. The Influence of Developments in the Natural, Environmental and Engineering Sciences on Strength, Space, Time and Information as Factors for Military Strategy

Since the 20th century, we have seen complete weapons system solutions being deployed that are capable of providing the most complete picture of what is happening on the battlefield and also in terms of attacking a target. One of the most significant developments in the 20th century was the development of missiles and nuclear weapons. These weapons were already embedded in a complex system of subsystems. This is why an *offset strategy* was first referred to in the 1970s, the idea being to combine various subsystems in one whole system (e.g. a defence system against intercontinental missiles). Many of the considerations of the military weapons developers were focused – influenced by the political realities of the Cold War – on regular armed forces. As a result of the significant technological advances made in the Second World War in particular, programmable, self-propelled ground-to-ground and air-to-ground missiles, which are also referred to today as cruise missiles, were continuously developed after the end of the war (cf. Sapolsky, Friedman, & Green 2009, pp. 158ff. Recent decades have seen a shift from conflicts between countries to conflicts within countries. This means that today there is an ever more complex battlefield on which there are a large number of parties moving within the civilian population, which requires protection. Any deployment of weapons is therefore a major political challenge. The use of unmanned systems (such as unmanned drones) to generate C4ISTAR data[2] or to protect one's own forces is becoming increasingly prevalent. In addition, for Western armies, preventing casualties among their own military and civilian populations is the top priority. The weapons systems which have previously been dominant, such as tanks and the air planes, but also traditional missiles or cruise missiles, are being supplanted or assigned new roles in military operations (cf. Jordan & Kiras, pp. 1ff). Cruise missiles and traditional missiles share one thing in common: once they are programmed and launched at a specific target, these guided missiles are very difficult to control. However, in modern conflict scenarios you need a system which can be deployed for as long as possible, and operates ideally unmanned, in a specific theatre for reconnaissance, and also carries the weapons that allow you to strike instantly. The development of armed and unarmed drones means that for the first time reconnaissance and impact, as well as unmanned remote control, have been realised in a weapons system family. At the same time, further semi-autonomous armed and unarmed systems, which look highly promising from a military perspective, are currently being developed for use on land and at sea (cf. Scharre 2015a)).

Maxim: The objective of the offset strategy is to combine different subsystems that affect security in one overall system. Increased importance is attached to C4ISTAR data (Command, Control, Communications, Computers, Intelligence, Surveillance, Target Acquisition, Reconnaissance).

The end of the 20th century saw a change in the traditional pattern of conflict that had previously existed. Today it seems that wars waged between countries by conventional means will increasingly become the exception. But the start of the 21st century is bringing further developments, whose impacts are much more significant and whose dimension is currently inestimable. Digitalisation and the development of highly capable information technology has created the conditions for a revolution in warfare. One crucial factor in this development has been the increasing automation and autonomy of military weapons systems. Nowadays international armed forces with modern equipment have weapons systems which make it possible to strike with lethal effect anytime, anywhere in the world and without endangering their own personnel. There has been a great shift in the boundaries of space and time for military

---

[2] C4ISTAR = Command, Control, Communications, Computers, Intelligence, Surveillance, Target Acquisition and Reconnaissance. (Cf. ALBERS et al. 1999; Cf. NATO 2005, p. 5)

operations. This means that the familiar parameters for military operational thinking – strength, space, time and information – are beginning to change and, as far as the deployment of resources is concerned, new possibilities are also emerging at the strategic level (cf. Lonsdale 2008, pp. 39ff). In contrast to the nuclear missile, with its devastating impact over a wide area, armed forces now have access to a range of unmanned weapons carriers and weapons systems, which promise to deliver an unprecedented level of precision in deploying effective weapons in the air, on land and at sea. Man-made advances allowing unmanned, semi-autonomous, robot-like weapons systems to be used herald the next stage in the evolution of warfare (Scharre 2015b). The human operator currently still controls the deployment of such systems, but science and technology are already in the process of implementing the next step in developing the technology and making it possible to factor out the (remote) operator. However, this (decisive) factor needs to be examined in greater depth, taking account of the possible consequences this may entail. In modern irregular and asymmetric confrontations, at least one of the conflicting parties is usually forced to engage in unconventional warfare. One party's superiority in technology and weapons capability in a battle against another well-equipped party forces the technologically inferior party in the conflict to engage in unconventional warfare. It is difficult, for example, to successfully win a battle against a heavily armed tank if you have only light weaponry. Conversely, it is almost impossible to defend yourself against aerial bombardment without anti-aircraft defences (cf. Münkler 2013).

Maxim: The technological paradox of modern wars is that the more advanced the technology used, the more the technologically inferior opponent is forced to operate covertly and embedded in the civilian population. This leads to an apparent imbalance in the way that resources are deployed in battle. There is also a lack of desire within Western societies to sacrifice their soldiers. This is where the advantage of deploying unmanned systems is clearly evident.

Electronic information warfare has in turn presented completely new challenges for (military) strategy. Alongside the traditional domains of *land, sea, air, and space*, rapidly developing information technology has now also created the *cyber* or *information* domain. Data and information can now be sent anywhere in the world at lightning speed. The weapons used are now tools of information technology to carry out attacks on the electronic links and on computerised systems or to prevent such attacks with appropriate mitigation measures. The term cyberwar is used to describe this kind of warfare. It is, therefore, a horror scenario for all those in charge of security when critical infrastructure is suddenly disrupted by cyberattacks – for example a blackout caused by a failure of the power supply – and as a result all human interactions and utilities are affected in a defined area. The objective here is to have a destabilising impact on the civilian population, which is to be made reject, and become distrustful of, its own government through fake news and inflammatory rhetoric on blogs. Cyberwar primarily involves material attacks (disrupting/interrupting cable, antenna and satellite links) or software attacks, for example social engineering, espionage (infiltrating external computer systems to steal confidential information), or denial-of-service attacks (disrupting the enemy's services for a short or longer period of time). The first cyberwar was the war in Kosovo in 1999 (cf Chase 2020, pp. 135ff).

Maxim: The biggest potential threat at present comes from cyber and information warfare. This permeates all other domains of warfare. As conventional collective use of force, formerly referred to as war, is avoided at all costs, indirect warfare in various forms is becoming increasingly important for achieving (military) strategic objectives.

The particular characteristics of this emerging new form of warfare imply that unmanned weapons systems in particular have become the preferred means of deploying resources. From a military point of view, armed and unarmed drones are highly effective. The combination of the *in time* perspective and *in time* impact (achieved through the concept of *network centric warfare* (cf. Albers et al. 1999), which is practised in many modern armed forces) makes it possible to destroy a potential target with high precision and a high probability of achieving the first hit. This significantly increases the performance capability of modern armed forces. The level of autonomy in operating these systems is steadily increasing. This means that in the medium term the human operator will be reduced purely to monitoring the action. The modern *joint targeting* process (cf NATO 2010) defines the objective of military operations as identifying and attacking a selected target with as much precision as possible. High priority is assigned in particular to complying with the need to deploy weapons proportionately in accordance with international law. The increasing use of precise weaponry is not just a direct consequence of these requirements or obligations, but in particular also a product of the technical developments that are enabling the military to deploy more and more precise weapons systems. This makes it possible to achieve a high level of efficiency. It means that a military target can be hit much faster and at lower cost than before (cf. Macgregor & Willamson, 2015). The unmanned reconnaissance and weapons systems used at present are still all semi-autonomous. However, the processing of large amounts of complex data is increasingly being outsourced to artificial intelligence, which performs arithmetic operations at lightning speed and provides the operator with options for action.[3]

Maxim: The strategic factor of time is proving to be essential in the 21st century. The conduct of modern military operations substantially depends on having a comprehensive and timely ISTAR picture of the situation. Unmanned systems make a significant contribution to this. The higher the degree of autonomy, the faster the system is able to respond.

3. Disruptive Developments – The Art of Considering Their Impact in Strategic Thinking

A new potentially disruptive threat emerged during the First World War in the form of chemical weapons. Initially envisaged as a deterrent to prevent wars or end them due to their devastating effect, toxic chemical warfare agents were nevertheless initially deployed on the Western Front (cf. Haber 1986). This chemical warfare occurred for the first and last time in the Austro-Hungarian Empire on the South-Western Front in the defining battle of Flitsch/Piezzo/Bovec-Tolmein/Tolmino/Tolmin as part of the 12th Battle of the Isonzo on 24 October 1917. When the commander-in-chief, Emperor Charles I, saw the dreadful consequences, he forbade any further use of toxic gas. This also meant a change in military strategy. In a broader sense, chemical weapons also include incendiaries (napalm), smoke agents and also defoliants (herbicides) and nettle agents. Chemical weapons are among the weapons of mass destruction (chemical, biological, radiological and nuclear weapons) that are outlawed and therefore banned by the U.N. In the Vietnam War, the USA used the defoliant *Agent Orange* to deny Viet Cong members any cover for their infrastructure. This use of chemicals over a wide area was problematic due to the toxic and carcinogenic side effects and its direct and indirect consequences for the environment, as Agent Orange contains large amounts of dioxin. But at that time, it formed part of the prevailing military strategy. Biological weapons are targeted against people, livestock, crops or materials. Their impact often cannot be limited, particularly in the case of infectious

---

[3] *Hoffmann concludes „A seventh revolution, the autonomous revolution, looms ahead of us. By combining machines and computers in ways thus far envisioned mostly through science fiction, this era will merge the changes generated by the Industrial Revolution and the Information Age with potentially significant alterations in how war is conducted. Of particular salience in this new era are developments in artificial intelligence, especially machine learning and deep-learning AI, combined with unmanned systems"* (Hoffmann 2017).

pathogens. The risk of disease means that these weapons are targeted particularly at civilian targets, whereas soldiers are less at risk because of their training and equipment (gas masks, protective suits, etc.) However, the corona-virus crisis in 2020 has clearly shown how susceptible our closely interwoven modern service-based society is with its global links and the danger posed by pandemics. This presents overriding lessons, firstly, for the national defence system (political system) and for national, European and international security structures, and secondly, for military strategy. The Atomic Age began with the test dropping of a plutonium bomb as a part of the Manhattan Project to develop nuclear weapons on 16 July 1945 by a B-29 bomber of the USAAF at the Alamogordo test range in New Mexico/USA, and of two atomic bombs dropped during the Second World War on the Japanese cities of Hiroshima on 6 August and Nagasaki on 9 August 1945 (cf. Walton 2008, pp. 379ff).

Maxim: The chemical warfare (poisonous gas) used in the First World War and the atomic/nuclear warfare (atomic bombs) deployed in the Second World War once again presented new aspects for military strategy to consider. CBRN warfare still presents a realistic threat today and is therefore one of the basic parameters of military strategy.

The space age began on 4 October 1957 with the successful launch of the world's first artificial satellite, Sputnik 1, from the Soviet Baikonur Cosmodrome. Today, information transmission, tracking and navigation, observation of the Earth and the atmosphere and monitoring by manned and un-manned near-Earth space travel are key applications of modern space technology. They are of global (military) strategic but also practical importance for both civilian and military uses. The objectives and expansion of terrestrial and orbital space infrastructure were originally dictated predominantly by military policy, but today economic interests are increasingly also having a bearing. To support their own national (security) policy and armed forces, modern countries of all sizes today also utilise all options for obtaining, establishing and maintaining (military) strategic advantages over other states in the space sphere. With the end of the global political bipolarity of the 20th century, this has become all the more relevant in this 21st century. The treaties governing the legal aspects of how space should be used, which were concluded internationally and between states in the last century, are increasingly being eroded. Their primary objective was to promote peace. At the same time, the intention was to prevent or at least thwart the creation and emergence of other rival states. It is becoming increasingly difficult to reach military targets in or via near-Earth space in a legally compliant way within the framework of applicable international (space) law. New technical developments have opened up possibilities that powerful states do not want to forego in military terms. The ever-growing reliance of global military (and also civilian) power projection on space-based infrastructure raises the question of its vulnerability. This has already been demonstrated – in terms of military strategy – with *anti-satellite weapons*, which have successfully conducted kinetic strikes on orbital targets with rocket-propelled effectors. The clouds of debris produced present and will for a long time continue to present a constant hazard to all – civilian and military – satellites in orbit, including the permanently manned International Space Station (ISS) (cf. Walton 2008, pp. 379ff). The political resistance that is growing internationally following such displays is therefore today making the military increasingly interested in developing suitable energy weapons (lasers, particle beams) for dazzling and interference purposes as options for a military strategy against orbital infrastructure. The military interest, which was keenly pursued both theoretically and experimentally around the turn of the millennium, in altering the connecting medium between the Earth's surface and space, the atmosphere in the ionosphere, artificially for a limited time and in a limited space, so that electromagnetic message propagation between terrestrial and orbital transmitters and receivers is suppressed (*ionospheric mirrors*) is also worth mentioning. Attacks on the trans-ionospheric channel of propagation between the Earth's surface and space are attractive in principle, because they permit, for instance, attacks to be disguised as natural phenomena, deny the enemy the ability to directly detect an attack, do not cause lasting damage to functionally crippled infrastructure and are very difficult to trace (cf. Bauer 2002). An example of another, smaller application of the physics of *ionospheric mirrors* is *plasma antennas*, which disappear from radar as soon as they stop operating (Ashley 2008, p. 16). The advantages of space technology for military strategists, such as the ability to deploy available resources relatively rapidly, as well as global oversight and mobility, are increasingly being challenged by the vulnerability in space of expensive infrastructure components, which cannot be replaced at short notice and can only be replenished in volume to a very limited extent. The dominance of information superiority can only be eliminated in space, as this is where the most important communication nodes converge (cf. Walton 2008, 379ff).

Maxim: Multidisciplinary space technologies are today key technologies alongside biotechnologies and are therefore of essential for (military) strategy. They include information transmission, tracking and

navigation, observation of the Earth and the atmosphere as well as monitoring by manned and unmanned near-Earth space travel.

Human control of manned and unmanned weapons systems is performed via network structures in cyberspace. If the enemy succeeds in gaining control of these networks, optional strategies of attack or defence need to be developed. Restricted communication means that these strategies can only involve a higher degree of software and hardware autonomy. In the *Cyber domain*, work is already actively taking place to develop semi-autonomous programmes (Cunningham 2020, p. 135ff). They are designed to perform different *Computer Network Operations* (CNO). However, semi-autonomy is just an interim goal here. One example of this is the development of a program called *MonsterMind* for the US National Security Agency (NSA). The purpose of the program is to detect and neutralise possible cyber-attacks on the USA at an early stage. The high speed at which such operations are performed means that the aim is to deploy the program fully autonomously. Fully autonomous software, that is to say an active system which is equipped with artificial intelligence (AI) in the sense of a technological singularity (as well as cyber-programs, for example also a Lethal Autonomous Weapon System, LAWS), could revolutionise warfare in a decisive way. The decision regarding a person's right to live or physical safety would be taken away from a human, who would be relegated to a mere spectator (cf. Zeter 2014). The leap to developing a fully autonomous robot does not necessarily have to be made first by the military, but may also be accomplished by civilian research. Fully autonomous systems have a series of advantages. First is the fact that humans need time to negotiate their decision-making loop (Observe, Orientate, Decide and Act, the OODA loop (cf. Marra & Mcneil 2016). This time period can be largely marginalised by a fully autonomous system. Unmanned reconnaissance and weapons systems, in which a human being is in or on the loop, have the disadvantage that the uplink and downlink communication that needs to take place between the unmanned system and the control station takes time. One of the stated objectives of the military is to overcome this drawback. Another factor is that with defence systems in particular, for example, the human response time is too slow to be able to guarantee an effective defence mechanism. There are in fact already a whole host of systems that boast a high level of automation or autonomy (cf. Singer 2015, 45ff). It is only possible to prevent any unwanted developments from taking hold through appropriate transparency. It is not just the military, but in particular also civilian research, that has a responsibility to do this. However, the fact remains that at present the efforts of state actors in terms of arms are aimed at breaking the predominant stalemate between *nuclear deterrence* and *information superiority* (cf. Singer 2015).

Maxim: It can be assumed in the longer term that ultimately, at the end of a corresponding process of development, fully autonomous reconnaissance and weapons systems will be capable of autonomously resolving situations with a moderate degree of complexity (e.g. unarmed reconnaissance or armed patrols in a defined area that is designated as such). The development of such systems, which is currently being expedited, their advantages and disadvantages, need to be clearly presented to the wider public by military and political decision-makers.

4. Outlook

The change in modern warfare, the increase in the threats posed by phenomena, such as international terrorism, and the fact that Western societies in particular are no longer prepared to risk their armed forces in protracted conflicts with heavy casualties means that we should expect to see a steady increase in the deployment of unmanned reconnaissance and weapons systems. However, in modern asymmetric, irregular and hybrid conflicts, there is a tendency for the technologically superior party in the conflict to exploit legal grey areas to deploy their weapon technologies against organised non-state actors outside their area of control. Non-state actors (including terrorist groups) are increasingly also using semi-autonomous systems. In the future, the provisions of international humanitarian law will also need to be complied with when semi-autonomous systems are used. With appropriate application and control, these provisions could even be met better by using unmanned systems. Reconnaissance with unmanned systems helps to generate an extremely precise picture of a possible target. On the other hand, a fully autonomous robot equipped with artificial intelligence would be able to collect information about its environment by independently using its sensors. As the robot increasingly gains in experience, it will be more and more able to optimise itself. The effectiveness of its actions will steadily rise. The possible use of weapons is no longer proportionate, but rather becomes more efficient. The robot's software operates solely on the basis of mathematical calculations and ignores any moral or ethical trade-offs and considerations. This creates a *fighting machine* (or killer robot), which has no inhibitions and which can only be stopped by a technical fault or destruction or (ideally) an external command. The question of human responsibility must always be asked when developments such as this are employed. Wrong action on the part of a human operator in or on the loop may result in a breach of international law. By contrast, with a potential fully autonomous system (AI, off the loop), this could either have been programmed from the outset in violation of international law, or misguided action may have been the result of a technical defect. The countries developing such systems are therefore also urged to comply with the standards of international law seriously in the future, and to allow for human intervention in software developments (cf. Reisner 2018, 311ff). If you have the right financial means, today it is possible to kit yourself out with all kinds of weapons on the booming black market. Our high educational standards and extremely simple technologies also make it possible for people to develop highly effective weapons themselves and procure the components that are required by mail order. Although this does not especially change the threat level, it does of course also change the strategies of the military (and the police) to allow them to counter such a threat at an early stage. The new biotechnologies and microbiology in particular present entirely new threats and therefore challenges for the security services. They are key technologies today and, alongside space technologies, they are the key areas of concern for (military) strategy. Quantum mechanics is one of the key pillars of modern physics. Complementing classical physics, it forms the basis for describing the phenomena of atomic physics, solid-state physics and nuclear and elementary particle physics, but also related sciences, such as quantum chemistry. The practical applications of this theoretical knowledge and the consequences for the security domain can currently only be speculated on. From the point of view of military strategy, it is very much advisable to keep a close eye on these developments in the natural sciences, so that no unwelcome surprises arise. The development of small nuclear weapons for specific means implies that a nuclear war involving nuclear and radiological weapons (weapons whose effect is primarily due to their radiation) is certainly feasible from a military point of view, but the risks and long-term repercussions are very difficult to predict. However, the deployment of a nuclear or radiological weapon remains a military strategic option for the world's official and unofficial nuclear powers.

5. References

Albers, D. S., Garstaka, J. J, Stein, F. P., et. Al. (1999). Network Centric Warfare – Developing and Leveraging Information Superiority. In US Department of Defense (Ed.). *C4ISR Coopera0tive Research Program (CCRP)*.

S. Ashley. (2008). Aerial Stealth – Plasma antennas disappear when shut off. In *Scientific American*, February 2008.

Bauer. S. J. (2002). *Die Abhängigkeit der Nachrichtenübertragung, Ortung und Navigation von der Ionosphäre*. Vienna: Verlag der Österreichischen Akademie der Wissenschaften.

Cunningham, C. (2020). *Cyber Warfare – Truth, Tactics, and Strategies*. Packt Publishing.

Drews, R. (2020): *The End of the Bronze Age. Changes in Warfare and the Catastrophe ca. 1200 B.C.* 3rd Ed. XII. Princeton: University Press.

Haber, L. F. (1986). *The Poisonous Cloud. Chemical Warfare in the First World War*. Oxford University Press, Oxford.

Hoffmann, F. G. : *Exploring War's Character & Nature Will War's Nature Change in the Seventh Military Revolution?*. Retrieved from: https://ssi.armywarcollege.edu/pubs/Parameters/issues/Winter_2017-18/Vol47No4.pdf (29.03.2018)

Jordan, D. & Kiras, J. (Eds.). (2008). *Understanding Modern Warfare*. New York: Cambridge University Press.

Lonsdale, D. (2008) Strategy. In Jordan, D. & Kiras, J. (Eds.): *Understanding Modern Warfare* (pp. 19-38). New York: Cambridge University Press.

Macgregor, K., & Willamson, M. (2015). *The Dynamics of Military Revolution 1300-2050*. New York.

Marra, W. C., & Mcneil, S. K. (2016). *Understanding "The Loop" – Regulating the next Generation of War Machines*. Retrieved from: https://www.law.upenn.edu/live/files/3895-marra-and-mcneil-understanding-the-loop- (10.01.2016)

Morris, I. (2013). *War – What is it good for?*. Profile Books Ltd.

Münkler, H. (2013). Neue Kampfsysteme und die Ethik des Krieges. In: Heinrich Böll Stiftung (Ed.): *High Tech Kriege – Frieden und Sicherheit in Zeiten von Drohnen, Kampfrobotern und digitaler Kriegführung*, Band 36. Berlin.

North Atlantic Treaty Organization. (2005). *NATO Intelligence, Surveillance, and Reconnaissance (ISR) Interoperability Architecture (NIIA),* Volume 4: NIIA Terms and Definitions, AEDP-2 (Edition 1). Mons.

NATO. (2010). *Allied Command Operation (ACO) Directive (AD) 80-70. Campaign Synchronization and Joint Targeting in ACO*, II-1-1. Mons.

Ogarkov, N. (Ed.). (1983). *Voennyj ènciklopedičeskij slovar'*. Moskva: Voennoe Izd. [in Russian, Military Encyclopedia, Keyword Military Technological Revolution]

Partington, J. R. (1960). *A History of Greek Fire and Gunpowder*. Cambridge: Heffer. Republished: (1998) The Johns Hopkins University Press.

Reisner, M. (2018). *Robotic Wars*. Berlin. Miles-Verlag.

Sapolsky H., Friedman, B., & Green, B. (Eds.). (2009). *US Military Innovation since the Cold War – Creation without Distruction.* New York.

Scharre, P. (2015a) *Robotic on the Battlefield – Part I: Range Persistence and Daring:* Retrieved from: http://www.cnas.org/range-persistence-daring#VrpKzdKG-uI (23.12.2015)

Paul Scharre. (2015b*). Robotic on the Battlefield – Part II: The Coming Swarm.* Retrieved from: http://www.cnas.org/sites/default/files/publications-pdf/CNAS_The Coming Swarm_Scharre.pdf (23.12.2015).

Singer, P. W. (2009). *Wired for War – The Robotic Revolution and Conflict in the 21st Century.* New York.

Singer, P. W. (2015). The Five Deadly Flaws of Talking About Emerging Military Technologies and the Need for New Approaches to Law, Ethics, and War. In: Bergen, P. L., & Rothenberg, D. (Eds.). *Drone Wars, Transforming Conflict, Law and Policy.* New York.

Tuck, C. (2008). Land warfare. In: Jordan, D. & Kiras, J. (Eds.): *Understanding Modern Warfare* (pp. 81-127). New York: Cambridge University Press.

Walton, D. (2008). Weapons of Mass destruction. In: Jordan, D. & Kiras, J. (Eds.): *Understanding Modern Warfare* (pp. 377-404). New York: Cambridge University Press.

Zeter. K. (2014). *Meet MonsterMind, the NSA Bot That Could Wage Cyberwar Autonomously.* Retrieved from: http://www.wired.com/2014/08/nsa-monstermind-cyber-warfare/ (10.02.2016).

6.   Further Reading

Cole, A., Singer, P. W. (2020). *Burn-In: A Novel of the Real Robotic Revolution.* Houghton Mifflin Harcourt Publishing.

Cunningham, C. (2020). *Cyber Warfare – Truth, Tactics, and Strategies.* Packt Publishing.

Jordan, D., Kiras, J. D., et al, (2016). *Understanding Modern Warfare.* (2nd ed.). Cambridge University Press.

Reisner, M. (2018). *Robotic Wars.* Norderstedt. Miles-Verlag.

Scharre, P. (2019). *Army of None: Autonomous weapons and the Future of War.* W. W. Norton and Company.

Chapter 9: Strategic Communication(s)

Mag. Herbert Kullnig, Col Mag. Bernhard Lauring, Mag. (FH) Dr. Gerd Hiess, MSc

Keywords: Strategic Communication; Military Doctrine; Narrative; NATO; Information Warfare; Framing; EU;

0.   Abstract

Strategic communication(s), known as StratCom or SC for short, should be understood as a concept that has been used in governmental contexts for around two decades. It has now also been embraced as a subject of study for communication science, economics and political science. However, there is not yet any consistent understanding of what it is; state practice instead adopts different approaches which at times closely resemble traditional public relations models. This text will advocate StratCom that needs to be planned and organised with a national approach, with great importance attached to shaping the narrative as well as being aware of the information environment and synchronising words and deeds. However, the claimed impact of StratCom (influence) that is often postulated cannot be achieved with communication tools alone. It should be noted, however, that at the time this volume went to press, the war in Ukraine was raging, and it is not possible to predict what new insights will emerge for the field of research as a result of the scholarly reappraisal of the war. For this reason, the authors also refrain from giving examples, cross-references, or initial derivations that might result from the first "Tik-Tok conflict."

1.   Introduction

"While I was there, I saw the Iraqi soldiers coming into the hospital with guns and go into the room where 15 babies were in incubators. They took the babies out of the incubators, took the incubators and left the babies on the cold floor to die" (Williams, 1992), 15-year-old Nayirah sobbed into the microphones which had been set up for her testimony before the US Congressional Human Rights Caucus in October 1990. With huge media publicity, the girl recounted atrocities committed by Iraqi soldiers at Al Adan Hospital in Kuwait City as millions of Americans watched and listened to her testimony on TV. However, what the public did not know at this time: Nayirah's incubator story was a downright lie, orchestrated by the US agency Hill & Knowlton, which started its work immediately following the invasion of Iraq in August

1990. The PR agency was funded by a group called Citizens for a Free Kuwait; they were lobbying in the USA on behalf of the Kuwaiti Government, as McArthur (1992) subsequently revealed in the New York Times. The girl Nayirah turned out to be the daughter of the Kuwaiti Ambassador to the USA, Saud Nasir al-Sabah. Hill & Knowlton successfully achieved its aim of portraying Iraq as the evil enemy and preparing the ground for a US invasion, as we now know.

CUT TO: Germany. Berlin, 31 August 2015 – the Chancellor's summer press conference: With the brief phrase "We have achieved so much – we can do this!" Angela Merkel encapsulated her refugee policy. Whether she intended to or not – and authors and filmmakers speculate in equal measure about this today (Connolly, 2020; Oltermann, 2017), Merkel's words became strategically significant, because they created a draw that went on to entice millions of war refugees and economic migrants to Western Europe (Europäisches Parlament, 2019; Presse- und Informationsamt der Bundesregierung, 2015). Even though today it is known that the former German Minister of Economic Affairs Sigmar Gabriel had previously uttered these words, Chancellor Merkel put her stamp on her "We can do this" (Frankfurter Allgemeine Zeitung, 2016), especially as her words were also always followed by actions – specifically in the form of impressive pictures that went around the world, for example: Merkel surrounded by migrants taking selfies with her. Even Germany's Chancellor would later admit that a year like 2015 must not be repeated (Spiegel Online, 2016). The phenomenon: nowadays, state actors (and also non-state ones) are able to develop their own narratives which support or even actually enable them to achieve their own political strategy aims faster and with greater impact than ever before – and often this extends beyond the simple communication component that has just been described, for instance with deliberate disinformation, deception or a state-organised lie.

This is what happened in the early summer of 2017: The world witnessed an unusual power struggle in the Gulf: In a surprise coup, Saudi-Arabia and its allies, the United Arab Emirates, Bahrain and Egypt, for example, managed to isolate the neighbouring Gulf emirate of Qatar as a rogue state at first. The alliance broke off diplomatic relations with the Gulf state of Qatar and imposed a total economic blockade – on land, at sea and in the air. And it also demanded for example that the rulers in Doha must cool their relations with Iran, cut all links to terrorist organisations, and close the Qatari news channel Al Jazeera (Gambrell, 2017). The strategy of the alliance partners: orchestrated strategic communications! The obvious operational tactic employed here: deliberate disinformation as a result of computer network attacks designed to publicly humiliate Qatar's head of state, Tamim Bin Hamad Al

Thani. The American news network CNN initially held Russian hackers responsible: it stated that at the end of May 2017, they had hacked the Qatari news agency and social networks such as the Qatari YouTube channel and official Twitter account and linked the Emir of Qatar to compromising statements, so that Hamas should be viewed as the legitimate representatives of the Palestinian people or that Shiite Iran was an Islamic power that must not be ignored. Although Qatari officials immediately and vehemently denied these reports in the media and dispelled them as fake news, Saudi-Arabia and its allies were outraged and they publicly declared that they felt this vindicated all their suspicions that Qatar was supporting terrorism, with its close ties to Iran. The Washington Post later cited sources from the US Secret Service in reporting that the United Arab Emirates were instead primarily responsible for the orchestrated campaign of disinformation against Qatar (DeYoung & Nakashima, 2017; Perez & Prokupecz, 2017). This episode revealed a feud that the monarchies of the Gulf had been waging against one another for many years. These feuds are based on concrete political interests that are pursued not just by actors on the Arabian Peninsula, but in a broader context between the United States and Russia and not least the regime in Tehran: examples are the way in which Iran's revolutionary model and its attempts at export present a threat to the Saudi-inspired power politics, or the fact that the Iranian nuclear programme and Iran's support for Shiite groups in Lebanon, Yemen, Iraq and Syria are a thorn in the side of the Saudi Sunni rulers in Riyadh. What is more: from the point of view of Saudi-Arabia and its neighbours in the Gulf, Qatar has been a source of irritation since the 1990s – not least because of the news channel Al Jazeera, whose critical reporting sometimes enrages the autocratic rulers in the region. In addition, Qatar has been close to Iran for many years – also because both countries lay claim to and jointly exploit one of the world's largest gas fields in the Persian Gulf (al-Saleh, 2017; Kündig, 2017).

From the problem that is described here back to the phenomenon that sparked this crisis in the Persian Gulf: Saudi-Arabia and its allies have attempted in this post-truth age (Scheer, 2016) to assert political interests using strategic communications tools which extend way beyond their element of communication. The motto here is: if you can persuade, you establish facts – sometimes even alternative ones! As has already been stated above, such "factoids" are often based on deliberate disinformation, deception or state-organised lies. This is not an entirely new phenomenon. However, in their specific orchestration with other tools and in light of the global interconnection and interdependence of business, politics and society, it is presented in a completely new guise: it is more effective than ever before, employed at a strategic level, and in combination with new communications technologies and tools they are also more dangerous than ever. The rise of social networks coupled with the dwindling importance of traditional journalism is only fuelling this development – and people's lack of awareness about the flow of information in cyberspace is playing its part.

These three examples can today all be assigned to the frame of reference and action of the artificially coined term (Paul, 2011) strategic communication(s), although it should be stated at the outset that a uniform understanding does not yet exist – as is shown not least by the scenarios that have just been described. This is why the authors intend, initially in a synopsis, to highlight how selected states and confederations of states deal with questions of strategic communication and how strategic communication has developed in a governmental context. In addition, the question arises as to how science is addressing this field of research and what nuances can be seen in the way it is implemented in societies in practice. Furthermore, an attempt will be made to capture and at least outline the essence of comprehensive strategic communication(s) for the reader. Finally, it is key to explain what level of impact should be ascribed to the tools of strategic communication, especially as the examples in the introduction suggest that strategic communication is capable not just of establishing impact requirements, but also satisfying them.

2. On the Origin of the Term Strategic Communication(s)

Strategic communication or strategic communications (StratCom, SC) – the term is used synonymously in English-speaking countries in both the singular and plural – only became established as a field of research in the academic landscape in the second decade of the 21st century – in particular starting with communication science research in North America. In this context, emphasis should be placed first and foremost on the works of Hallahan et al. (2007), Zerfass (2009) as well as Holtzhausen and Zerfass (2013, 2015a), which apart from providing basic definitions also discuss institutional and organisational aspects and applications of strategic communications, although they mostly examine the research subject from a communication science perspective – practitioners would probably say: from a public relations perspective. Speaking of public relations: it should also be noted here that the corporate world in the US had been using the term StratCom for a decade or two previously, where in a less subtle and very non-specific way it represents almost anything demanding a modern, progressive touch in relation to product promotion (Brooks, 2011). But back to the academic discourse. StratCom has now also become established in English-speaking countries as an umbrella term in economic disciplines and also in the broadest sense in political science, whereas for Asia and Australia Holtzhausen and Zerfass state the following: "In Asia and Australia, strategic communication is a concept used in the professional field, in education and in literature alike ..." (2015b, 559). In this context, mention should also be made of Bentele and Nothhaft (2010), who highlight a European perspective, although in Europe in particular – not least in German-speaking countries in Europe – there is a clearly discernible trend towards approaching the research topic mainly from an economic or business point of view. The focus is always on companies and organisations as reference objects, with StratCom being understood fundamentally as integrated marketing and corporate communications whose communication paradigms are subject to the many technologically driven developments (social networks, Industry 4.0, etc.). This is also evident in the definition which Bruhn, Esch et al. propose in this context by stating that StratCom is to be understood as "the firm focus in the medium to long term on the overall communication of the company or a reference object of the company and on the use of the individual communication tools" (2016, p. 25). However, the communication scientists Gehrau et al. (2013) criticise the fact that the emphasis on business is associated with a distinctly instrumental understanding of StratCom, which almost ignores its social context; rather, strategic communications should primarily be viewed as a communication tool which one can use merely to seek to realise specific corporate interests.

But before communication science, economic science or political science discovered the notion of strategic communication(s) as a subject for research in its own right, it had long been a domain of governments and armed forces, first and foremost the US Government and its military. This is because the artificially coined term strategic communication(s) was used in the current context as early as at the start of the 2000s in Pentagon working groups, which can very much be interpreted as a consequence of the terrorist attacks on September 11, 2001, especially given that in the "aftermath of 9/11" the US administration was quick to recognise that having a coordinated communication policy in all communication channels was the way to go (Office of the Under Secretary of Defense for Acquisition, Technology, and Logistics, 2001). The first sources to cite are Paul (2011) and Farwell (2012), who presented fundamental works with more of a practical/normative focus in which they ultimately advocate comprehensive strategic communications extending way beyond the element of communication. This is also the context in which to understand all reports and concepts relating to strategic communications written and published by the US Department of Defense (and also the British Ministry of Defence) and the United States Armed Forces (Office of the Secretary of Defense, 2004; Office of the Under Secretary of Defense for Acquisition, Technology, and Logistics, 2001; U.S. Government Accountability Office, 2012; UK Ministry of Defence, 2012). To provide guidance, a wide-ranging definition of strategic communication is cited as a working term introduced by the US Government in Barack Obama's first term in office as a "whole of government approach", with the intention of clearing up any differences in understanding and interpretation and associated misunderstandings in relation to the term, which had become popular:

> *"By ‚strategic communication(s)' we refer to: (a) the synchronization of words and deeds and how they will be perceived by selected audiences, as well as (b) programs and activities deliberately aimed at communicating and engaging with intended audiences, including those implemented by public affairs, public diplomacy, and information operations professionals"* (The White House, 2010, p. 2).

Moreover, in the US Department of Defense, StratCom was officially defined as a wide-ranging sphere up until 2017:

> *"Focused United States Government efforts to understand and engage key audiences to create, strengthen, or preserve conditions favorable for the advancement of United States Government interests, policies, and objectives through the use of coordinated programs, plans, themes, messages, and products synchronized with the actions of all instruments of national power. Also called SC"* (Department of Defense, 2017, p. 223).

However, StratCom was removed from the Defense Department's range of terminology from 2018. This was down to an ideological disagreement over many years within and between various US agencies, as Brooks (2012) records. Critics argue that StratCom was initially viewed as a tool for synchronising communications across different agencies under the control of the White House (Deputy National Security Advisor for Strategic Communications). Instead, additional levels of management and organisation were created, roughly increasing the amount of bureaucracy, and in most cases StratCom turned out to be public affairs (PA) anyway (USA Today, 2012). StratCom should therefore be replaced with the much more accurate term "communication synchronization", as G. E. Little (personal communication, November 28, 2012) stated many years previously. The following is stated in the US Defense Department's official Dictionary of Military and Associated Terms:

> *"commander's communication synchronization — A process to coordinate and synchronize narratives, themes, messages, images, operations, and actions to ensure their integrity and consistency to the lowest tactical*

level across all relevant communication activities. Also called CCS" (Department of Defense, 2020, p. 44).

Despite this, the White House continues to appoint experts in strategic communications. Ben Rhodes, for example, performed the role of "Deputy National Security Advisor for Strategic Communications" until the end of Obama's term of office in 2017. And in April 2020, Trump appointed Alyssa Farah as "Director of Strategic Communications" (The White House, 2020). Conclusion: The "hype" surrounding StratCom in a governmental context seems to have been demolished for the time being, in the USA at any rate.

In this context, it is also worth looking at NATO, especially as the "North Atlantic axis" between the USA and the UK is regarded as being particularly influential in the defence alliance: NATO – 27 European countries are NATO members today – has been working since as far back as 2009 on a detailed definition of strategic communications:

> *The coordinated and appropriate use of NATO communications activities and capabilities – Public Diplomacy, Public Affairs (PA), Military Public Affairs, Information Operations (InfoOps) and Psychological Operations (PSYOPS), as appropriate – in support of Alliance policies, operations and activities, and in order to advance NATO's aims* (Private Office of the Secretary General, 2009, p. 2).

And yet despite this, even in NATO there was a debate for almost ten years about StratCom with turf wars and special interests in which traditional thinking and old habits clashed with new challenges in order to establish exactly what StratCom is, what it should be and what it should do or whether it actually has a right to exist, as Laity (2018) describes. This process was accelerated at any rate from 2014 onwards by the Russian intervention in Ukraine. And this belatedly focused the attention of an initially surprised NATO on Russia's "new approach to defence" – at least with a Western interpretation. "What it showed was that we should have been less surprised than we were because what the Russians did they had been talking about for years" (Laity, 2018, p. 70).

In this context, you are inevitably confronted with the oft-quoted "Gerasimov Doctrine". A brief digression here: At the end of February 2013, the weekly Voenno-Promyšlennyj Kur'er (VPK) – a trade newspaper of the Russian military-industrial complex – published an article by Russia's Chief of the General Staff Valery Gerasimov (Gerasimov, 2013). The article was based on excerpts from a speech which Gerasimov gave to the Academy of Military Sciences at the beginning of 2013 and in which he states how and why one can and must wage a hybrid – in Russian parlance – non-linear war nowadays. At first, it was articles from Scandinavia and the Baltic which focused on this text; although they were received in specialist circles, they were initially not available to a wider public. However, when Russia annexed Crimea in the spring of 2014 and a short time later triggered a war in the Donbass region, Coalson (2014) from Radio Free Europe/Radio Liberty posted on his Facebook page a first English translation of the Gerasimov speech, which Galeotti (2014) commented on in his blog "In Moscow's Shadows" and for journalistic reasons gave the snappy title "The 'Gerasimov Doctrine' and Russian Non-Linear War". "It was a mistake I will regret forevermore, because even though in the text I explicitly stated that it wasn't a doctrine and wasn't even necessarily Gerasimov's thinking, it turned out that a snappy headline is much more influential than the actual detail written beneath it" (Galeotti, 2020). For example, Bilban and Grininger (2019) also describe the "Gerasimov Doctrine" as a myth because a doctrine in the traditional sense does not exist in this form. Yet, following Russia's intervention, it appeared to many authors and commentators as if Russia's most senior officer had actually spelled out what was in store for the West. However, one can also interpret the specialist article which Russia's Chief of the General Staff probably did not even compile himself at the time as a Russian manifestation of a (hybrid) projection of power which really emanated from the USA and NATO. This is because for the Kremlin the popular uprisings of the Arab Spring and the coloured revolutions seen in Georgia, Ukraine or Kyrgyzstan were not simply responses to corrupt and authoritarian regimes, but the result of secret, Western destabilising campaigns, according to Galeotti (2020). Viewed in this way, the narrative concerning the "Gerasimov Doctrine" as a blueprint for a new kind of Russian warfare (keyword: hybrid warfare) can also be classified as skilful strategic communications by the West which came into play once the state of shock that paralysed NATO and the West over the Russian intervention in Ukraine had been overcome. "The irony is, that even while railing against the 'Gerasimov Doctrine' meme, Moscow itself helped it spread" (Galeotti, 2020). On the other hand, this may also mean that Russia's strategic communications then cleverly took up the baton and deliberately stoked this public perception further in order to appear more threatening than it actually was at the time, which in turn seems to have served its interests as a state actor on the international stage, as in the conflict in Syria, for example.

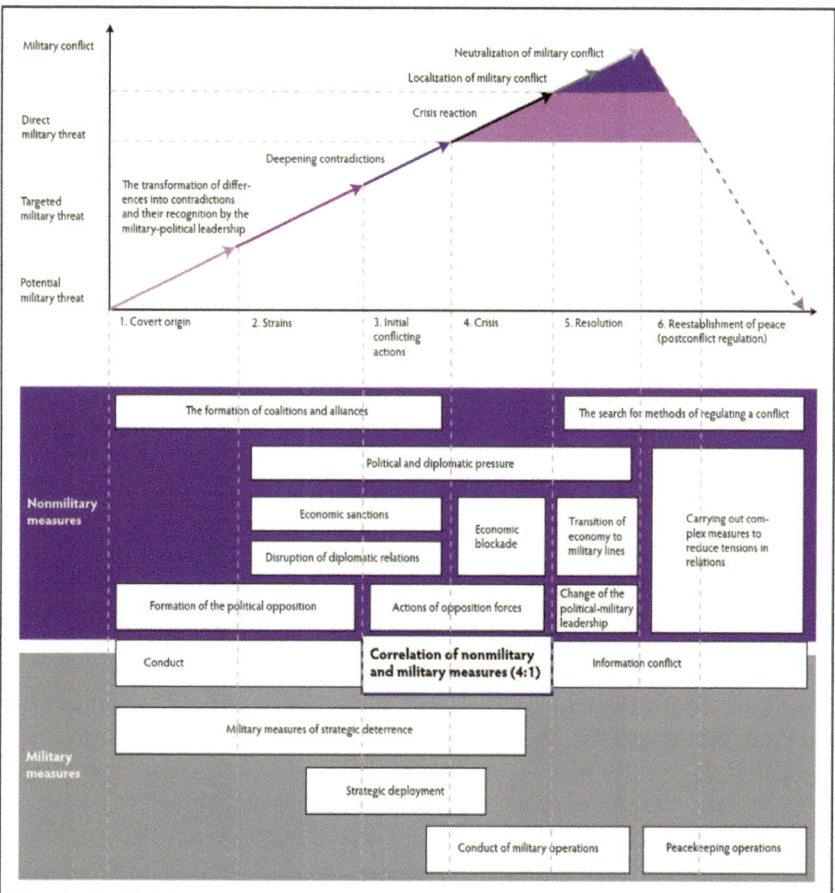

Figure 1 Diagram from the Gerasimov article in the Voenno-Promyšlennyj Kur'er; translated for Military Review by Charles Bartles (Gerasimov, 2016).

In the present context, the following can at least be gleaned from the Gerasimov article: Great importance is attached to the information space. For example, Figure 1 also shows six phases of modern conflicts, with the information conflict being conducted continuously in all stages. In addition, it is also conducted with non-military and military measures. This aspect particularly reflects the influence of the Arab Spring, as is documented here in the first English translation of the article:

> *"The information space opens wide asymmetrical possibilities for reducing the fighting potential of the enemy. In north Africa, we witnessed the use of technologies for influencing state structures and the population with the help of information networks. It is necessary to perfect activities*

205

in the information space, including the defense of our own objects" (Coalson, 2014).

Fridman (2020) comes to the conclusion that this concept of a continuous information conflict can be described as Russia's strategic communications, which it seeks to use to influence specific target groups in an information space. And although the term StratCom is now frequently used in business, politics and academia, so far it has not been mentioned in any official documents in Russia. But:

> *"Most generally, strategic communication is the state's projection of certain vital and long-term values, interests and goals into the conscience of domestic and foreign audiences. It is effectuated by means of adequate synchronization of multifaceted activities in all domains of social life, commonly with professional communication support"* (Pashentsev, 2019a, 694–695).

Back to the NATO debate on StratCom: from the Western perspective, as well as the direct experiences in Afghanistan the operations in China (key phrase: Three Warfares) and the rise of Islamic State (IS) are also driving the evolution of strategic communications within NATO. There were two milestones that firmly established StratCom in the North Atlantic Alliance: firstly the establishment of the NATO Strategic Communications Centre of Excellence in Riga in 2014 and secondly MC 0628, the strategy document which the North Atlantic Council and the Military Committee of NATO approved in 2017 as the new "Military Policy on Strategic Communications (StratCom)".

> *"Under this policy, the communication capabilities and the information staff function (StratCom, Mil Public Affairs (PA), Info Ops, PSY-OPS) are to be grouped together under a Chief StratCom/Director of Communications (or similar title). This individual will have coordination and integration authority, in accordance with the Commander's Intent, to issue appropriate Direction and Guidance in order to ensure StratCom's integration within every aspect of the HQ's activities"* (North Atlantic Military Committee, 2017, p. 1).

According to Laity (2018), MC 0628 ultimately removed a number of crippling areas of conflict within NATO and there has since been more money, staff and training for StratCom. However, the information environment is still not yet a domain of operations in a NATO context. According to MC 0628, StratCom is in essence based on a few basic principles:

All activity is founded on NATO's values
Activity is driven by objectives derived from Narrative, Policy and Strategy issued within a framework of political-military direction
Credibility and trust are vital attributes and must be protected
Words and actions must be aligned
The IE must be understood
Communication is a collective and integrated effort
Focus is on achieving (a) desired effect(s) and outcome(s)
Communication is empowered at all levels

Figure 2 Basic principles of StratCom according to MC 0628; own list based on (North Atlantic Military Committee, 2017, p. 4).

And this is how it is now defined: "StratCom, in the context of the NATO military, is the integration of communication capabilities and information staff function with other military activities, in order to understand and shape the Information Environment (IE), in support of NATO aims and objectives" (North Atlantic Military Committee, 2017, p. 4). NATO attaches a great deal of importance to always developing a narrative that strengthens its own credibility and only taking actions that are consistent with its fundamental set of values. For NATO has learned from mistakes it made in the past (such as Afghanistan); this is because there was a lack of detailed understanding of the specifics of the information environment, which is why support for its own objectives was usually lacking. NATO now has a tool at its disposal which it refers to internally as the StratCom framework. This is an efficient means of coordinating NATO's communication and mission objectives, topics and areas of focus in advance precisely and in a manner appropriate to the situation – essentially "a kind of StratCom mission command linking all levels" (Laity, 2018, p. 73).

Let's now turn from NATO to the European Union (EU) which, following Russia's intervention in Ukraine as well as IS propaganda activities, has only placed StratCom high up on its agenda since 2015/16. The European Council initially set up an East StratCom Task Force (ESTF) with the intention of detecting Russian campaigns of disinformation, and instructed the High Representative of the EU for Foreign Affairs and Security Policy, Federica Mogherini, to work with the EU institutions and member states to come up with an action plan for StratCom (European Council, 2015). The action plan was published in the middle of 2015 (High Representative of the Union for Foreign Affairs and Security Policy, 2015); it is designed primarily for the EU member states in eastern Europe and for eastern partner states such as Armenia, Azerbaijan, Georgia, Ukraine or Moldova. It is in these regions in particular that the EU wants to strengthen its communication, expose independent media and Russian narratives to bolster the resilience of these countries. In subsequent years, the ESTF, which is set up alongside the Communication Policy and Public Diplomacy group in the European External Action Service (EEAS), remained clearly focused on uncovering disinformation activities originating in Russia. The EU underlined this approach when at the end of 2018 the European Council approved an action plan to combat disinformation which confirmed the mandate of the ESTF of 2015 (European Commission, 2018). However, the EU has so far failed to provide any definition of what exactly it understands the umbrella term StratCom to mean, which is why the StratCom of recent years has been more akin to a development of the public relations efforts of EU foreign policy (European Commission, 2016; Fotyga, 2016; P8_TA(2016)0441, 2016).

In summary, the following is at any rate apparent: the world of science has adopted the field of research of strategic communication with different levels of intensity and with different areas of focus, usually as a single discipline in individual scientific fields, and therefore expanded the state of research overall, but always based on a different interpretation and understanding of the concept. StratCom has certainly been defined in multiple ways, but it has not been differentiated either logically or uniformly, nor has there so far been any attempt to follow a comprehensive and interdisciplinary approach. In addition, StratCom is implemented in normative-practical terms in different social areas of action and subsystems and also shares the same fate of highly inflationary use as is seen in business, for example. There is also the question of how StratCom can be tied to societal, social, media and organisational theories, especially as the phenomenon must also be considered across different types of organisation and areas of action (Gehrau et al., 2013, pp. 347–348). The literature on this is at least not consistent enough; in summary, this is because firstly, there is not yet an overview of the variety of terminology and secondly, StratCom is still waiting for a general definition which ideally could be logically and comprehensibly deduced from a theoretical foundation. There is a gap in the research here, but it could be closed with an independent piece of work. This is because when specialist scientific terms have made their way into everyday language, conceptual clarity in conjunction with a systematic-analytical and yet problem-oriented approach does at least seem sensible, states Sarcinelli (2010, p. 267).

In a governmental context, a similarly inconsistent understanding of terminology and applications of strategic communication is revealed, in particular the noticeable "squabbling" around questions of structure and workflow. Whereas over the years the United States (and United Kingdom) and NATO have applied a rather extensive, multidimensional understanding of StratCom (Brooks, 2012; Farwell, 2012; Le Page, 2014; Pashentsev, 2019b; Paul, 2011; S. A. Tatham, 2008; S. Tatham, 2013; S. Tatham & Le Page, 2014), the EU and many of its member states have tended to adopt a one-dimensional approach with a focus on the mass media for strategic communications (development of public relations), which from the EU's point of view is intended to counter any propaganda that the EU sees itself subjected to (Die Zeit, 2015, 2016; EU Institute for Security Studies, 2016a, 2016b; Ogrysko, 2016; Roth, 2017). Russia in turn pursues a multidimensional concept which reflects the essence and claimed impact of strategic communications. However, the term has not yet been mentioned in any official documents.

3. On the Essence of StratCom

For clarification: The authors assume here that there is a comprehensive understanding of the term StratCom which in the military context as in the government setting in general at least extends beyond the communication element. Accordingly, StratCom is more than just an "enhanced" form of public relations. So anyone who advocates comprehensive StratCom must present it and understand it as a whole-of-government approach; this very substantially corresponds to the basic idea which in the USA at least has developed over more than a decade and has also been propagated by the key authorities (Borg, 2008, pp. 5–10). The essence of this StratCom is the narrative around which the operational planning and execution must be oriented. The narrative is commonly understood nowadays to symbolise the persuasive force of a message, as a dramatic element, as a narrative unit or meaningful framework or as a simple package around complex content. Hardly any term has been placed under more strain in recent years than this one. Müller and Precht (2019) describe minimal conditions which Gerald Prince set back in the early 1970s for defining a narrative, stating that a narrative logically has to satisfy four conditions, specifically: initial state, transformation, end state and a constant as the reference point. The authors use the famous Trump election slogan "Make America Great Again" to explain one possible way of interpreting this approach. The United States should be viewed as the reference point. Although America was once "great" in the past, today this is evidently no longer the case (initial state). Accordingly, something needs to happen (transformation) for America to be "great" again (end state). It is now worth first explaining what significance narratives have in the present context and what "power" emanates from them.

3.1 The Power of the "Narrative"

The following section will seek to explore what effect narratives have on us. To be able to understand the significance of the narrative for strategic communications, you first need to look at the key determinants for why narratives can shape people. The effect of a narrative shapes people from an early age and accompanies them through to when they die.

The fundamental element of a narrative is the word, which in turn forms the basis of language. Wiegand (2018) states the following in relation to the importance of words and language: "The spoken word defines the world all around us and has a power that is stronger than any weapon. If you have a good command of language, you will be more successful in the world of work." One institution that is always mindful of the previously described importance of words and language, in particular in the context of measures designed to de-escalate any tension during demonstrations, is the police (Stecken, n.d.; Verwaltungs-Berufsgenossenschaft [VBG], n.d.). In this context, there has been a focus for quite some time on the nature and impact of words.

In the area of psychology, narratives have a long tradition and significance as they allow people to access narrated personal experiences (Lucius-Hoene, 2017). This also applies to the same extent to psychotherapy, which depends on narratives (Boothe, 2011). These narratives are based in particular on narrative reconstruction. This can be used in two different ways. Firstly, episodes in people's lives can be depicted in narrative form through people's cognitive emotions or communication activities. This establishes continuity and coherence and other people are able to understand or comprehend these experiences. On the basis of this narrative structure, a corresponding significance can be attached to the experience in time. This form of reconstruction can be used, for example, to substantiate actions and decisions in genetic terms. Secondly, it allows people to process experiences emotionally and work on both their own identity and their own biography. Narrative reconstruction is also used as a method for content analysis and structural or interaction-based analysis of verbal experiences. Various methods (for example text-analytical or hermeneutic methods) may be applied (Lucius-Hoene, 2020).

Thanks to this method, it is once again possible to illustrate very strikingly that narratives follow part of our lives. But what are narratives based on and why are we so preoccupied by them, and why do they have such an influence on our life (experience) and behaviour? Another question that arises in particular in relation to the influence of the narrative on strategic communications is, what happens to the target audience as a result of narratives? What effect do narratives have on the particular target audience?

In order to answer these questions, you need to look at the processes that occur in our brain because of narratives.

A key factor in this context is our memory. Our memory processes information in two different ways. We have firstly an episodic memory and secondly a semantic memory that stores factual knowledge. The episodic memory is defined in particular by narrative structures. This is where experiences, events, adventures or autobiographical aspects are processed. Factual knowledge is based on formal information and data. This is where in particular factors, formal tests, details or knowledge in general play a role (Erlach & Müller, 2020, p. 15).

Other factors that influence our memory are the subdivisions into short-term memory and long-term memory. The Short-term memory covers time spans ranging from seconds up to no more than a few minutes. The long-term memory, on the other hand, extends from minutes and hours, days, weeks through to years (Markowitsch & Staniloiu, 2015, p. 53).

The long-term memory is in turn divided up into five so-called long-term memory systems. The first one to mention here is the procedural memory. This subsumes mechanical or motor-related skills. The second system in this context relates to what is known as priming. Priming means a higher probability of recognising stimuli that have previously been perceived in a similar or identical way. Both the processes in the procedural memory and the processes of the priming system occur in our memory in an unconscious (anoetic) way. This contrasts firstly with the perceptual memory. This features processes relating to the recognition of stimuli based on things we already know; familiarity judgements are also made in this memory. The unconscious processes contrast secondly with the long-term memory, which is also known as the semantic memory or knowledge system. This relates to experiences or processes in the present. In this connection, the semantic memory represents context-free facts. Both systems, the perceptual and the semantic memories, relate to conscious processes. The fifth long-term memory system is assigned to the episodic-autobiographical memory. Self-conscious processes, known as autonoetic processes, are assigned to this system. It is understood to be the conjunction of autonoetic consciousness, the experiencing self and subjective time (Markowitsch & Staniloiu, 2015, p. 55).

Consequently, in relation to the effect of the narrative in the context of strategic communications, it is necessary to consider two concepts: the concepts of framing and of storytelling.

The concept of framing can originally be traced back to the sociologist Ervin Goffman (Kempf, 2020). However, the definition of the term used today is attributable to Robert Mathew Entman (1993). Entman understands it to mean "[...] that in a communication text certain aspects of reality are selected and made salient in a way that encourages a certain definition of a problem, assignment of root cause, moral assessment and/or way of dealing with the subject that is outlined" (Kempf, 2020).

The concept of storytelling is a narrative method. This approach already has a long tradition in respect of its application in psychology and psychotherapy. Explicit and implicit knowledge is recounted here for example in the form of fables, histories, metaphors, sentences or stories (Wirtz, 2020). Various regions in the brain are activated as a result. In relation to fact-based information, the regions activated are firstly Broca's area, which is responsible for processing language and understanding, and secondly Wernicke's area, which is responsible for language comprehension. When we absorb information in the form of stories, additional regions of the brain are also activated. These include the motor cortex, which is responsible for arbitrary movements, controlling emotions, processing smells, developing emotions and our own memories when we identify with the protagonist of the story. It can therefore be stated overall that the brain is comprehensively activated by stories (Jäger, 2016).

In summary, it can therefore be stated for the area of strategic communication that the type and form of narratives are key determinants. Our brain thinks in stories. Experiences are stored in narrative structures in the brain. Stories are processed by the brain (almost) like experiences (Erlach, Müller, & Thier, 2020, p. 16). When disseminating content (that is to be conveyed), the rule is therefore: the more certain factors or regions of the brain are addressed, the better the lasting effect and thus the success of strategic communications on the target audience.

3.2   Understanding the Information Environment

With regard to the essence of a narrative, there are at least two further, basic aspects that influence StratCom – firstly having a deep understanding of the information environment (IE) and secondly the orchestration or coordination of StratCom. First, in relation to the information environment: NATO understands the information environment logically to mean people and their cognitive processes, systems and organisations in physical or virtual spaces and their receipt, processing and transmission of information (North Atlantic Military Committee, 2017, p. 3). Having a deep understanding of the IE is essential for designing effective StratCom. For if you cannot get to grips with the complexity of the information environment, you will scarcely ever be able to develop effective narratives. "In many of our conflicts our grasp of culture, understanding of the audience and general awareness of the environment has been lacking, and we have paid the price in our inadequacies in gaining and maintaining support", states Laity (2018, p. 73) in summing up past NATO deployments, and in particular he means the North Atlantic Alliance's overall mediocre mission in Afghanistan. Mullen (2009), who was once the most senior US officer, uses other words to indicate how important it is to understand the IE: "We've come to believe that messages are something we can launch downrange like a rocket, something we can fire for effect. They are not. Good communication runs both ways. It's not about telling our story. We must also be better listeners."

How can the complexity of an information environment be unravelled particularly in an era in which societies are facing an unprecedented level of socio-technical change, in which traditional mass media have lost their monopoly as the exclusive brokers of information, in which social media is shaping social processes and in effect everyone is carrying digital media around with them all day long? So how can information environment analysis (IEA) take place? First of all, it is well known that solid language skills and an in-depth understanding of the history and culture of an area and its people (intercultural skills) are required. And then there are two more things in particular: first, professional handling (which since the Cambridge Analytica affair especially is compliant with the law) of big data, continuous processing of large amounts of different data and data streams from a large number of internal and external sources – as well as analysing this data. Even though big data analytics is currently still mostly designed to be descriptive (what has happened?) and explanatory (why did it happen?) – and there are many different reasons for this (unresolved questions of law or legal ethics, lack of expertise, cost factor, etc.), the biggest potential for these analyses is probably forecasting (what is going to happen?). Second, attention is being paid to automation

> *"to feed algorithms for creating and delivering content, and not only for analytics or decision-making. The huge potentials have been shown in political communication, for example, in the data-driven election campaign by President Obama in 2012 (…) or in 2016 with the increased usage of bots and automation"* (Wiesenberg et al., 2017, p. 95).

In a series of studies, researchers from Oxford University discovered that roughly a tenth of the Twitter posts that they recorded during the 2016 US election campaign originated from bots or that 45 per cent of all Twitter activity in Russia is not produced by human beings, but rather by computer algorithms (Woolley & Philip N. Howard, 2017). All in all, Wiesenberg et al. (2017) at any rate establish the following: the full potential of comprehensive data analyses and algorithms has so far not been fully exhausted.

3.3 The Orchestration of StratCom

In short, effective StratCom requires lean but strong structures and processes, which need to be coordinated and always take place with a national approach. There is no place for any vanities, solo action or specific sensitivities of individual agencies and their representatives. One sentence, calmly uttered, because such developments sometimes start with heads of state – and the examples already mentioned demonstrate: in practice, states, authorities or organisations repeatedly fail to synchronise their words and actions. Although the concept of the US Ministry of Defense from 2010 (see Figure 3) may seem idealistic, the orchestra metaphor does reflect what really matters for comprehensive StratCom: it is all about the harmonious "interaction" of all stakeholders, even if their tasks may be secretive in nature (Magen, 2017).

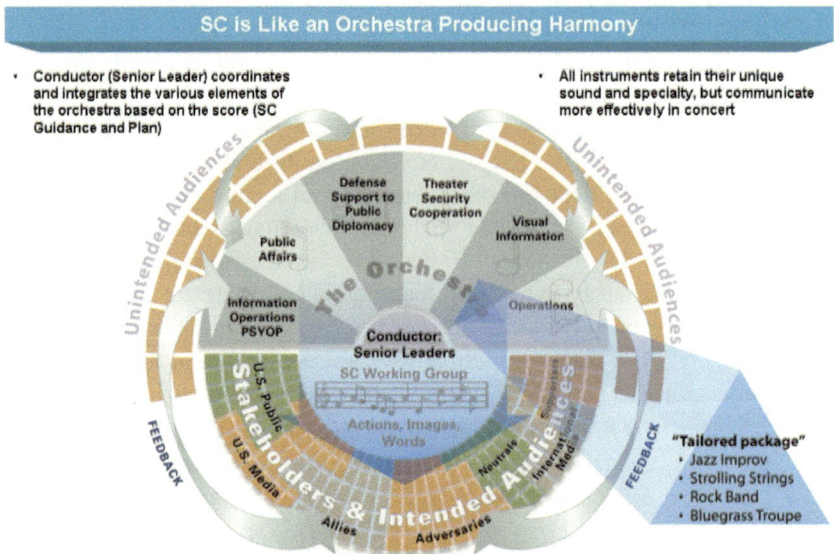

The selection, timing, and emphasis of SC instruments help orchestrate the message to stakeholders consistent with a desired effect or commander's intent. The conductor must continuously adapt the score based on stakeholder feedback.

Figure 3 The StratCom Orchestra (Joint Warfighting Center, 2010, p. 32).

For as Mullen (2009) writes: "To put it simply, we need to worry a lot less about how to communicate our actions and much more about what our actions communicate."

4.   The Impact of StratCom

The world has changed dramatically since the end of the Cold War – and it will continue to do so. In today's information environment, state and non-state actors are able to create and spread their own narratives within a continuous, global information cycle. "As a part of this change, decision-making systems as well as perceptions, attitudes and behaviours of groups and individuals are being continually influenced" (North Atlantic Military Committee, 2017, p. 2). This is why the speed and effectiveness of StratCom needs to be constantly adjusted and improved, states the North Atlantic Military Committee (2017), for example in its most recent strategy paper on StratCom, before adding: "It does this on a continuous basis in support of Alliance aims and is a primary tool of the commander to appropriately inform and influence audiences through actions and words" (North Atlantic Military Committee, 2017, pp. 5–6). Or, as it is stated in the Commander's Handbook for Strategic Communication and Communication Strategy: "Strategic communication must be at the heart of U.S. Government efforts to inform and influence key audiences in support of U.S. national interests, policies, and objectives" (Joint Warfighting Center, 2010, p. 2). Because this "informing" and "influencing" is repeatedly mentioned as a requirement for having an impact in the field of strategic communication, this inevitably throws up the question of the extent to which perceptions, attitudes and the behaviour of individuals or groups of people can actually be influenced. If one follows the examples in the introduction, these measures do at least appear to be undisputed.

In seeking an underlying scientific context, you will quickly come across attitude research and therefore one of the most studied concepts of social psychology. "From a socialisation theory perspective, attitudes may have affective, behavioural, and cognitive causes, producing the ABC of attitudes. What this means: We develop our own attitudes from what we feel, think or do" (Rudolph & Kim, 2018, p. 80). However, there has been very little research into the development-related dynamics of how attitudes are acquired. In addition, the function of attitudes in guiding actions is at the core of attitude research, especially as psychology and the related academic disciplines such as sociology have particularly pursued the aim of understanding and predicting human behaviour, according to Rudolph and Kim (2018, pp. 80–81). This is why at this point one should ask how and by what means attitudes and behaviours can actually be influenced or even changed. In the field of StratCom, open sources at any rate largely refer to measures in this context which can be planned and put in place using one's own or external communication tools and channels. This aspect then leads us to another related academic discipline: to the field of communication science and in particular to its "supreme discipline", media impact research, although this text in no way claims to consider this field of research in an all-encompassing way. However, one thing is clear: in popular discourse in particular and in socio-political discourse in general, "the media" is often considered to have an extraordinary impact. There is sometimes talk of the media being the fourth power in the state or even having total influence. This perception dates back to findings obtained by researchers in the 1930s and 1940s when they assumed that the media (popular press, radio) had a strong and direct influence – in particular in political communication (propaganda) and in commercial advertising.

The communication scientist Burkart, who is now retired, stated in a journal article on research into the impact of the media almost 20 years ago (before the advent of social networks) that this conclusion was simply incorrect from an (academic) perspective. Rather, in spite of various findings, mass communication research has not managed to provide a clear answer to the question of what impact the media has. However, while relativising the notion of the impact, one also cannot assume that all media are, as it were, ineffectual (2003, pp. 5–7). Is it now possible for an institution, an organisation, to persuade individuals, groups of people or sections of the public to change their attitude and their behaviour through targeted communication measures? In short, the initial answer to this specific, closed question must be No, because simple stimulus-response patterns between media (active communicators) and media users (passive recipients) are now outdated. However, without an explicit or at least implicit assumption of impact, any impact research would border on the absurd, which is why the following clarification should be made: media impacts are rather demonstrable under certain conditions, although the question of how an individual processes media messages cognitively and affectively is always important. Instructive explanatory models can be found for these heterogeneous interdependencies in long-established psychological phenomena such as cognitive dissonance and selective perception (for example: how a passionate smoker processes results of research into lung cancer that are circulated in the mass media) or also in proven models of the research into media use such as that of the uses and gratification approach (almost any media content can be used or processed in almost any way by the respective media recipient) or in that of opinion leading. The latter – and this makes the complex relationships even clearer – "is incidentally a relatively safe result of relevant research: direct, personal conversations influence our opinions, attitudes and actions much more than receiving media content" (Burkart, 2003, p. 6).

Taking these individual, "subjective" aspects into consideration, the "power" of the mass media therefore lies more in its role in providing information and guidance (disseminating knowledge) and less in the expected impact of directly influencing the attitudes and behaviour of defined individuals or groups. But a relativising criterion must also be cited in this regard: Tichenor et al. (1970) conclude in a long-term study that a higher information density benefits in particular those consumers of media who, as a result of their education or their socio-economic status, already had a higher level of information, which leads to a knowledge gap in society. Research into the knowledge gap hypothesis does show the following: there are relevant intervening variables which limit the impacts of media on the recipient and therefore indirectly have an impact on society.

Back to the role of the mass media in providing information and guidance. Its ability to highlight issues and place them in a specific context (emphasis, rating) should also be mentioned: In the last five decades, hardly any approach has therefore received more attention from impact research than that of agenda setting; it can be traced back to Cohen (1963), who, with his central thesis that media tended to dictate more of what people reflected on than what they thought (p. 13), sparked a research agenda which was first picked up by McCombs and Shaw (1972) with their oft-quoted Chapel Hill study. The essence of the agenda-setting hypothesis is that mass media have an impact on people by essentially deciding, through what they report, which topics will enter their thought agenda, although the following has now become clear:

> *"The fact that agenda-setting effects are less pronounced at a micro level than can be demonstrated in aggregate or just for specific issues can be explained by individual people's different predispositions that produce different effects"* (Bulkow & Schweiger, 2013, p. 186).

This merely illustrates that, in relation to assumed media impacts, what level of impact is actually meant must also always be taken into account: the micro level (individual), the meso level (social groups or fields) or the macro level (society). After all, a correlation between two variables which is measured at the aggregate level sometimes does not exist or is weaker at the micro level because there it is displaced by other variables (Schweiger, 2013, p. 29).

Furthermore, it is known from advertising that stimulus frequency (repetition) can influence a recipient's recall and recognition. This is the focus of George

Gerbner's cultivation theory, which – although it has since been heavily critiqued as a theoretical model – focuses on regular viewers (in light of the boom in TV at the end of the 1960s and 1970s), whose perception of the world Gerbner views as being increasingly "cultivated" by watching television.

Noelle-Neumann (2001) describes with her "spiral of silence" how people developed an instinct for registering when opinions were increasing or decreasing in a social setting. Those whose opinion is on the rise feel particularly compelled to speak out publicly, whereas those whose opinion places them in the minority start to remain silent for fear of isolation. The real strengths thus become blurred: some people occasionally seem stronger than they actually are and others, who apparently are weaker, are caught in a spiral of silence. The hypotheses, which in Noelle-Neumann's research still relate in particular to the impact of television, can also be applied to the online world of the 21st century, as Hampton et al. (2014) demonstrate.

Finally, in the context of the impact of StratCom, research into the effects of media priming and media framing should also be highlighted; this is one of the newest areas in the field of media impact research. In Europe in particular, priming (elaborates the agenda setting and describes a decidedly affective influence of the media agenda) and framing ("journalistic" selection/highlighting of specific snapshots of reality at the expense of others, using cleverly chosen figurative language) are becoming the focus of social discourse not least as a result of the controversial public discussion of the migration crisis in 2015/16. And on Germany's media scene, the issue recently bubbled up in 2019, when it became public knowledge that the public broadcaster ARD had prepared a customised framing manual even though it is fundamentally required by law to maintain strict objectivity and balance in its reporting (Biazza, 2019). With priming and framing, it is also apparent that the effects are linked to preconditions, for example the previous knowledge or attitude of the recipients.

> *"For example, framing and priming effects manifest themselves both through cognitive responses (e.g. 'foreigners are criminals') and through affective responses (e.g. 'antipathy towards foreigners'). In other words, stereotypical depictions in the media can stimulate in recipients both stereotypes or other cognitive responses, and also affective responses. Other studies illustrate that media framing can also trigger specific emotions (e.g. sadness or anger), and that these emotions can have very different consequences for judgement formation (...)"* (Schemer, 2013, p. 165).

If one summarises the statements made above, there must be some doubt at least from a communication science perspective that simple stimulus-response patterns produce the effect that is self-imposed by StratCom in particular with the requirement to have an influential impact. However, if one takes another look at the examples which were described at the beginning, it is apparent that strategic communication measures have at least a temporally limited impact, even though the "incubator lie" was quickly revealed, or Germany's Chancellor soon had to reverse her "We can do this", and to the present day Qatar is not only successfully defying the blockade of the Saudis, but has also increased its profile internationally. This leads to the conclusion that StratCom cannot have a powerful impact with communication measures alone, but rather only in "orchestration" with the strategic tools that extend well beyond the simple element of communication.

5.   Conclusion

All sorts of things are "sold" nowadays under the umbrella term StratCom; but often what is revealed is merely a fraction of what the term actually promises to deliver. For example, StratCom is sometimes merely viewed as an enhanced form of public relations. In a governmental context, the United States in particular has in the past devoted a great deal of attention to StratCom and, despite significant wrangling, has generally speaking developed a profound understanding of StratCom which extends far beyond the element of communication and, for example, seeks to orchestrate diplomatic or military measures in the same way as intelligence or commercial ones. The same is true of NATO. Such StratCom is essentially based on carefully chosen narratives that, with all parties and actors working together in harmony, create a strategic guideline so that set objectives can be achieved quickly and in their entirety. All mechanisms of action generally follow more complex patterns than simple stimulus-response models. Final remarks: the authors are aware that this text also leaves open many questions, not least for reasons of space – and has therefore created plenty of scope for follow-up work on this topic. Questions that remain unanswered include: How can StratCom be created and executed lege artis? What defensive measures can be taken to combat StratCom and promise to be successful? Where do the limits of strategic communication lie, in particular in functional states governed by the rule of law?

6. References

al-Saleh, H. (2017). *How Qatar and Iran's hardliners are very much alike politically.* https://english.alarabiya.net/en/features/2017/05/29/ANALYSIS-How-Qatar-and-the-Khomeinis-are-very-much-alike-politically.html

Bentele, G., & Nothhaft, H. (2010). Strategic Communication and the Public Sphere from a European Perspective. *International Journal of Strategic Communication, 4*(2), 93–116. https://doi.org/10.1080/15531181003701954

Biazza, J. (2019). *Kampf um den Deutungsrahmen.* https://www.sueddeutsche.de/medien/ard-framing-manual-rundfunkbeitrag-sprache-1.4335445

Bilban, C., & Grininger, H. (Eds.). (2019). Schriftenreihe der Landesverteidigungsakademie. Mythos „Gerasimov-Doktrin": Ansichten des russischen Militärs oder Grundlage hybrider Kriegsführung?

Boothe, B. (2011). *Das Narrativ: Biografisches Erzählen im psychotherapeutischen Prozess* (1. Auflage). Stuttgart: Schattauer. Retrieved from http://d-nb.info/1002141400/04

Borg, L. J. (2008). *Communicating With Intent: The Department of Defense and Strategic Communication.* Center for Information Policy Research. http://pirp.harvard.edu/pubs_pdf/borg/borg-i08-1.pdf

Brooks, R. (2011, July 12). "Ten Years On: The Evolution of Strategic Communication and Information Operations since 9/11": Testimony before the House Armed Services Sub-Committee on Evolving Threats and Capabilities. http://indianstrategicknowledgeonline.com/web/Brooks.pdf

Brooks, R. (2012). *Confessions of a Strategic Communicator: Tales from inside the Pentgaon's message machine.* http://foreignpolicy.com/2012/12/06/confessions-of-a-strategic-communicator/

Bruhn, M., Esch, F.-R., & Langner, T. (Eds.). (2016). Springer Reference Wirtschaft. Handbuch Strategische Kommunikation: Grundlagen - Innovative Ansätze - Praktische Umsetzungen (2. Aufl.). Springer Fachmedien Wiesbaden GmbH; Springer Gabler.

Bulkow, K., & Schweiger, W. (2013). Agenda Setting – zwischen gesellschaftlichem Phänomen und individuellem Prozess. In W. Schweiger & A. Fahr (Eds.), *Handbuch Medienwirkungsforschung* (pp. 171–190). Springer VS.

Burkart, R. (2003). Medienwirkungsforschung – ein Einblick. *Medienimpulse, 12*(46), 5–8.

Coalson, R. (2014, June 21). *Russian Military Doctrine article by General Valery Gerasimov [Facebook].* Facebook. https://www.facebook.com/notes/robert-coalson/russian-military-doctrine-article-by-general-valery-gerasimov/10152184862563597/

Cohen, B. C. (1963). *Press and Foreign Policy.* Princeton University Press. https://doi.org/10.1515/9781400878611

Connolly, K. (2020). *Film on Angela Merkel's role during refugee crisis set for screening.* https://www.theguardian.com/world/2020/mar/30/film-on-angela-merkels-role-during-refugee-crisis-set-for-screening

Department of Defense. (2017). *DOD Dictionary of Military and Associated Terms, March 2017.* http://www.dtic.mil/doctrine/new_pubs/dictionary.pdf

Department of Defense. (2020). *DOD Dictionary of Military and Associated Terms, March 2017.* https://www.jcs.mil/Portals/36/Documents/Doctrine/pubs/dictionary.pdf

DeYoung, K., & Nakashima, E. (2017). *UAE orchestrated hacking of Qatari government sites, sparking regional upheaval, according to U.S. intelligence officials.* https://www.washingtonpost.com/world/national-security/uae-hacked-qatari-government-sites-sparking-regional-upheaval-according-to-us-intelligence-officials/2017/07/16/00c46e54-698f-11e7-8eb5-cbccc2e7bfbf_story.html?utm_term=.00db9c125a76

Entman, R. M. (1993). Framing: Toward Clarification of a Fractured Paradigm. *Journal of Communication, 43*(4), 51–58. https://doi.org/10.1111/j.1460-2466.1993.tb01304.x

Erlach, C., & Müller, M. (2020). Geschichten: Der Stoff, aus dem Organisationen sind. In C. Erlach, M. Müller, & K. Thier (Eds.), *Narrative Organisationen: Wie die Arbeit mit Geschichten Unternehmen zukunftsfähig macht* (pp. 13–35). Berlin, Heidelberg: Springer Gabler. in Springer Fachmedien Wiesbaden GmbH. https://doi.org/10.1007/978-3-662-60721-3_2

Erlach, C., Müller, M., & Thier, K. (Eds.) (2020). *Narrative Organisationen: Wie die Arbeit mit Geschichten Unternehmen zukunftsfähig macht.* Berlin, Heidelberg: Springer Gabler. in Springer Fachmedien Wiesbaden GmbH.

EU Institute for Security Studies. (2016a). EU strategic communications with a view to counteracting propaganda.

EU Institute for Security Studies. (2016b). *Strategic communications: East and South.* https://www.iss.europa.eu/sites/default/files/EUISSFiles/Report_30.pdf

Europäische Kommission. (2016, April 6). *Security: Eu strengthens response to hybrid threats* [Press release]. http://europa.eu/rapid/press-release_IP-16-1227_en.htm

Strategische Kommunikation der EU, um gegen sie gerichteter Propaganda von Dritten entgegenzuwirken (2016). http://www.europarl.europa.eu/sides/getDoc.do?pubRef=-//EP//TEXT+TA+P8-TA-2016-0441+0+DOC+XML+V0//DE

Europäisches Parlament. (2019). *Asyl und Migration: Zahlen und Fakten.* https://www.europarl.europa.eu/news/de/headlines/society/20170629STO78630/asyl-und-migration-zahlen-und-fakten

European Commission. (2018). *Action Plan against Disinformation.* https://eeas.europa.eu/sites/eeas/files/action_plan_against_disinformation.pdf

European Council. (2015). *European Council meeting (19 and 20 March 2015) – Conclusions.* http://www.consilium.europa.eu/en/meetings/european-council/2015/03/european-council-conclusions-march-2015-en_pdf/

Farwell, J. P. (2012). *Persuasion and Power: The Art of Strategic Communication.* Georgetown University Press. https://books.google.at/books?id=kvXy5Yg445AC

Ausschuss für auswärtige Angelegenheiten (2016, October 14). Plenarsitzungsdokument A8-0290/2016.

Frankfurter Allgemeine Zeitung. (2016). *Flüchtlingskrise: „Wir schaffen das" stammt nicht von Merkel.* http://www.faz.net/aktuell/politik/fluechtlingskrise/fluechtlingskrise-wir-schaffen-das-ist-von-sigmar-gabriel-14415508.html

Fridman, O. (2020). 'Information War' as the Russian Conceptualisation of Strategic Communications. *The RUSI Journal, 165*(1), 44–53. https://doi.org/10.1080/03071847.2020.1740494

Galeotti, M. (2014, July 6). *The 'Gerasimov Doctrine' and Russian Non-Linear War.* https://inmoscowsshadows.wordpress.com/2014/07/06/the-gerasimov-doctrine-and-russian-non-linear-war/

Galeotti, M. (2020). *"The Gerasimov Doctrine".* https://berlinpolicyjournal.com/the-gerasimov-doctrine/

Gambrell, J. (2017). *AP News Guide: What to know about the Qatar crisis.* https://www.washingtonpost.com/d7095bce-99db-11e7-af6a-6555caaeb8dc_story.html?utm_term=.ac80ac94cb2a

Gehrau, V., Röttger, U., & Preusse, J. (2013). Strategische Kommunikation: alte und neue Perspektiven. In U. Röttger, V. Gehrau, & J. Preusse (Eds.), *Strategische Kommunikation* (pp. 347–356). Springer Fachmedien Wiesbaden.

Gerasimov, V. (2013). Cennost' nauki v predvidenii. *Voenno-Promyšlennyj Kur'er*(8). https://vpk-news.ru/sites/default/files/pdf/VPK_08_476.pdf

Gerasimov, V. (2016). The Value of Science Is in the Foresight: New Challenges Demand Rethinking the Forms and Methods of Carrying out Combat Operations. *Military Review*, 23–29. https://jmc.msu.edu/50th/download/21-conflict.pdf

Hallahan, K., Holtzhausen, D., van Ruler, B., Verčič, D., & Sriramesh, K. (2007). Defining Strategic Communication. *International Journal of Strategic Communication*, *1*(1), 3–35. https://doi.org/10.1080/15531180701285244

Hampton, K. N., Rainie, L., Lu, W., Dwyer, M., Shin, I., & Purcell, K. (2014, August 26). *Social Media and the 'Spiral of Silence'*. Washington, DC. Pew Research Center. http://www.pewinternet.org/files/2014/08/PI_Social-networks-and-debate_082614.pdf

(2015, June 22) Ares(2015)2608242 - 22/06/2015.

Holtzhausen, D., & Zerfass, A. (2013). Strategic Communication – Pillars and Perspectives of an Alternative Paradigm. In A. Zerfaß, L. Rademacher, & S. Wehmeier (Eds.), *Organisationskommunikation und Public Relations* (pp. 73–94). Springer Fachmedien Wiesbaden. https://doi.org/10.1007/978-3-531-18961-1_4

Holtzhausen, D., & Zerfass, A. (Eds.). (2015a). Routledge handbooks. The Routledge Handbook of Strategic Communication (Kindle Edition). Routledge.

Holtzhausen, D., & Zerfass, A. (2015b). Strategic Communication: Opportunities and Challenges of the Research Area. In D. Holtzhausen & A. Zerfass (Eds.), *Routledge handbooks. The Routledge Handbook of Strategic Communication (Kindle Edition)* (Pos. 552–1044). Routledge.

Jäger, S. (2016). Storytelling - Das Gehirn will Geschichten. Retrieved from https://www.wissenskurator.de/storytelling-das-gehirn-will-geschichten/

Joint Warfighting Center. (2010). *Commander's Handbook for Strategic Communication and Communication Strategy*. http://www.dtic.mil/doctrine/doctrine/jwfc/sc_hbk10.pdf

Kempf, W. (2020). Framing. In M. A. Wirtz (Ed.), *Dorsch – Lexikon der Psychologie*. Bern. Retrieved from https://portal.hogrefe.com/dorsch/framing/

Kündig, M. (2017). *Saudis verhandeln im Geheimen. Welche Rolle spielt Israel im Katar-Konflikt?* Schweizer Radio und Fernsehen (SRF). https://www.srf.ch/news/international/welche-rolle-spielt-israel-im-katar-konflikt

Laity, M. (2018). NATO and Strategic Communications. *The Three Swords Magazine*(33), 66–73. http://www.jwc.nato.int/images/stories/threeswords/NATO_STRATCOM_2018.pdf

Le Page, R. (2014, October 22). *Understanding NATO Strategic Communications.* https://www.cmdrcoe.org/download.php?id=335

Lucius-Hoene, G. (2017). Narrative Analysen in der Psychologie. In G. Mey & K. Mruck (Eds.), *Springer Reference Psychologie. Handbuch Qualitative Forschung in der Psychologie.* Wiesbaden: Springer.

Lucius-Hoene, G. (2020). Narrative Rekonstruktion. Retrieved from https://portal.hogrefe.com/dorsch/narrative-rekonstruktion/

MacArthur, J. R. (1992). *Remember Nayirah, Witness for Kuwait?* https://www.nytimes.com/1992/01/06/opinion/remember-nayirah-witness-for-kuwait.html

Magen, C. (2017). Strategic Communication of Israel's Intelligence Services: Countering New Challenges with Old Methods. *International Journal of Strategic Communication, 11*(4), 269–285. https://doi.org/10.1080/1553118X.2017.1334207

Markowitsch, H. J., & Staniloiu, A. (2015). Neuropsycholologie und Hirnbildgebung des mnestischen Blockadesyndroms. In C. E. Scheidt & A. Aurnhammer (Eds.), *Narrative Bewältigung von Trauma und Verlust,* pp. 52–63. Stuttgart: Schattauer.

McCombs, M. E., & Shaw, D. L. (1972). The Agenda-Setting Function of Mass Media. *The Public Opinion Quarterly, 36*(2), 176–187. www.jstor.org/stable/2747787

Mullen, M. G. (2009). From the Chairman: Strategic Communication: Getting Back to Basics. *Joint Force Quarterly*(55), 2–4.

Müller, M., & Precht, J. (Eds.). (2019). Narrative des Populismus: Erzählmuster und -strukturen populistischer Politik. Springer VS.

Noelle-Neumann, E. (2001). *Die Schweigespirale: Öffentliche Meinung - unsere soziale Haut* (6., erw. Neuaufl.). Langen Müller.

North Atlantic Military Committee. (2017). *MC 0628: NATO Military Policy on Strategic Communications.* http://stratcom.nuou.org.ua/wp-content/uploads/2020/01/NATO-MILITARY-POLICY-ON-STRATEGIC-COMMUNICATIONS.pdf

Office of the Secretary of Defense. (2004, September 23). *Report of the Defense Science Board Task Force on Strategic Communication.* https://fas.org/irp/agency/dod/dsb/commun.pdf

Office of the Under Secretary of Defense for Acquisition, Technology, and Logistics. (2001). *Report of the Defense Science Board Task Force on Managed Information Dissemination.* https://www.acq.osd.mil/dsb/reports/2000s/ADA396312.pdf

Ogrysko, V. (2016). Russian information and propaganda war: some methods and forms to counteract. http://www.stratcomcoe.org/download/file/fid/5969

Oltermann, P. (2017). *Germany devours book on Angela Merkel decision to open borders.* https://www.theguardian.com/world/2017/apr/06/germany-devours-book-on-angela-merkel-decision-to-open-borders

Pashentsev, E. (2019a). Strategic Communication in EU-Russia Relations. In E. Pashentsev (Ed.), *Strategic Communication in EU-Russia Relations [Kindle-Version]: Tensions, Challenges and Opportunities* (628–1382). Springer International Publishing.

Pashentsev, E. (Ed.). (2019b). Strategic Communication in EU-Russia Relations [Kindle-Version]: Tensions, Challenges and Opportunities. Springer International Publishing.

Paul, C. (2011). *Strategic Communication: Origins, Concepts, and Current Debates.* Praeger. https://books.google.at/books?id=VIxuxcmt5qQC

Perez, E., & Prokupecz, S. (2017). *CNN Exclusive: US suspects Russian hackers planted fake news behind Qatar crisis.* http://edition.cnn.com/2017/06/06/politics/russian-hackers-planted-fake-news-qatar-crisis/index.html

Presse- und Informationsamt der Bundesregierung. (2015). *Sommerpressekonferenz von Bundeskanzlerin Merkel.* https://www.bundesregierung.de/breg-de/aktuelles/pressekonferenzen/sommerpressekonferenz-von-bundeskanzlerin-merkel-848300

Private Office of the Secretary General. (2009, September 29). *NATO Strategic Communications Policy.* http://stratcomhellas.weebly.com/uploads/5/1/6/5/51658901/nato_stratcom_policy_2009.pdf

Roth, A. (2017). *Pro-Putin bots are dominating Russian political talk on Twitter.* https://www.washingtonpost.com/world/europe/pro-putin-politics-bots-are-flooding-russian-twitter-oxford-based-studysays/2017/06/20/19c35d6e-5474-11e7-840b-512026319da7_story.html?utm_term=.0f33fc9c9857

Rudolph, U., & Kim, M. (2018). Einstellung, soziale. In J. Kopp & A. Steinbach (Eds.), *Grundbegriffe der Soziologie* (12th ed., pp. 79–82). Springer Fachmedien Wiesbaden.

Sarcinelli, U. (2010). Strategie und politische Kommunikation. Mehr als die Legitimation des Augenblicks. In J. Raschke & R. Tils (Eds.), *Strategie in der Politikwissenschaft* (pp. 267–298). VS Verlag für Sozialwissenschaften. https://doi.org/10.1007/978-3-531-92209-6_12

Scheer, U. (2016). „*Postfaktisch*": *Die Faktendämmerung hat eingesetzt*. Frankfurter Allgemeine Zeitung GmbH. http://www.faz.net/aktuell/feuilleton/faktendaemmerung-postfaktisch-ist-das-wort-2016-14530776.html

Schemer, C. (2013). Priming, Framing, Stereotype. In W. Schweiger & A. Fahr (Eds.), *Handbuch Medienwirkungsforschung* (pp. 153–169). Springer VS.

Schweiger, W. (2013). Grundlagen: Was sind Medienwirkungen ? – Überblick und Systematik. In W. Schweiger & A. Fahr (Eds.), *Handbuch Medienwirkungsforschung* (pp. 15–37). Springer VS.

Spiegel Online. (2016, December 6). *Angela Merkel beim CDU-Parteitag: "Eine Situation wie im Sommer 2015 darf sich nicht wiederholen"*. http://www.spiegel.de/politik/deutschland/angela-merkel-bei-cdu-parteitag-fluechtlingskrise-darf-sich-nicht-wiederholen-a-1124599.html

Stecken, J. (o.J.). Die schärfste Waffe der Polizei. Retrieved from http://www.cpv-online.org/impulse/16-die-schaerfste-waffe-der-polizei.html

Tatham, S. (2013). U.S. Governmental Information Operations and Strategic Communications: A Discredited Tool or User Failure? Implications for Future Conflict (ARMY WAR COLLEGE CARLISLE BARRACKS PA STRATEGIC STUDIES INSTITUTE). http://www.dtic.mil/cgi-bin/GetTRDoc?AD=ADA589976&Location=U2&doc=GetTRDoc.pdf

Tatham, S., & Le Page, R. (2014). *NATO Strategic Communication: More to be Done?* Riga. Center for Security and Strategic Research. http://www.stratcomcoe.org/rita-lepage-steve-tatham-nato-strategic-communication-more-be-done

Tatham, S. A. (2008). *Strategic communication: A primer. Special series: 08/28*. Defence Academy of the United Kingdom, Advanced Research and Assessment Group.

Tichenor, P. J., Donohue, G. A., & Olien, C. N. (1970). Mass Media Flow and Differential Growth in Knowledge. *The Public Opinion Quarterly, 34*(2), 159–170. www.jstor.org/stable/2747414

U.S. Government Accountability Office. (2012, May 24). *DOD Strategic Communication: Integrating Foreign Audience Perceptions into Policy Making, Plans, and Operations*. Washington, D.C. http://gao.gov/assets/600/591123.pdf

UK Ministry of Defence. (2012). Joint Doctrine 1/12: Strategic Communication: The Defence Contribution.

USA Today. (2012). *Pentagon drops 'strategic communication'*. https://www.usatoday.com/story/news/nation/2012/12/03/pentagon-trims-strategic-communication/1743485/

The White House. (2010). *National Framework for Strategic Communication: White House response to Sec. 1055 of NDAA for FY09.* https://mountainrunner.us/wp-content/uploads/2012/03/2010-NSC-White-House-Strategic-Communication-1055.pdf

The White House. (2020). *President Donald J. Trump Announces Additions to White House Staff.* https://www.whitehouse.gov/briefings-statements/president-donald-j-trump-announces-additions-white-house-staff/

Verwaltungs-Berufsgenossenschaft (VBG) (o.J.). „Die stärkste Waffe ist das gesprochene Wort". Retrieved from https://www.certo-portal.de/sicher-arbeiten/artikel/deeskalation-fuer-sicherheitskraefte-die-staerkste-waffe-ist-das-gesprochene-wort/

Wiegand, E. (2018, December 21). Wenn Sprache zur stärksten Waffe wird - Werte und Wandel. Retrieved from https://werteundwandel.de/inhalte/wenn-sprache-zur-staerksten-waffe-wird/

Wiesenberg, M., Zerfaß, A., & Moreno, A. (2017). Big Data and Automation in Strategic Communication. *International Journal of Strategic Communication, 11*(2), 95–114. https://doi.org/10.1080/1553118X.2017.1285770

Williams, N. B. [J.]. (1992). *Mideast : Kuwait Story of Babies Removed From Incubators Refuses to Die.* https://www.latimes.com/archives/la-xpm-1992-03-06-mn-3337-story.html

Wirtz, M. A. (2020). *Dorsch - Lexikon der Psychologie* (19., überarbeitete Auflage)

Woolley, S. C., & Philip N. Howard. (2017). *Computational Propaganda Worldwide: Executive Summary.* http://comprop.oii.ox.ac.uk/wp-content/uploads/sites/89/2017/06/Casestudies-ExecutiveSummary.pdf

Die Zeit. (2015). *Die EU zieht in den Propagandakampf.* http://www.zeit.de/politik/ausland/2015-03/russland-propaganda-eu-strategie-informationskrieg/komplettansicht

Die Zeit. (2016). *Europäische Union: EU-Parlament warnt vor russischer Propaganda.* http://www.zeit.de/politik/ausland/2016-11/europaeische-union-anti-eu-propaganda-russland-europaparlament-populismus

Zerfass, A. (2009). Institutionalizing Strategic Communication: Theoretical Analysis and Empirical Evidence. *International Journal of Strategic Communication, 3*(2), 69–71. https://doi.org/10.1080/15531180902810205

7. Further Reading

Britz, M. et al (eds.). (2018). *European Participation in International Operations. The Role of Strategic Culture.* UK: Palgrave Macmillan.

Paret, Peter (1986). *Makers of Modern Strategy from Machiavelli to the Nuclear Age.* New Jersey: Princetown University Press.

Matlary, J.H. (2018). *Hard Power in Hard Times. Can Europe Act Strategically?* London: Palgrave Macmillan.

Mejer, H. and Wyss, M. (2018). *The Handbook of European Defence Policies and Armed Forces.* Oxford: Oxford University Press.

Nye, Joseph (1990). *Bound to Lead: The Changing Nature of American Power.* New York: Basic Books.

Paret, Peter (1986). *Makers of Modern Strategy from Machiavelli to the Nuclear Age.* New Jersey: Princetown University Press.

De Wijk, R. (2004). *The Art of Military Coercion: Why the West's Military Superiority Scarcely Matters.* Amsterdam: Mets & Schilt.

Carola Hartmann Miles-Verlag

Wiener Strategie-Konferenz

Wolfgang Peischel (Hrsg.), *Wiener Strategie-Konferenz 2016 – Strategie neu denken,* Berlin 2017.

Wolfgang Peischel (Hrsg.), *Wiener Strategie-Konferenz 2017 – Strategie neu denken,* Berlin 2018.

Wolfgang Peischel (Hrsg.), *Wiener Strategie-Konferenz 2018 – Strategie neu denken,* Berlin 2019.

Wolfgang Peischel (Hrsg.), *Wiener Strategie-Konferenz 2019 – Strategie neu denken,* Berlin 2021.

Sicherheitspolitik

Wolf Graf v. Baudissin, *Grundwert: Frieden in Politik – Strategie – Führung von Streitkräften, herausgegeben von Claus von Rosen,* Berlin 2014.

Dirk Freudenberg, *Theorie des Irregulären – Erscheinungen und Abgrenzungen von Partisanen, Guerillas und Terroristen im Modernen Kleinkrieg sowie Entwicklungstendenzen der Reaktion, (3 Bände),* Berlin 2017.

Markus Reisner, *Robotic Wars – Legitimatorische Grundlagen und Grenzen des Einsatzes von Military Unmanned Systems in modernen Konfliktszenarien,* Berlin 2018.

Helmut Fiedler, *Military Assistance – eine moderne Einsatzart zwischen Anspruch und Wirklichkeit,* Berlin 2019.

Pascal Riemer, *Von der russischen Kriegskunst. Eine Untersuchung der dialektischen Zusammenhänge von Staatsidee und Militärwesen am Beispiel der Sowjetunion und der Russischen Föderation,* Berlin 2021.

Georg Kunovjanek, *Cyber – Die Domäne der vernetzten Unsicherheit. Eine kritische interdisziplinäre Analyse des Krieges der Zukunft und seiner normativen Grundlagen,* Berlin 2021.

Joachim Weber (Hrsg.), *Konfliktraum Arktis. Die Großmächte und der Hohe Norden,* Berlin 2021.

Thomas Jäger, Ralph Thiele (Hrsg.), *Der Politische Islamismus als hybrider Akteur globaler Reichweite. Die liberale demokratische Ordnung muss ihre Resilienz stärken,* Berlin 2021.

Uwe Hartmann, *Die Nato. Mächte und Menschen in der transatlantischen Allianz,* Berlin 2021.

Dirk Freudenberg, *Wehrhaftigkeit der Medienordnung – Rechtliche und rechts-politische Probleme vor dem Hintergrund der Konzeption Zivile Verteidigung (KZV),* Berlin 2022.

Carsten Rechtien, *Trumps Amerika – Eine geopolitische Revolution? Tradition und Neuausrichtung der US-Außenpolitik in der beginnenden Ära Trump,* Berlin 2022.

Hans-Peter Weinheimer, *Bevölkerungsschutz 2030 – Anleitung zur Überwindung eines "bewährten" Systems,* Berlin 2022.

Jahrbuch Innere Führung (seit 2009)

Uwe Hartmann, Reinhold Janke, Claus von Rosen (Hrsg.), *Jahrbuch Innere Führung 2020. Zur Weiterentwicklung der Inneren Führung: Themen und Inhalte,* Berlin 2020.

Uwe Hartmann, Reinhold Janke, Claus von Rosen (Hrsg.), *Jahrbuch Innere Führung 2021/22. Ein neues Mindset Landes- und Bündnisverteidigung?,* Berlin 2022.

Uwe Hartmann, Reinhold Janke, Claus von Rosen (Hrsg.), *Jahrbuch Innere Führung 2022/23. Zeitenwende und Kriegsbilder,* Berlin 2023.

Standpunkte und Orientierungen

Daniel Giese, *Militärische Führung im Internetzeitalter – Die Bedeutung von Strategischer Kommunikation und Social Media für Entscheidungsprozesse, Organisationsstrukturen und Führerausbildung in der Bundeswehr,* Berlin 2014.

Uwe Hartmann (Hrsg.), *Lernen von Afghanistan. Innovative Mittel und Wege für Auslandseinsätze,* Berlin 2015.

Klaus Beckmann, *Treue.Bürgermut.Ungehorsam. Anstöße zur Führungskultur und zum beruflichen Selbstverständnis in der Bundeswehr,* Berlin 2015.

Uwe Hartmann, *Hybrider Krieg als neue Bedrohung von Freiheit und Frieden. Zur Relevanz der Inneren Führung in Politik, Gesellschaft und Streitkräften,* Berlin 2015.

Hartwig von Schubert, *Integrative Militärethik. Ethische Urteilsbildung in der militärischen Führung,* Berlin 2015.

Martin Sebaldt, *Nicht abwehrbereit. Die Kardinalprobleme der deutschen Streitkräfte, der Offenbarungseid des Weißbuchs und die Wege aus der Gefahr,* Berlin 2017.

Uwe Hartmann, *Der gute Soldat. Politische Kultur und soldatisches Selbstverständnis heute,* Berlin 2018.

Helmut Jermer, *Innere Führung kompakt. Eine Zusammenschau als Lehr- und Lernhilfe,* Berlin 2019.

Martin Sebaldt, *Das Elend der Strategen. Warum die deutsche Militärpolitik versagt,* Berlin 2020.

Hannes Wendroth, *Gute Führung – (k)ein Selbstgänger. Kleine Führungshilfe mit praktischen Hinweisen und persönlichen Anmerkungen,* Berlin 2022.

Hans-Christian Witthauer, Thomas Saller, *Führung und das 3 Alpha Prinzip. Militärisches Handwerkszeug für den zivilen Führungsalltag,* Berlin 2023.

Militärgeschichte

Eberhard Kliem, Kathrin Orth, *"Wir wurden wie blödsinnig vom Feind beschossen". Menschen und Schiffe in der Skagerrakschlacht 1916,* Berlin 2016.

Hans Frank, Norbert Rath, *Kommodore Rudolf Petersen. Führer der Schnellboote 1942–1945. Ein Leben in Licht und Schatten unteilbarer Verantwortung,* Berlin 2016.

Eckhard Lisec, *Der Völkermord an den Armeniern im 1. Weltkrieg – Deutsche Offiziere beteiligt?,* Berlin 2017.

Joachim Welz, *Erfolgsstory oder Trauma – die Übernahme von Armeen. Lehren aus der Übernahme des österreichischen Bundesheeres in die Wehrmacht 1938 und der Reste der NVA in die Bundeswehr 1990,* Berlin 2018.

Georg Neuhaus, *Am Anfang war ein Speer. Eine Chronographie der Kriegs- und Militärtechnologien,* Berlin 2018.

Hans-Werner Ahrens, *Die Transportflieger der Luftwaffe 1956 bis 1971. Konzeption – Aufbau – Einsatz, (Reihe Schriften zur Geschichte der Deutschen Luftwaffe, Band 8),* Berlin 2019.

Jobst Reller, *Die Anfänge der evangelischen Militärseelsorge,* Berlin [2]2020.

Eberhard Frhr. v. Senden, Friedrich Frhr. v. Senden, *Der Erste Weltkrieg 1914–1918. Erlebnisse eines jungen Leutnants,* Berlin 2020.

Hans-Günter Behrendt, *Flugabwehr in Deutschland. Stationierungsorte und Systeme 1956-2012,* Berlin 2021.

Harald Fritz Potempa, *Balkan 1914-1945. Raum und Kleiner Krieg als militärhistorische Kategorien in der Wahrnehmung deutscher Streitkräfte,* Berlin 2021.

Stephan Horn, *Französische und wallonische Freiwilligenverbände im Zweiten Weltkrieg. Politische Implikationen militärischer Kollaboration,* Berlin 2021.

Jörg Beining, *Streng geheim! Elektronische Kampfführung im Kalten Krieg. Die EloKa der Bundeswehr und NATO aus östlicher Perspektive,* Berlin 2021.

Gerd Bolik, *NATO-Planungen für die Verteidigung der Bundesrepublik Deutschland im Kalten Krieg,* Berlin 2021.

Martin Kutz, *Die Schlacht als Männerballett oder Mythos und Militär,* Berlin 2022.

Olaf Rönnau, *Eine totale Institution als Zwischenspiel. Die Kadettenschule der NVA von ihrer Gründung 1956 bis zu ihrer Auflösung 1961,* Berlin 2022.

Stephan Maninger, *Für einige Morgen aus Eis und Schnee – Großbritanniens Kampf um Nordamerika 1754-1763,* Berlin 2022.

Einsatzerfahrungen

Artur Schwitalla, *Afghanistan, jetzt weiß ich erst...,* Berlin 2010.

Sascha Brinkmann, Joachim Hoppe (Hg.), *Generation Einsatz. Fallschirmjäger berichten ihre Erfahrungen aus Afghanistan,* Berlin 2010.

Rainer Buske, *KUNDUZ. Ein Erlebnisbericht über einen militärischen Einsatz der Bundeswehr in Afghanistan im Jahre 2008,* Berlin 2015.

Marcel Bohnert, Andy Neumann, *German Mechanized Infantry on Combat Operations in Afghanistan,* Berlin 2016.

Alois Bach, Carola Hartmann (Hrsg.), *Unbekannte Helden des Alltags. Soldaten und Ehefrauen berichten über Verantwortung, Humanität und Belastung im Auslandseinsatz,* Berlin 2020.

Kurt Helmut Schiebold, *99 Tage in Afghanistan. Wie der deutsche Einsatz 2003 im Nordosten Afghanistans begann. Aus meinem Tagebuch,* Berlin 2022.

www.miles-verlag.jimdo.com